S A N C R I S T Ó B A L

Voices and Visions of the Galisteo Basin

SAN CRISTÓBAL

Voices and Visions of the Galisteo Basin

Christina Singleton Mednick

Office of Archaeological Studies
Museum of New Mexico
Santa Fe, New Mexico

Editor: Robin A. Gould
Production Manager: Jim Mafchir Publications and Graphic Services
Designed and typeset on QuarkXPress by Jim Mafchir

Library of Congress Cataloguing–in–Publication Data is available from the publisher:

Office of Archaeological Studies
Museum of New Mexico
P.O. Box 2087
Santa Fe, New Mexico 87504–2087

Printed by Palace Press in Hong Kong

05 04 03 02 01 00 99 98 97 96

10 9 8 7 6 5 4 3 2 1

CONTENTS

Foreword by Polly Schaafsma *vii*

Foreword by Tim Maxwell *ix*

Acknowledgments *xi*

PROLOGUE 2

1. THE EARLY GALISTEO BASIN 6

2. THE SOUTHERN TEWA 20

3. PETROGLYPHS 60

4. SPANISH *ENTRADAS* 80

5. A REMOTE COLONY 100

6. A MEXICAN GRANT 130

7. AN AMERICAN TERRITORY 152

8. THE COWBOY TRADITION 172

9. A TWENTIETH–CENTURY RANCH 192

EPILOGUE 230

Citation and Quotation Credits *237*

Photograph and Illustration Credits *247*

References Cited *251*

Index *257*

FOREWORD

IN NEW MEXICO between the Sandia Mountains and the Sangre de Cristo Range and the Rio Grande and the High Plains, lie the great expanses of the Galisteo Basin and the San Cristóbal Ranch. The rolling grasslands, the low mesas with their scrubby forests of piñon and juniper, dissected by canyons and arroyos, have been home to many peoples and cultures over the last several millennia. They have all left their traces.

Burned and ashy soil and cracked rocks of an ancient hearth, a mano and slab metate, dart and arrow points, and fragments of chipped obsidian and chert mark places where the first people camped, hunted, and gathered wild foods. Scattered potsherds and large mounds formed by the collapsed stone walls of ruined rooms mark the large towns of the later Pueblo Indians. These Southern Tewa farmers planted corn fields, and the landscape is dotted with small cairns that marked their shrines and sacred places. The many petroglyphs and rock paintings they made near the old villages, on prominent topographic features and in secluded shelters, are symbols that condense a Pueblo perception and description of the cosmos. These symbols describe supernaturals, the need for rain for fields, and sources of strength in war and conflict. In some cases these figures contribute to the power of the supernatural forces believed to reside in the places where they are pictured. The landscape was an integral part of the Pueblo world.

With the discovery of the New World and eventual settlement of New Mexico by the Spanish in the seventeenth century, the Pueblo way of life was significantly disrupted. After the Pueblo Revolt of 1680—against oppressors who had foisted upon them economic burdens and a new ideology at the expense of the old—the Pueblos fled the Galisteo Basin. The following years were tumultuous and unsettled, and marauding bands of Comanches were among those who wandered through. Although Tewas resettled at Galisteo in 1706, they were plagued by disease and Comanches, finally leaving after 1782. It wasn't until 1799 that the first Hispanic settler put down roots in the Galisteo Basin, and in 1827 the San Cristóbal Grant was established. The rolling grasslands became pasture for herds of sheep, goats, and cattle, and stone–walled animal pens are still extant. Since 1851, the lands of the San Cristóbal Grant have been in Anglo hands, and today it is staged by cattle ranchers. A major highway divides the ranch lands, which are defined by barbed wire and handsome steel gates that parallel the pavement. Except for a few families who maintain the ranch, the land is empty of people. Fences partition the land into large pastures. Small earthen dams catch runoff, and windmills reached by dirt roads provide water for the cattle that now wander through the washes and over the grassy plains and rolling hillsides under the ever–watchful eyes of the petroglyphs.

This changing kaleidoscope of human history within the boundaries of the San Cristóbal Ranch, the rich human drama that has taken and is still taking place in the Galisteo, is the subject of Christina Mednick's story. This story describes a succession of events through time acted out by contrasting cultures, presided over by different gods, and motivated by diverse goals. This is no dry history but a search into the complex cultural heritage that goes straight to the heart of the people themselves who were and are creators of the story of the Galisteo Basin. Mednick's saga is enlivened by the inclusion of Tewa poetry, songs, and prayers, quotes from the journals of explorers and travelers, cowboy lyrics, and personal accounts. Thus the past becomes the present.

The history that unfolds in this volume is a microcosm of New Mexico's history. In one sense it might be viewed as another approach to telling New Mexico's story. By focusing on a single locale, Mednick explores the past and present of this state in depth. As she develops her account through time, she uses the threads that reach out beyond the ranch to tie San Cristóbal's history into the larger historical context.

Yet it is a story about a place, sensitively written. It is the spirit of the place, too, that has been important in the lives and thinking of the Tewas, the Hispanics, and the ranchers, all the people who have lived and continue to live within these boundaries and whose horizons have been marked by the same mesas and mountains from time immemorial.

Polly Schaafsma
Spring 1995
Santa Fe, New Mexico

I AM PLEASED TO INTRODUCE CHRISTINA MEDNICK'S BOOK on the prehistory and history of the San Cristóbal Ranch as our first in a series of books on past life in New Mexico. The San Cristóbal Ranch possesses the essence of natural beauty, archaeological marvels, and historic events that define the Galisteo Basin. Christina illustrates these elements through striking photographs and gives an account of past and present life on the ranch through the use of anthropological and historical studies as well as personal observations. The tale that follows was eight thousand years in the making—from the first hunters and gatherers roaming through the region to the communities and ranches of today. Set against a backdrop of incredible terrestrial beauty, the story is both sad and remarkable.

In addition to her colorful photographs of the ranch and its environs, Christina's work is the first to summarize the history of the people who have lived, and those who still dwell, in the Galisteo Basin. As a researcher who is forever looking for historical accounts of small New Mexico communities and regions that rarely receive full coverage by scholars, I am delighted to publish a book that will allow others to easily read the story of this important area of the state. The story is made even more cordial through Christina's perceptive photographs which give the historical narrative a sense of place. I hope that the reader finds her work as informative and enjoyable as I have.

Tim Maxwell
Director, Office of Archaeological Studies
Spring 1995
Santa Fe, New Mexico

ACKNOWLEDGMENTS

Many People helped create this book. I am grateful to John Ware, David Noble, Albert Schroeder, Alfonso Ortiz, and Orlando Romero for their generous help in guiding my research. Polly Schaafsma, Frances Levine, and Richard Lang all provided invaluable criticism and comments as the manuscript progressed. Ken Scott, Wesley Layman, and Toby Herbst shared their acute observations and knowledge about San Cristóbal's rich flora, fauna, and topography, and were teachers as well as guides. My thanks to those who gave their time freely to answer questions and tell me about their lives: Harper and Elsie McFarland, Jeff Bilberry, José Ortiz y Pino III, Arlin and Teri Talbot, and Terry, Jerrie, and T. C. Pilley.

I have been extremely fortunate to work with the staff and associates of the Museum of New Mexico's Office of Archaeological Studies. I am indebted to Tim Maxwell for his early interest in the manuscript and his unflagging support and help throughout. Robin Gould, as editor, has made contributions above and beyond the call of duty. I have learned much from her knowledge, discriminating eye, committment to the project, and negotiating skills. Deborah Reade has contributed beautiful and precise cartography, and Jim Mafchir's dedication, design, and production skills have been essential.

Many friends supported and encouraged the effort to complete this book: Laura Bank Forest and Kay Calvin; Charlotte Evans Scavone, Sharon Chang Redfern, Edward Wagner, Betty Luboff, and Cathy Layman; Blanche Mednick, Audrey Denenberg, and Marvin Mednick.

It is not possible to acknowledge each person in my community of like–minded friends, but I am indebted to all of them. I especially wish to thank our teachers.

I am grateful to my siblings, John Singleton, Will Singleton, Jim Singleton, Diana Singleton, and Pamela Clinton Singleton, and to my aunt, Anne Wood, for their interest and caring. A special thanks to Diana for her early research, which laid the groundwork for my own, and to Will, for being my first photography teacher and introducing me to the technique and beauty of this medium.

My husband, Murray Mednick, has given me a real gift through his supportive faith in me all through this project.

And finally, my great appreciation goes to my parents, Carolyn and Henry Singleton. My father first suggested the idea of a photographic book about San Cristóbal back in 1987; the project grew from that. The support and encouragement of both my parents made this book possible; and this one good idea has led to a multitude of other adventures and worlds; for this, and more, I will always be grateful.

SAN CRISTÓBAL

Voices and Visions of the Galisteo Basin

PROLOGUE

THE SKY IS A BRILLIANT BLUE and the "cloudbeings," as the Tewa called them, are moving in from the north, stately and white over the Sangre de Cristo Mountains. My 4-wheel-drive van bumps over the dry red road as I look for the marker, a sign on a large boulder at the foot of this rocky outcrop that will point the way. There it is, small but clear, a spiral with its tail pointing up, pecked into the sandstone slab hundreds of years ago. It seems to call, "Up! Here!" I climb out of the van and hike up through the craggy rocks, now and then seeing other small markers: a snake, a face, a simple star. The sunlight is clean and strong, unfiltered by smog, and a light breeze keeps the insects away.

Reaching a grassy ledge, I pause to catch my breath and look around in the silence. To the west is the Cerro Pelón, with Sandia Mountain and the Ortiz range behind it. To the south and east the mesas and meadows of the Galisteo Basin, dotted with piñon and juniper, ripple with summer grass. I turn back to the north, following a faint dirt path up to my first resting place, a smooth boulder where I can sit facing a vertical 8-foot slab completely covered with crea-

tures, signs, and symbols. There are snakes, lightning bolts, one and two-horned masks, turkeys, cornstalks, lizards, and stars. All were laboriously etched into the rock between 1,500 and 300 years ago. No one really knows what they mean. Many call them art; some call them writing. Most agree that their meaning is often religious. Theories abound, and even the modern Tewa, those who will communicate with researchers, admit that much of the old knowledge has been lost, and stand speculating before the mystery along with the rest of us.

As I continue along the path I come to other walls covered with unknown beings: here a zig-zag serpent with a horned head, there a robed figure in a tall, pointed hat like an Egyptian pharoah's. The path turns steep, and I step over a face with a grimacing mouth, full of pointed teeth. Finally I round the bend that reveals the "painted cave." It is actually a shallow hollow of pale sandstone, with faded red and yellow stars and masklike faces haloed by ochre feathers. The cave is up above the path, accessible only with great difficulty. Someone from the recent past has evidently surmounted the odds; his name is scrawled near the faces. Perhaps he has desecrated a holy place; perhaps he has only made himself part of a larger story.

My favorite place to sit is just southwest of this cave. It's a cluster of massive, dark boulders that overlook the pale green valley, the mesas and bluffs that stretch off to the horizon, the ribbon of highway appearing between the hills. The Tewa pueblo below, buried so long that only gentle oblong mounds show its shape, is just out of view.

I love this place, not only because it is beautiful and wild and still, but because I feel the spirit of others who loved the land and sky in a much deeper and more consistent way than I am capable of. They honored the land, and the forces that created and sustained it, with their whole lives. Of course, "Anglos" who wax enthusiastic about the Indian way of life are frequently called romantics. Perhaps this accusation is true. But I think that the idealization of Native American life may spring from an instinctive recognition that this culture had something very real at its core: a profound understanding of our human connection to the earth and the forces of the universe, an understanding that we of the twentieth century have somehow lost.

If we could regain even the rudiments of this Native American perspective, becoming visionary not as impractical romantics but as pragmatists concerned for our own survival, perhaps we might find a way back to the wholeness we long for.

CHAPTER 1

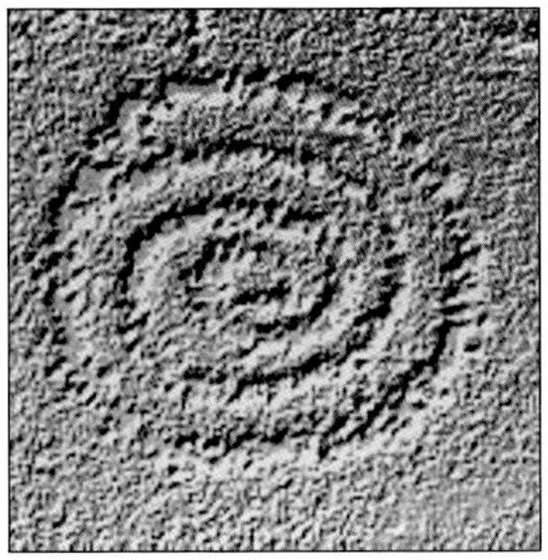

THE EARLY GALISTEO BASIN

San Cristóbal Ranch has carried many names. In nineteenth-century America it was called the E. W. Eaton Grant; in Mexican times, the *Rancho del Pueblo de San Cristoval*. Earlier it bore the names of Pueblo villages, like *Yam-p'-ham-ba*[1] and *Tze-man Tu-o*; earlier still it was a nameless roaming ground for great extinct mammals. It has been home to Native Americans, Spaniards, Mexicans, Hispanics, and now, Anglo-Americans.

About 22 miles south of Santa Fe, New Mexico, and 35 miles east of the Rio Grande, the San Cristóbal lands are part of the Galisteo Basin. The terrain of the basin varies from rugged mesas and arroyos to meadows and rolling plains. The land transforms itself seasonally: in July and August, violent thunderstorms drench the red earth; in autumn, brilliant green grasses and patches of purple and yellow wildflowers appear; in winter, snowstorms hang the piñon and cedars with icicles; and in spring, the land dries to brown under a cloudless sky.

San Cristóbal Ranch embraces the remains of many cultures. Perhaps most significant are six Southern Tewa pueblos buried on the land. These are San Cristóbal Pueblo, Pueblo Colorado, Pueblo Largo, Pueblo Shé, Colina Verde, and an unnamed recent discovery. Five of these villages flourished and declined

Editor's note: *All bibliographic citations to the narrative and to the footnotes are located at the end of the volume and are referred to by page number or footnote number.*

1. *Yam-p'-ham-ba* was the original Tewa name for San Cristóbal Pueblo. It may mean "narrow belt or strip of willows." *Tze-man Tu-o* was the Tewa name for Pueblo Colorado, another of the ancient villages on what is now ranch land. As written, *Tze-man Tu-o* is untranslatable, however Harrington states that *Tsemanto'i* means "place where the eagle's hand or claw is inside or in."

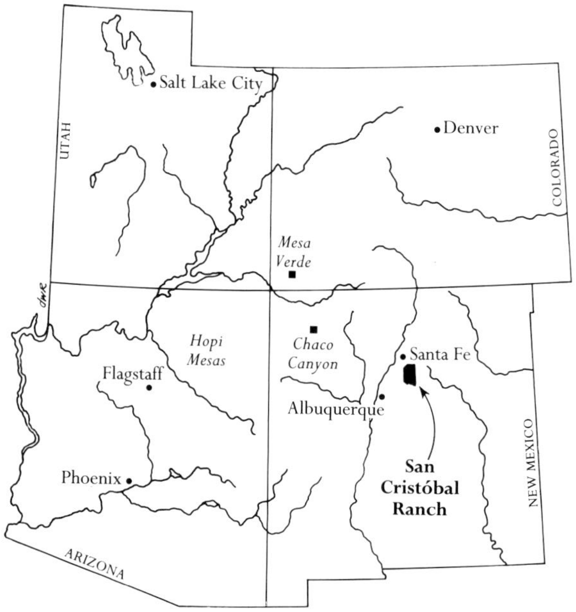

before Europeans ever arrived; San Cristóbal Pueblo was the only one to survive into the Spanish era. Still, thousands of Pueblo Indians, many generations, once lived in these adobe dwellings. Since the Indians' departure, no other group has settled the land in such numbers, and the ruined homes and kivas of these people remain largely unexplored. (Beyond the borders of the ranch lie three other major towns of the Southern Tewa: Galisteo, San Lázaro, and San Marcos.)

All of San Cristóbal's inhabitants have left their traces here. Some are easy to identify, like Tewa pottery sherds or the ruined Spanish chapel. Others, such as the crumbling stone walls near several pueblos, need more archaeological research to determine their makers. And some, such as certain rock art images, are fairly easy to attribute to specific cultural groups or time periods, but leave us baffled as to meaning. Because this intriguing land is still so unspoiled, layers and layers of the past lie waiting for the careful observer.

The story of San Cristóbal began a long time ago. Herds of now-extinct animals—mastodons, mammoths, great bison, and sloth—lived all over what is today New Mexico and roamed the Galisteo Basin in a wetter and cooler environment than that of today.

Current scientific opinion holds that the first humans reached the Southwest about 12,000 B.C. Many scholars believe early Paleoindians crossed over the Bering Straight when it was a passable land bridge several times between 23,000 and 8000 B.C., and that these people probably migrated southward over many centuries. But some contemporary Native Americans[2] say that according to their traditional oral histories, their ancestors have been here much longer. (The radiocarbon dating techniques that determined scholars' time estimates have also been questioned recently, and publicized evidence has shown that these techniques have produced results that may be off by as much as 3,500 years.)

Paleoindians were clearly in the Galisteo Basin by 6000 B.C. or even earlier; future research may provide more precise information about their time of arrival.[3] (Hunting sites elsewhere in New Mexico have revealed primitive weapons and mammoth bones that date back as far as 9500 B.C.)[4] Archaeologists discovered what appears to be a bison lookout station here that may date from around 6000 B.C.; they believe buffalo may still have roamed the basin then.

By 3000 B.C. a few small bands of hunter-gatherers were living in the basin. These nomadic people followed the herds of mule deer and antelope, making regular base camps along the Galisteo Creek where they foraged for wild plants. Elsewhere in the Southwest, many tribes were interacting and expanding, but the basin population increased only gradually. Seed grinding tools appeared

2. I have chosen to use both names—Native Americans and Indians—for the original inhabitants of North America.

3. Richard W. Lang, noted archaeologist and anthropologist, and authority on the Galisteo Basin, comments, "Earlier Paleoindians were likely in the ranch area prior to this time [6000 B.C.], but the earliest artifact known *is* the broken Eden point from a hunting overview site. An even earlier point (Agate Basin—7500–6500 B.C.) has been identified from the uplands fairly close to Ojo de la Vaca [the northern boundary of the ranch] along the margin of Glorieta Mesa. A. H. Warren informed me that she found chipped stone artifacts diagnostic of the Llano Culture (Clovis Complex, 9500–9000 B.C.) in a rock shelter now buried under the fill of the Galisteo Dam."

4. Evidence of man that has been radiocarbon dated between 33,000 and 15,000 B.C. has been found in Sandia Cave northeast of Albuquerque. This evidence has been disputed, however. Both archaeology and anthropology are currently undergoing self-questioning and changes in methodology and approach, and new discoveries are always being made; with this in mind, it is probably safe to say that our present conclusions will be modified, or possibly even turned upside down.

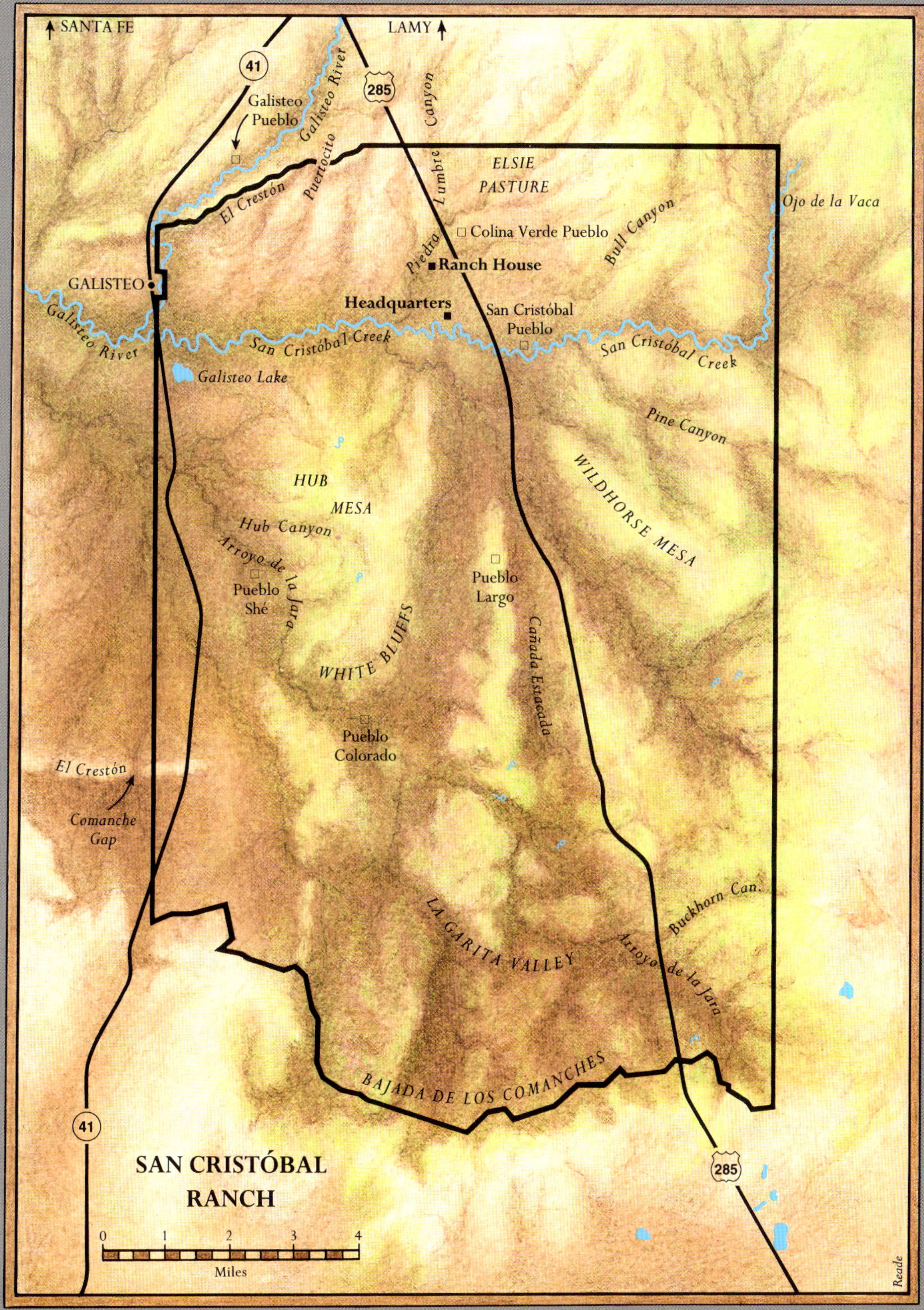

The original description of the grant's boundaries is as follows: "On the north, by the summit of the crestón; on the east, by the Ojo de la Vaca; on the south, by the Bajada de los Comanches; on the West, a point opposite the middle crestón" (translated from the original Spanish document).

San Cristóbal Canyon in July.

Broken pieces, or sherds, of prehistoric Pueblo pottery litter the ground near Pueblo Shé.

around 2500 B.C., and obsidian tools were found from the period 1800–1500 B.C. Basin people may have obtained or bartered these from Jemez Mountain bands to the northwest.

Around 1500 B.C. farming practices spread into the area, and the agricultural revolution began. But life in New Mexico changed very slowly, and it was several centuries before farming took firm root. (The adoption of agriculture used to be viewed as a natural part of the "evolution" of societies, but scholars have shown that hunter-gatherers actually invest less time and labor in subsistence activities than do agriculturalists; this may partially explain the slow change in the Southwest.) As the population grew, the people gradually turned to farming, perhaps initially to supplement gathered foods in lean years.

Much of the Galisteo Basin has yet to be explored archaeologically, so our knowledge of its early history remains sketchy. As of this writing, very few sites show evidence of people before 1500 B.C. But from 40 B.C. to A.D. 400, there are numerous hunting lookout stations, camps with stone hearths, and possible shrines. Many of these are in the San Cristóbal area. Basin expert Richard Lang believes that ancient tribes here moved seasonally, growing crops in spring and summer at established campsites, hunting and gathering wild plants all year round. These people may have created the oldest petroglyphs in the basin, and Lang says their later art (about A.D. 200–700) reveals "strong cultural ties with the Desert Mogollon peoples" who lived to the south, in what is now southern New Mexico, eastern Arizona, and northern Mexico.

Still, the Galisteo Basin seems to have been a relatively remote area during these centuries. Until about A.D. 1050, people in surrounding areas used the basin mainly as an alternate place to hunt and forage, and as a trade route, possibly for the turquoise, malachite, and lead they mined in the Cerrillos hills at this time.

Meanwhile, less than 200 miles to the northwest, an advanced tribal culture was coming into full flower. Its people, called the Anasazi,[5] would eventually leave their mark on many nearby areas, including the Galisteo Basin. The Anasazi towns began as small villages of pithouses (partly subterranean round or oval structures) around the fifth century A.D. The Anasazi grew beans, squash, corn, and cotton, and made ceramics, bows and arrows, and fine wickerwork (which inspired the earliest Anasazis' anthropological name, Basketmakers). Sometime in the ninth century they started to build the first true pueblos, rectangular stone and adobe buildings like those of today.[6]

Soon after this, there was a sudden burst of activity in architecture, engineering, trade, and social organization; it continued nearly 300 years. In New Mexico's Chaco Canyon, the Anasazi built many pueblos, eight of them up to five stories in height; scholars believe they housed thousands of people at Chaco's peak. The Chacoans created dams, canals, huge kivas (ceremonial cham-

5. The term "Anasazi" comes from a Navajo word introduced in 1936 by archaeologist A. V. Kidder. He mistakenly understood that the term meant "old people." The word actually translates as "enemy ancestors," which, from the Navajo point of view, makes sense, but from the Pueblo perspective seems an unfortunate choice of names.

6. Richard Lang has pointed out that, "by the A.D. 500s, at least, the culture of the Rio Grande from the vicinity of Albuquerque northward was also Anasazi, albeit with some minor Mogollon elements derived from their neighbors to the south and southwest. They were, of course, rustics by comparison with peoples of the major culture centers of the west and northwest, like Chaco."

bers), and an extensive and unusual road system to link their towns and "great houses" to the surrounding villages. It is possible that the advanced cultures of Mexico and Central America may have somehow been linked to the Anasazi flowering. Several of these ancient states evolved trade networks that extended over vast distances; perhaps much of their technological knowledge and many religious beliefs came north in this way.

But in about A.D. 1125, a prolonged drought began and, for reasons we still don't fully understand, the Anasazi slowly abandoned their communities. Initially they abandoned only their lower-elevation towns, moving to higher sites where more rain seemed likely.[7] The drought persisted and by A.D. 1300 both Chaco Canyon and Mesa Verde (another large cluster of Anasazi villages and religious centers, many built on the mesas and cliffs of southwestern Colorado) were empty.

Where did the Anasazi and all their knowledge go? No one knows exactly, though many scholars have concluded that both the Hopi and the Keresan-speaking Pueblos are their descendants. Lang states that "there is really no question at this point that the Anasazi and the early historic Pueblos of New Mexico and Arizona form one continuum. The question is which prehistoric cultures hook up with which historic peoples and how?" Some believe that Mesa

A prehistoric hunting lookout station overlooking San Cristóbal Creek.

A natural or man-made rain collector atop the White Bluffs.

7. Archaeologist Fred Plog theorizes that the abandonment was caused partially by the drought, but also by a combination of disease and warfare. As the population centralized in the larger cities, the economy became strained, and the Anasazi built larger and larger systems for water and erosion control. The whole social structure became heavily dependent on this agricultural system, yet, as Plog says, "variation in rainfall is simply too great in the area for intensive agriculture." A vicious cycle probably began as drought and nomadic raiding forced more and more people into the great centers, straining the system even more, and finally the area was abandoned for locales nearer to water.

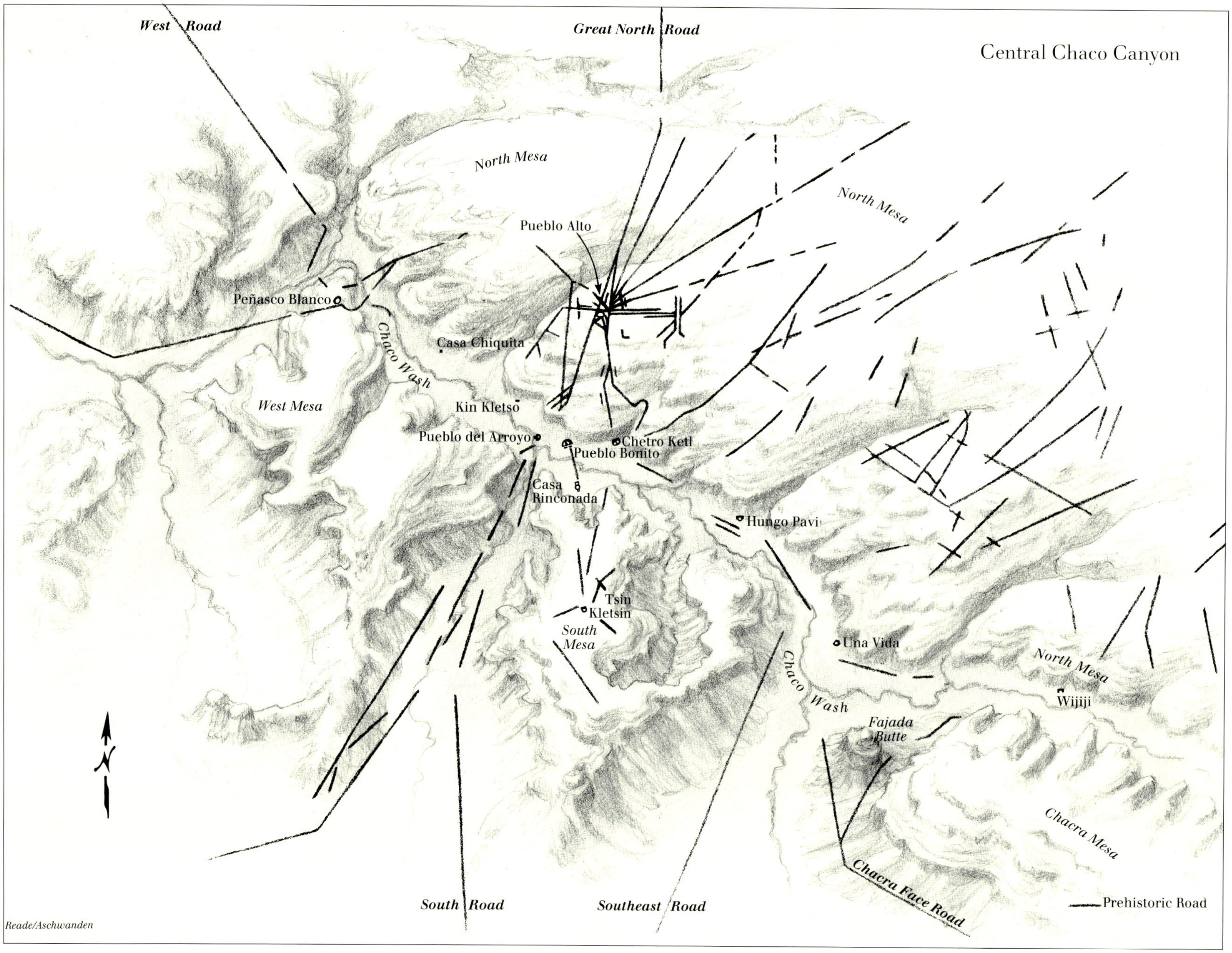
Central Chaco Canyon
West Road
Great North Road
North Mesa
North Mesa
Pueblo Alto
Peñasco Blanco
Chaco Wash
Casa Chiquita
West Mesa
Kin Kletso
Pueblo del Arroyo
Chetro Ketl
Pueblo Bonito
Casa Rinconada
Hungo Pavi
Tsin Kletsin
South Mesa
Una Vida
North Mesa
Chaco Wash
Wijiji
Fajada Butte
Chacra Mesa
Chacra Face Road
South Road
Southeast Road
Prehistoric Road
Reade/Aschwanden

The Chaco Phenomenon

Some scholars now believe that Chaco was a powerful ritual and economic locus for the Anasazi, a center for thousands of surrounding villagers who may have made periodic pilgrimages there. Of the many mysteries surrounding this culture, the Anasazi roads may be the most puzzling. Fanning out from Chaco Canyon in wide and absolutely straight lines, there are over 400 miles of them. What might have been their purpose in a time when there were neither wheels nor draft animals?

In *New Light on Chaco Canyon*, the prehistorian W. James Judge presents a fascinating theory. He believes (as do several other scholars) that Chaco Canyon was not a permanent residence but rather a powerful ritual and economic locus where goods were redistributed. This would explain the scarcity of burials in the area. Apparently, Chaco was a center for turquoise artifact manufacturing, as huge amounts of turquoise in different phases of processing have been discovered there, along with turquoise workshops. Judge theorizes that this control of the turquoise trade helped Chaco to evolve into a major center, with turquoise assuming religious importance. Archaeologists have also discovered evidence of large feasts and ritual use of imported ceramic vessels.

More support for Judge's argument is the fact that the amount of available farm land was nowhere near enough to support the numbers of people who would have occupied all the Chaco residences. Judge believes that the apartment complexes were built rather "to accommodate periodic influxes of large numbers of people," that is, pilgrims from all the surrounding areas who were dependent on Chaco as a cultural and economic capitol (as many as seventy communities). These villagers must have contributed their labor to the system, helping to construct the intricate stone walls of the central pueblos, hauling the 200,000 beams that went into them, and building the roads themselves. The roads, Judge believes, were intended not for transportation per se, but for formal pilgrimages from all the outlying areas. Thus, the precise rayed pattern of the roads would have had religious significance, and their width would have accommodated large processions.

Wall at Pueblo Bonito, Chaco Canyon (Charles Lummis, photographer).

Kivas at Pueblo Bonito, Chaco Canyon (photographer unknown).

- Pueblos
  - Rio Grande
    - Keresan (unique): San Felipe, Santa Ana, Zia, Cochiti, Santo Domingo, Laguna, Acoma
    - Tanoan (Kiowa-Tanoan family)
      - Tiwa (Northern and Southern): Isleta, Sandia, Taos, Picuris
      - Tewa (Northern and Southern): Nambe, Tesuque, San Ildefonso, San Juan, Santa Clara, Hano (on Hopi First Mesa)
      - Towa: Jemez
      - Piro (extinct)
  - Zuni (unique)
  - Hopi (Shoshonean language of the Uto-Aztecan family. There are 8 Hopi villages on 3 Hopi Mesas, not including Hano.)

The diverse Pueblo languages evolved over thousands of years. Some seem to be unique and unrelated to any others, while some are clearly linked to areas as geographically distant as Central Mexico. The Tanoan languages are part of the Kiowa-Tanoan family. Linguists do not know where the original speakers lived, but many believe it was in the northern United States, in line with Pueblo tradition of a northern origin. Kiowa speakers split off from the other Tanoan groups about 3,000 years ago; roughly 500 years later the three branches of Tiwa, Tewa, and Towa had evolved. Tewas then split into northern and southern groups, but their language remained common, differing only in dialect.

Keresan is a distinct language with little similarity to any other tongue. Zuni, too, is unique. The place of origin for both is unknown, but some believe it to be the Four Corners area.

The Hopi language is part of the Uto-Aztecan family, which many scholars believe originated around the Arizona-Sonora border, then spread both north and south.

Verdeans migrated into the Galisteo Basin, merging with the Tanoan-speaking peoples already there.[8] Scholars have had great difficulty tracing these migration paths because, as Fred Plog explains it, "people, not cultures, moved" and in such disruptive times as the abandonment of great centers "individuals, families, groups, and communities probably moved in incredibly complex patterns."

In any case, just as the Anasazi settlements were being abandoned, there was a major influx of people into the Galisteo Basin. At first the newcomers built small pithouse or pueblo-style villages, planting their crops nearby. Gradually people began to coalesce into the larger villages. As their pueblos grew, often expanding out from central plazas, the villagers built water-control systems, too. Lang believes that all these developments had a strong "Anasazi cast" and that the rock art of the period also mirrors the Anasazi culture.

Between A.D. 1100 and 1300, several different tribes lived in or passed through the basin, slowly creating an intricate web of cultures. This long process is still a mystery to scholars, with only a few clues, most of which lead straight to new puzzles. But after about 1300, the picture comes into sharper focus. By this time the primary inhabitants of the Galisteo Basin (and the San Cristóbal Ranch area) were clearly the Southern Tewa, a Pueblo tribe.

Originally the Southern Tewa and their relatives, the Northern Tewa, had been all one linguistic group, but at some prehistoric time they split into two tribes. After the split, the Southern Tewa lived mostly in the Galisteo Basin. The Northern Tewa lived close to the Rio Grande, north of what is now Santa Fe. But even after they separated, the Northern and Southern Tewa continued to speak the same language and live in much the same way, with similar customs and ceremonies. In early historic times, the Southern Tewa were also called Tanos. Tano is a Tewa word meaning "near the sun," or loosely interpreted, "Tewa who live nearer the sun," that is, to the south. Numerous Spanish documents, in particular, refer to the Southern Tewa as Tanos.

Exactly where the Tewas as a whole originated is another mystery. Theories abound, but some scholars now believe that ancestors of the Tewas have been in the Rio Grande Valley for at least 2,000 years.

Tewas still live in the Rio Grande Valley today, in the pueblos of Nambe, San Ildefonso, Santa Clara, San Juan, Tesuque, and elsewhere. However, the majority of these people are Northern Tewa. The Southern Tewa of the San Cristóbal Ranch area had a tumultuous history in the seventeenth century, and many did not survive. Disease, famine, war, and persecution took a heavy toll on their tribe, and events finally forced them to leave the Galisteo Basin and splinter into refugee bands who blended, to a greater or lesser extent, into other pueblos. Thus their descendants today all reflect a mixture of heritages. There is no pure Southern Tewa thread we can trace.

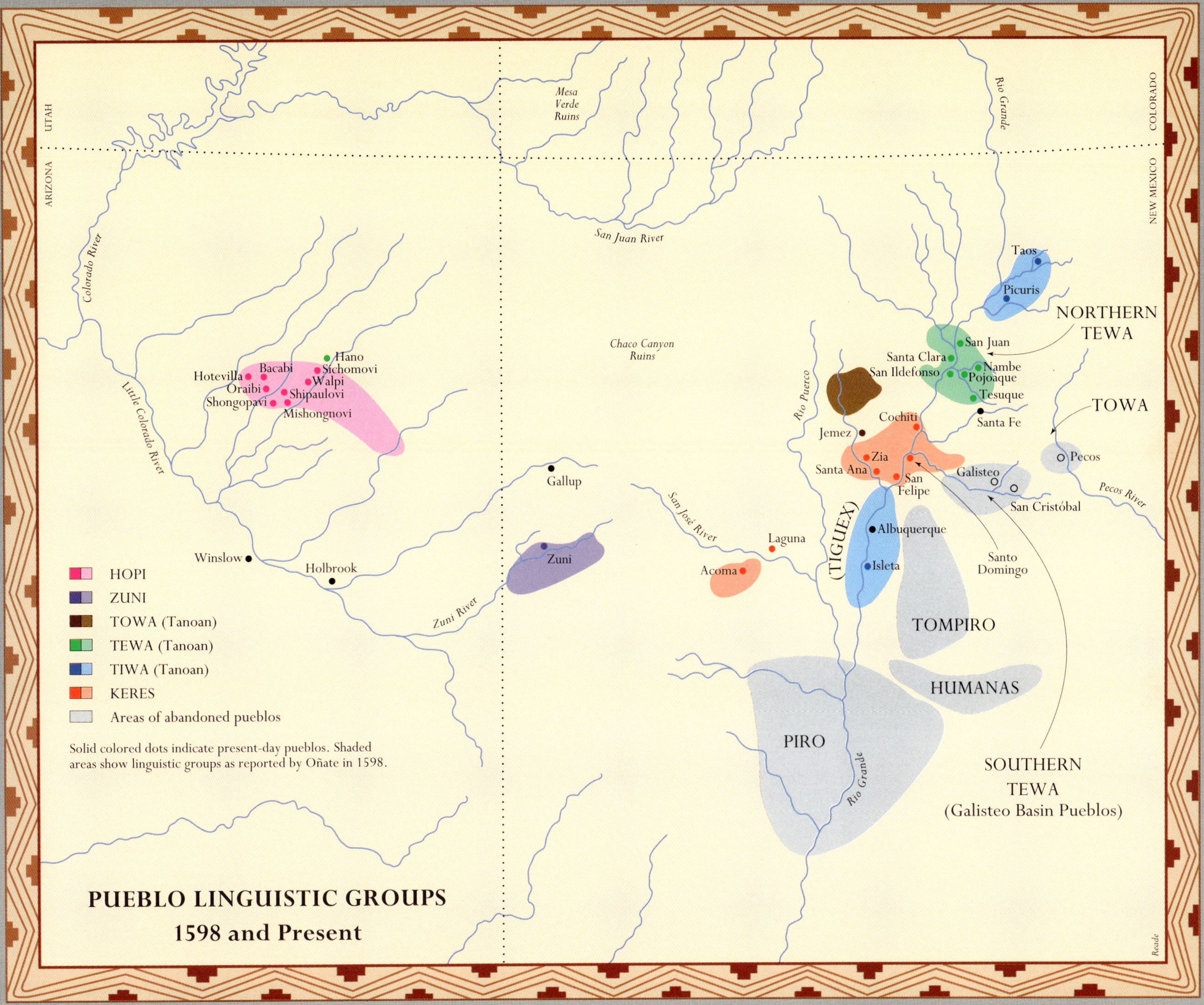

UTAH
ARIZONA
COLORADO
NEW MEXICO
Mesa Verde Ruins
San Juan River
Colorado River
Little Colorado River
Chaco Canyon Ruins
Rio Puerco
Rio Grande
San José River
Zuni River
Pecos River
Hotevilla
Bacabi
Oraibi
Shongopavi
Shipaulovi
Mishongnovi
Walpi
Sichomovi
Hano
Winslow
Holbrook
Gallup
Zuni
Acoma
Laguna
Jemez
Zia
Santa Ana
San Felipe
Cochiti
Santo Domingo
Albuquerque
Isleta
(TIGUEX)
Taos
Picuris
San Juan
Santa Clara
San Ildefonso
Nambe
Pojoaque
Tesuque
Santa Fe
NORTHERN TEWA
TOWA
Pecos
Galisteo
San Cristóbal
TOMPIRO
HUMANAS
PIRO
SOUTHERN TEWA
(Galisteo Basin Pueblos)
HOPI
ZUNI
TOWA (Tanoan)
TEWA (Tanoan)
TIWA (Tanoan)
KERES
Areas of abandoned pueblos
Solid colored dots indicate present-day pueblos. Shaded areas show linguistic groups as reported by Oñate in 1598.
PUEBLO LINGUISTIC GROUPS
1598 and Present
Reade

Around 1700, some of the San Cristóbal people, along with other Southern Tewas, migrated to First Mesa, now on the Hopi Reservation in Arizona. Their Tewa village, called Hano, is still there today. (The name Hano is probably a variation on the word Tano or, as it was sometimes spelled, Thano.) Tewa elements in Hano customs and ceremonies are pronounced, but sometimes it is difficult to see where Tewa influence stops and Hopi begins. So if we are looking for clues to the lives of the prehistoric San Cristóbal people, since there is almost no documentation of the Southern Tewa way of life, we are probably safest turning to the Northern Tewa tradition for information. As famed Pueblo scholar, Edward P. Dozier, says, "Historical and ethnological data indicate that there was little difference linguistically and culturally between the two Tewa groups [Northern and Southern]."[9] Therefore, in this book I will refer mostly to legends and rituals of the Northern Tewa.

As a result, the picture of Southern Tewa life that follows may not be accurate in every detail. Archaeological investigation holds the only real promise of more conclusive knowledge. Chapter Two is meant to convey a general approach to life common among the Eastern Pueblos.

8. Scholars have used several methods to try to trace the possible paths of migration. Some have tried to correlate past and present cultural features such as ceramics, tools, building styles, and farming methods; others have attempted to follow a linguistic trail. For example, Cordell notes that "at about 1300. . .the production of Galisteo Black-on-white ceramics, which resemble late Mesa Verde Black-on-white [began]."

9. Dozier's conclusion that the Northern and Southern Tewa cultures were very similar is supported by the many remnants of Tewa customs still observable among the people of Hano. In order to stay on course with a description that is likely to be true in most important respects, the following chapter steers away from specific detail and the intricacies of lineage.

CHAPTER 2

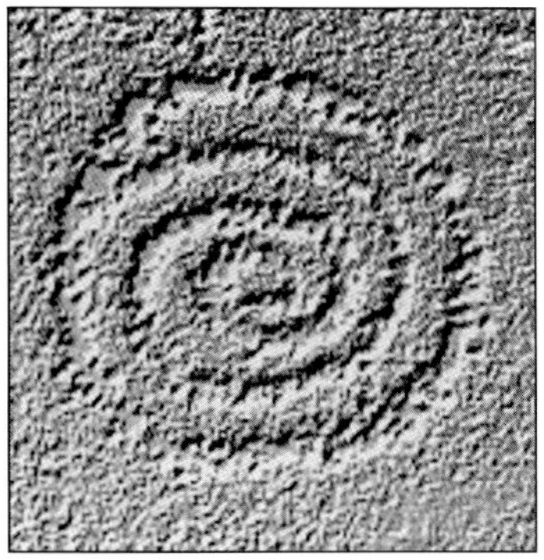

THE SOUTHERN TEWA

The Tewa who live in the Rio Grande Valley today say that they have been here for a long, long time. They, and all Pueblo people, believe that eons ago they emerged from lower worlds beneath the earth's crust. This origin story, which varies from tribe to tribe, resonates throughout every aspect of Pueblo culture and life. Pueblos say their original home was far to the north, and the Tewa call this place *Sipofene*. Here there was no death, and people, gods, and animals all lived together. The Tewa say they came up through this dark, wet underworld through a lake and then began their long migration south.

The story begins in this way: There were two original mothers of the Tewa, Blue Corn Woman and White Corn Maiden. One day they asked a man to find the way to the upper world. He tried each of the four directions but found that "the world above was still *ochu*, 'green,' or 'unripe'." Finally the man went straight up to the "above" where he met fierce animals who first attacked, then magically accepted him, giving him a bow and quiver of arrows. Through this experience he became the first Hunt Chief. The Hunt Chief then picked two

*Indian paint brush (*Castilleja *sp.), native to New Mexico. The root bark was used for black dye, especially for deer skins. The seeds prevent chile pods from spoiling.*

leaders, the Summer Chief and the Winter Chief, to care for the people. The Summer and Winter Chiefs then called upon six pairs of twin brothers, each a different color, called the *Towa é*. One after the other, the brothers went out to the six directions to explore. The blue pair went north, the yellow pair west, the red south, the white east, the dark to the zenith. The multicolored brothers went out last, and they come back describing a rainbow; at this good sign the people came up. When the Summer Chief stepped out onto the ground it was still too soft, but when the Winter Chief came up the earth hardened with frost and the people were able to emerge.

But as they traveled south they discovered that certain things were missing, and they had to return to *Sipofene* four times. On their first return a Medicine Man was created to cure those who had fallen sick. On the second, sacred Clowns (the *Kossa* and *Kwirana*) were brought into being to entertain the people when they grew weary or discouraged. Next the Scalp Chief was created, for warfare, and last, the Women's Society, to help the Scalp Chief.[1] Now they were finally complete, and as they set out again, the Hunt Chief divided them into Summer and Winter People. The Summer People followed their Chief down the west side of the Rio Grande, farming and gathering wild plants for food. The Winter People, who were hunters, went down the east side of the river. The Great Spirit guided both chiefs on these journeys.

The Tewa who told this story concluded, "Each group took twelve steps [made twelve stops] on this journey, and after each step they built a village and stayed for a day. In that time a day was one year." The two groups finally reunited near present-day Ojo Caliente, remaining there for several years. When an epidemic came they left, and six groups of combined Summer and Winter People founded the six present-day Tewa villages.[2]

This story tells much about the Tewas and their world. It reveals attitudes toward time and space which are very different from our present Western approach. For example, there were once *many* Tewa villages, both Northern and Southern, certainly more than six. But this sort of historical detail is not particularly significant to the Tewa. Also, most of the actions in the origin myth take place in groups of four or twelve purely because these numbers are sacred to the Tewa and serve to sanctify the events. (Such compression of fact also serves the purpose of drama and emphasis.) This tendency to compress time and events reveals a belief that symbols are as important as "reality," and perhaps more so. For Pueblos, the subjective dominates the objective, creating a "mythical ordering of life" whereby the significance of the past creates the present and the future.

If these people perceived time and space in a way so foreign to us, how then

1. "Until about a century ago when warfare was still a live activity, members of [the Women's Scalp Society] among the Tewa pueblos met a returning war party, took the enemy scalps from the victorious warriors and wildly chewed the scalps while emitting vindictive epithets at the enemy. Once at the pueblo, the returning warriors and the members of the Women's Scalp Society engaged in a frenzied dance of victory."

Many Native Americans believed scalps contained the enemies' souls. At Zuni, priests used scalp ceremonies to turn enemy spirits into rain-bringers. And "Tewa scalps are called Mist or Light Rain and foretell precipitation. People say, 'We are going to have a little rain, the Scalps are crying.'" Among the Plains Indians, the chief performed a ritual in which he thrust a pole on which scalps were suspended through the opening of his tipi. In this way the souls were released.

2. This simplified account of the Tewa origin myth is paraphrased from Ortiz. Other similar but slightly different accounts have also been recorded. There is great similarity in all Pueblo origin myths, even among tribes with mutually unintelligible languages.

did they see this land they lived on? With its mesas, streams, and arroyos, the San Cristóbal Ranch looks basically the same as it did when the Tewas grew their crops here. It seems to have changed very little over the centuries, especially in relation to the rest of America. But the way we see this country is subtly different than the way Tewas saw it 500 years ago. The land is seen with different eyes.

Can we see San Cristóbal through Tewa eyes?

Santa Fe thistle (Cirsium *sp.), native to New Mexico. This plant, also called "life medicine," is useful as an emetic, to bring down fever, and for smallpox.*

Oh our Mother the Earth, oh our Father the Sky,
Your children are we, and with tired backs
We bring you the gifts that you love.
Then weave for us a garment of brightness;
May the warp be the white light of morning,
May the weft be the red light of evening,
May the fringes be the falling rain,
May the border be the standing rainbow.
Thus weave for us a garment of brightness
That we may walk fittingly where birds sing
That we may walk fittingly where grass is green
Oh our Mother the Earth, oh our Father the Sky!

–*Song of the Sky Loom*[3]

The origin myth seeps into every part of Tewa life, as penetrating as water. Its characters and symbols reappear in the round of ceremonial activities which repeat year after year, forming an ever-turning wheel. At the heart of this cycle is a deep recognition that human beings are a part of the Earth and the forces of nature. From this understanding, a wish appears—a wish to honor and assist nature and the Great Spirit in all ways possible. Thus the highest Tewa ideal is to live in harmony with the world.

Knowledge about the prehistoric Tewa world can come from four directions. One is the accounts of the first Spanish visitors. Another is the body of records of historians, anthropologists, and ethnographers who have studied the group over the last 300 years. A third source is archaeology, both of the past and of the future; its potential in the Galisteo Basin is very promising. And the fourth is the stories, songs, and lives of Tewas today. Because the Pueblos are an extraordinarily traditional people, many basic elements of their village and ritual life today are unchanged since the time of the Spanish explorers.

3. The wish of this song, for a blessing from the Great Spirit so that the singers may "walk fittingly" on the earth, recalls many other Native American prayers, such as the one described by Black Elk in *The Sacred Pipe*: "Everything is *wakan* [holy] that is on our Mother, the earthly source of all life. . . . Help us to walk in a *wakan* manner pleasing to You!"

Overlooking Canyon Ceta and the Pueblo Colorado ruins (green mound at right), from the White Bluffs.

Still, if we are not Tewa ourselves, we can only see the bones of this society. Most likely we will never know its heart. The Tewas who still practice the traditional ways today generally do not wish to reveal what is left of their rituals and drama. For these traditionalists, the old ways are sacred, the core of who they are. Even in ancient times this knowledge was hidden, guarded, and only revealed to the initiated. And much was lost when, beginning about 300 years ago, Tewa priests and medicine men began to die without successors.

But from the bones, the rough outlines of this society now mostly vanished or hidden, we can get a glimpse of who these people were.

Imagine we are in Yam-p'-ham-ba (later called San Cristóbal Pueblo) in the year 1400, in a large town several stories high, spreading out from five plazas. Hills

San Cristóbal Creek after a heavy rain.

and mesas surround us in this alternately gentle and rugged basin land; a shallow creek runs a short walk from our home. There is timber on nearby mesas, land for farming, sandstone for building, and game—rabbit, deer, and antelope—nearby.

Life, however, is not idyllic. There are droughts and lean years, and fierce enemies from the Great Plains who swoop down on the village, plundering the storehouses of patiently gathered crops. Yam-p'-ham-ba is relatively near the plains, so it is a favorite target.

But there are many advantages to this location, and the people stay. Their ancestors have lived here for generations, and the sandstone hills near their pueblo are full of sacred places where they have chiseled powerful images into the rocks.

High on the mesas atop these hills, sentries keep lookout for enemies. From here they gaze down on their village, the center of the world. They see their pueblo as better than any neighboring town, their ceremonies, customs and language, as all superior. They watch the circles of shrines which radiate out from their village, all the beneficent forces which surround and support their world.

The outermost ring of this world is made of four sacred mountains in each of the four directions. Supernatural spirits dwell in lakes or ponds on each mountain, and at the very top of each one is an "earth navel," a powerful center with a tunnel-like connection to the underworld. The *Towa é*, sometimes known as the war gods, live within these mountains and watch over the pueblo from afar.

Closer in is another circle—of four sacred mesa-topped hills. Frightening creatures called *Tsave Yoh* live inside the caves and tunnels of these hills; they are the "masked whippers" who periodically descend on the town to enforce proper behavior.[4] Closest of all are the four shrines loosely bordering the northern, southern, eastern, and western edges of the pueblo. Each shrine is a pile of large rocks in a C–shaped arrangement (with the opening toward the pueblo), and each embodies a force or deity, such as Spider Woman or Ash Youth.[5] When Tewas leave offerings or prayer-feathers at any of these shrines, they must be the correct color: blue or green for the north shrine; yellow for the west; red for the south; and white for the east.

Within the village itself are the plazas where many dances and rituals take place. And at the very center of the pueblo, at its heart, is the "Earth mother earth navel middle place," the prime earth navel. At this holy place the medicine men communicate with the earth, ritually planting the seeds which will reawaken nature each spring.

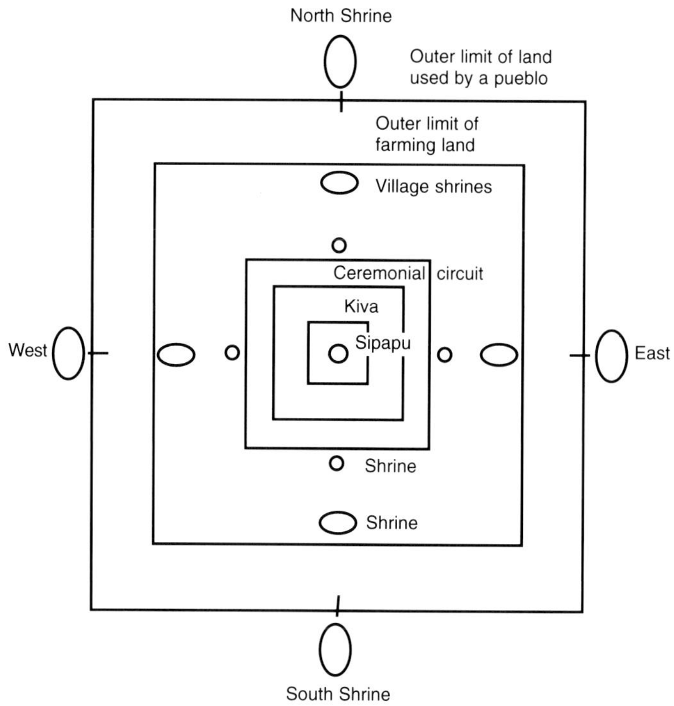

This diagram from Barton Wright's Pueblo Cultures *illustrates the organization of the pueblos in general.* Sipapu *has the same meaning as the Tewa word* Sipofene, *and is meant symbolically.*

4. Actually the *Tsave Yoh* are impersonated by selected village members, but children, and in some cases women, are encouraged to believe them to be real.

5. Ortiz reports that at San Juan Pueblo such shrines are piles of large rocks or a single stone. Lang comments that "at San Cristóbal they are large C-shaped arrangements of rock as well as simple rock pile shrines. Others [as yet undiscovered] may be present."

In the north the cloud flower blossoms,
And now the lightning flashes,
And now the thunder clashes
And now the rain comes down!
A-a-aha, a-a-aha, my little one.

In the west the cloud flower blossoms,
And now the lightning flashes,
And now the thunder clashes,
And now the rain comes down!
A-a-aha, a-a-aha, my little one.

In the south the cloud flower blossoms,
And now the lightning flashes,
And now the thunder clashes,
And now the rain comes down!
A-a-aha, a-a-aha, my little one.

In the east the cloud flower blossoms,
And now the lightning flashes,
And now the thunder clashes,
And now the rain comes down!
A-a-aha, a-a-aha, my little one.

–*The Cloud-Flower Lullaby*[6]

A child born into the Tewa world is welcomed in ancient ways.[7] Two midwives called "naming mothers" assist at its birth, then leave the mother and baby to stay quietly indoors for four days. When relatives come to visit they perform a short ritual with their hands, symbolically gathering in all the evil which could ever befall the child, then throwing it toward the country of their enemies. On the morning of the fourth day the chief naming mother rises before dawn to invoke the spirits of the six directions (north, west, south, east, above, and below) and call upon the *xayeh*, or ancestral spirits which inhabit certain sacred objects kept in her home. She asks the spirits to "make my heart right and guide my thoughts" for the ceremony she is about to perform. Then she and the other naming mother go to the home of the new baby, carrying it outside just as the sun is rising. This is the child's first glimpse of the outer world. The two women hold the child up to the six directions, gathering in blessings and praying to the dawn beings, winter spirits and summer spirits to bring the baby good fortune and fulfillment. Then the chief naming mother calls upon the original Tewa cre-

6. Parsons comments that Pueblo songs "have a magically coercive nature." So in a sense, this Tewa lullaby may be a kind of ritual blessing. The four directions are addressed and great natural forces are invoked to create rain and all its benefits. As in many Tewa songs, the present tense is used as a kind of affirmation: "And now the rain comes down!" As mentioned earlier, the Pueblo sense of time seems to be a kind of continuous present. Thus, "future" events are also described in the present tense.

7. This birth and naming description is adapted from *The Tewa World: Space, Time, Being and Becoming in a Pueblo Society* by Alfonso Ortiz.

Acoowa–Tsirah (Pelican Bird), a Tewa child from San Ildefonso, 1905, by Edward S. Curtis.

Woolly Indian wheat (Plantago *sp.), native to New Mexico. This plant was known as a cure for battle bruises and as a stomach tonic. The nearby Keres people found it allayed headaches and diarrhea. The seeds and leaves were used as food.*

ator mothers, Blue Corn Woman and White Corn Maiden (who give every child its soul at birth) to witness as she gives the child its name. The name could be that of a special ancestor or could recall some aspect of this season or even some quality of this particular morning. In this way the child is brought "in out of the darkness" to become part of the Tewa world.

Somewhere, somewhere
Far away,
What were you at *Sibopay* when you were born?
That is what I am asking,
What am I myself going to be?

I'm asking,
What am I?
Where am I going?
Where do I come from?

–Part of a long chant sung at Midwinter Ceremony in Hano, the Tewa village on First Mesa, Hopi[8]

Before a Tewa child is one year old, it joins either the Summer or Winter People, continuing the tradition begun on the emergence. If the baby's father is of the Summer People, his mother will bring him on a certain day in early spring to the home of the Summer Chief, where the Water-Giving Ceremony will be performed for all new Summer babies.[9]

The village Hunt Chief, dressed as the original Hunt Chief of the emergence myth, leads each mother and child into a special inner room in the Summer Chief's home. During the night the Summer Chief and his helpers have created a ceremonial sand painting on his sanctuary's earthen floor, and built an altar of sacred fetishes and Summer symbols. Black, green, and yellow (the colors of summer clouds, grass, and sun) dominate the room.

When all the mothers and babies are inside, the Chief's women helpers take the infants. The Chief then prays over the children one by one, giving each a drink of sacred water and medicine he has prepared. Every baby also gets a new name, but this name is only used much later in special ceremonial circumstances.

Now the child is more fully a part of this world where many things come in pairs—pairs of opposites, pairs of complements—always interacting and bal-

8. Albert Yava, a Tewa-Hopi author, says that the chant "repeats how you are born, how you grow into childhood and get to be mature, and how you are supposed to conduct yourself until the Great Spirit calls you." *Sibopay* is another variation on the name of origin previously referred to as *Sipofene*. In spite of the diversity of Pueblo languages, all the tribes' names for the origin lake are similar.

9. There is some question about the antiquity of the entire "water-giving" rite described here. Ortiz notes that Dozier describes this rite as either discontinued or never practiced at Santa Clara, a Northern Tewa village. But Ortiz goes on to say that there is evidence from early Spanish accounts that something very similar to the water-giving rite did exist at San Juan.

ancing each other. As she grows, she learns that the Summer Chief *(Poetunyo)* rules the pueblo from the spring to the fall equinox, and that the Winter Chief *(Oyike)* takes over the rest of the year, directing and guiding all the activities—social, political, and spiritual—of the villagers, his "children." Her people see all things as belonging to either Summer or Winter (or the middle); as either hot or cold. Winter and its people are said to embody qualities of the north, like masculinity, hardness, cold, the mineral world, and turquoise; Summer People are seen as more akin to the south, to softer plant life like squash, to warmth and femininity. Her elders believe that both are necessary to each other, that it is only natural that the people should be divided in this way, for such duality mirrors all life on earth.

Towards Leaf Lake we are going
Under the farthest lightning we are going,
Under the thunder we are going,
Under the rain and the dew we are going,
Even now we are arriving.

–Lake Song of the Tewa K'osa[10]

A newborn Tewa child comes to this world from the watery spirit realm; by age six or seven it has gradually become more human, or as the Tewas say, more *seh t'a.* All ordinary humans are known as *seh t'a*, which literally means "dry food" or "dry matter." This idea refers back to the time of the emergence when the world, at first green and unripe, hardened and dried as the people came out.[11]

As the child grows, it has various possibilities. It may remain one of the ordinary Tewas, who are also known as Weed or Trash People. When they die they become "Dry Food Who Are No Longer" and their souls are thought to inhabit the shrines around the village or the *xayeh* (sacred objects such as fossilized bones and seashells which people keep in their homes).[12]

But village elders select certain individuals from among the Dry Food People to become *Towa é*, which means "persons" or "youths." These people act as earthly representatives of the *Towa é* of the origin story, the six pairs of brother-gods who led the people out of *Sipofene* and now stand guard at the mountain earth navels. The human *Towa é* coordinate most of the pueblo rituals and must also protect the pueblo from outer and inner enemies; for example, they often stand guard on the plains during village ceremonies and they chastise anyone

10. This song is from the Tewa pueblo of Nambe, and is sung by the K'osa or Kossa, who are sacred clowns. All lakes lead down to the Underworld. It is described as "a very sad magic song of the Tewa K'osa which all the Indians know but are afraid to sing. It means the K'osa are going in under a sacred lake to the place where the rains and the lightnings are made . . ."

11. Ortiz makes interesting comments regarding the term *seh t'a*. He explains that *seh* means food and *t'a* means hardened or dry, but that in ritual use the meaning of *seh* is expanded to include all matter in general. Would this imply that the Tewa consider "matter" and "food" as interchangeable—that all matter is "food" on some level?

12. Ortiz says there is no firm consensus today on exactly where Dry Food souls go, perhaps because of the general agreement that it is unwise to remain a Dry Food person for life.

Grinding or water-collecting holes on a flat-topped boulder near San Cristóbal Pueblo.

suspected of being a witch. Just as in the creation myth, human *Towa é* always carry out actions in pairs.[13]

The *Towa é* act as helpers to the Made People (or *Patowa*), who represent the highest level of Tewa life on earth. *Patowa* literally means completed, instituted, or become; such Tewas are considered to be human bridges to the sacred. They represent the gods beneath the lake of origin and are said to have been "made" beneath the lake.[14]

Tewas become *Patowa* in several ways. Individuals may dedicate themselves to particular societies for a variety of reasons, or a person could be promised to a society before she were born. Less often someone is recruited because he has accidentally witnessed sacred activities of a group. Sometimes when a society's membership is low, new members will even be "trapped" by one method or another, such as the promise of a cure for illness. In each case, a long period of initiation is necessary.

There are at least eight societies of Made People. These are: the Summer and Winter societies (two select bands from the larger Summer and Winter groups), the Medicine or Bear Society, the *Kwirana* (cold clowns), the *Kossa* (warm clowns), the Hunt Society, the Scalp (or War) Society, and the Women's Society. Among the Southern Tewa the Kachina Society was also extremely important.[15]

The *Patowa* societies are responsible for keeping the cycle of seasons flowing smoothly and the pueblo in harmony with the spirits. They do this mainly by performing a series of "works" each year. During a "work," each society, in turn, secludes itself in its leader's home for a day and a night, praying, singing, and enacting special rituals connected with its aim. The first work of the year, in January, is called "To lessen the cold." This work is also known as "of moderation." The next is called "Bringing the buds to life." The works continue in this way all year long, assisting and honoring nature. Since all eight societies of *Patowa* must work, following each other at four day intervals, each work takes at least thirty-two days to complete. After a work is finished at least one ritual or dance follows, performed by either the Made People or the whole village.

The Made People are the guardians of all Tewa sacred knowledge; they acquire wisdom and powers which are often extraordinary. Their duties, however, are also extraordinary, and nearly continuous. They basically dedicate their entire lives, from the time of initiation onward, to the service of the spirits and the pueblo. At the turn of the fifteenth century in Yam-p'-ham-ba and for generations before and after this time, almost every adult Tewa joined one of these societies. Everyone knew that it was unwise to remain a Dry Food Person for life; to be truly adult, one must become *Patowa*. And each *Patowa* knew that at death, his spirit would return to the lake of origin to dwell with the gods and the cloud-beings.

13. This description of the *Towa é*, derived from Ortiz, is meant to portray them as they probably existed six centuries ago. The *Towa é* of the Tewa Pueblos today have been greatly influenced by Spanish political institutions. However, Ortiz emphasizes that the category of human *Towa é* definitely existed in prehistoric times. For a very thorough discussion of the *Towa é* today and their roots in tradition see Ortiz.

14. That the *Patowa* were "made" beneath the origin lake does not necessarily mean that they were created long ago. The Tewa also refer to a certain private ceremonial room as *Sipofene*. Initiations often occur in these rooms. This discussion of the Made People is adapted from Ortiz.

15. Ortiz describes the Northern Tewa today as having eight *Patowa* societies. Polly Schaafsma comments that rock art reveals the importance of a ninth *Patowa* group, the Kachina Society of the Southern Tewa (see Chapter 3).

May all tame animals increase and children all,
For little people are we all to be loved of the Gods
As far away as our Great Mother's sound of breathing
Reaches. Even to the Utes, Apaches, Navajos,
Kiowas, Comanches, Cheyennes, even to all of them!
To the Mexican people, even to them it reaches!
To the people of America, even to them the sound
Of our Great Mother's breathing reaches. So now
They are loved of the Gods and each by the other loved!
So that is why we hope to find our living here,
We mortal men! Then place good summers and
Good days and nights of harvest! For each
The same, place then good days and nights of harvest!

–A prayer, part of the Initiation Chant of one of the Tewa clown societies[16]

A Tewa placing a prayer feather near Nambe Pueblo (north of Santa Fe) in 1925. Edward S. Curtis called this portrait "An Offering at the Waterfall."

The Raingod Ceremony is a powerful blessing ritual which calls forth the rain-bearing spirits known as Kachinas, or as the Tewa call them, *Oxua.* All the Pueblos say that in former times Kachinas lived with the people and taught them the secrets of hunting, farming, and the arts. In those days the Kachinas themselves danced in order to bring rain. But once the people argued with the Kachinas, so the latter went away to the underworld lake, and only visit periodically now.

In ancient times Tewas performed the Raingod Ceremony at least four times a year, during initiation ceremonies or as a blessing for the whole pueblo. In her book, *Seeking Life,* Vera Laski describes a Raingod Ceremony as the Winter People of San Juan pueblo gave it in the late 1940s or 1950s. Clearly most of the elements of this Tewa ceremony originated centuries ago, though there are a few modern touches. The following is a condensed version of Laski's beautiful and detailed account.

On certain special evenings of the year, after seven nights of preparation by the Made People, all the villagers—men, women, and children—meet in the large kiva. (The kiva is a large circular structure, partly subterranean, entered by means of a ladder which protrudes from its roof.) As the people sit expectantly, the Summer and Winter Chiefs quietly recite the Smoke Prayer. Suddenly a thunderous commotion breaks out overhead. The people laugh, knowing that the clowns, masters of ceremony for the night, have arrived. They are on the roof, "making thunder" with their feet.

Slowly the two clowns come down through the central ceiling hole and sit on the top

16. This excerpt quotes the last thirteen lines of "The Initiation Chant of the Kwirana K'osa." From this title, it is unclear exactly which of the two Tewa clown societies the translator, H. J. Spinden, refers to. However, he comments that this chant "expresses the high spiritual purpose of these sacred clowns." This chant was obviously augmented in historical times.

A kiva entrance on one of the Hopi Mesas, ca. 1915. The kiva openings of San Cristóbal Pueblo were probably very similar to this (photographer unknown).

steps of a fireplacelike adobe structure where they have a good view of the crowd. They peer around at the people with curiosity.

First Clown: I wonder where we are, Little Twin Brother?
Second Clown: Oh, we are probably in hell. Look at all those devil heads around.[17]
First Clown (pointing at a woman): Look brother, that one over there is looking at me.
Second Clown: Maybe she is in love with you.

The people laugh and the clowns begin to walk around, one scrutinizing the men, who are all on one side, the other peering at the women. Most of the people hide under their blankets or shawls, hoping to avoid the clown's embarrassing remarks. Some children peek out curiously.

First Clown: You know, when people are traveling, they have to stop and eat, don't they?
Second Clown: You are right, Younger-Brother-Older-Than-I; people do. Let's sit down and eat.[18]

The clowns take off their sheepskin backpacks and sit down, unwrapping meat and bread. They throw small bits of the food to the ground, mumbling the Food Offering Prayer:

> You, who are souls departed,
> Partake of this food,
> To build your body's strength.

Then they start to eat.

First Clown: It is said that when people eat, they tell stories, don't they?
Second Clown: You start with a story, Little-Brother-Older-Than-I.
First Clown: Oh, the other day, when I was walking to the home of the refuse, I saw Flower Mountain going out to gather cowchips. And whom, do you think, did I see coming over to help her?
Second Clown: Bear Mountain, I guess.
First Clown: You said it, Little-Brother-Older-Than-I, and was he helping her, indeed!
Second Clown: And do you know what I saw when I went to the river last week?
First Clown: No, I haven't the faintest idea.
Second Clown: Well, I saw Big Mountain running after Cactus Blossom.
First Clown: Did he catch her?

17. This line shows the influence of Christianity. The clowns are lampooning European religion.

18. "Younger-Brother-Older-Than-I," "Little Twin Brother," etc., are ritual names ceremonially used between Made People.

Clowns at San Juan Pueblo in 1934 (photographer unknown).

The clowns continue to eat and tell jokes meant to embarrass the people in one way or another for twenty minutes or so.[19] *When they have finished they hand out small pieces of bread and meat to various people, saying, "Here, throw this away." Then they roll and tie their sheepskins carefully and lay them at the feet of the Winter and Summer Chiefs, saying, "Please, do not take care of this for me."*[20] *Then the second clown declares: "Now, let's get down to business."*

And they both begin their sacred task, which is to "see" and call the Raingods. The first clown cries, "Let's try our luck!" and gathers some ashes from one of the kiva fireplaces. He holds the ashes up and claps his hands, and a black ash cloud, symbol of the heavens, forms and disperses. Peering into the "cloud," he shades his eyes as if trying to see something far away. He is searching for the Raingods, but sees nothing. The other clown tries the same thing but he too sees nothing. Then they try in all four directions, always with the clapping gesture first, exhorting each other and comparing what they see. Finally one "sees" a far-off lake and bubbling, troubled waters. Then he sees a lone head emerging, then another, then another. Both clowns now see the Raingods emerging from a faraway lake, carrying with them the sacred Cloudflower, a beautiful cloud which holds abundance and power. The excited clowns relate their vision:

> And more and more of them [the gods] come out . . . bringing with them the power to make rain, the power to raise watermelon, the power to raise musk melon, the power to raise squash, wheat, and corn, the power to hunt deer, the power to hunt buffalo, and they keep coming out with the power to hunt rabbits and the power to kill skunks. (The people laugh.)

The clowns take turns describing how the Raingods travel: they float on to another lake, sink into its waters and rise again, bringing even more gods with them. The gods move on through four or five more lakes, each one nearer to the pueblo. Toward the close of this journey, many Raingods end up staying in the last lakes, so now only a few are approaching the pueblo. Anticipation and excitement build in the people as the clowns at last "see" the Raingods approaching the village refuse mound. (When this occurs, three priestesses rise and quietly prepare a sacred pathway around the kiva floor. They breathe on cornmeal, then sprinkle it around, slowly repeating the sanctifying prayer.)

Meanwhile the clowns report that the Raingods have now entered the pueblo and in fact have reached its center, the Earth Navel.

As they speak, Winter Men who had been standing near the kiva entrance slowly turn around and spread their blankets out behind them, forming a concealing screen. Masked Raingod impersonators, who have been waiting outside, then quietly descend the kiva ladder and stand hidden behind the screen. (The Made People who impersonate the

19. Affection is never publicly shown in Pueblo society, although as the Spanish discovered, moral codes were more flexible than among Europeans. The clowns, however, are the only ones with the license to discuss these things, or to voice other thoughts and emotions that are normally suppressed or frowned upon.

20. All manifestations in the spirit world are the opposite of what would occur in ordinary life. Since the clowns represent this other world, they say the opposite of what would conventionally be said. There may be other meanings and of course there is a humorous intent as well. Parsons points out that this kind of "backward speech"—saying the opposite of what is meant—"is the commonest form of Pueblo humor."

"Coming of the Longhorn," a 1990 painting by Duane Dishta depicting three Zuni kachinas.

Raingods have spent the last four days in seclusion, preparing and painting the sacred masks, praying, and listening to the stories and wisdom of the old men, who stay with them. As each one finally puts on the mask of his Kachina he relinquishes his own identity and takes on the spirit of the god. He is then considered to actually have become *the Raingod.)*

Now the nearly delirious clowns describe the approach of the Raingods: they are approaching the kiva, they are reaching the foot of the ladder, they are climbing the kiva steps, one by one, when at last . . .!

> *Second Clown*: And here they are with their thunder, their wind, their lightning, their bird songs, their cricket chirpings!
> *First Clown:* Here they are with their power of corn raising, of squash raising, of watermelon raising; with their deer-killing power . . . their power to bring fertility, and growth, and abundance, right here at the top opening of the kiva!

"Suddenly a deafening noise breaks loose from behind the blanket screen, filling men, women, and children with a feverish fascination. The closely packed, dimly lit kiva, hot and sticky from the crowd of huddled, squatting human bodies, is astir with joyful anticipation. There is a wild roar from the top of the kiva opening, and the gods seem to have dropped suddenly, bringing with them frightening thunder, lovely bird songs, and the rhythmic jingling of a hundred tiny bells attached to their writhing waists and their swiftly moving feet. The shrill hoots, the resounding whooping, and the weird piercing sounds which identify each individual Raingod intermingle."

A long "spirit" hand, painted white, reaches down through the kiva roof opening, throwing a blessing of piñon seeds and corn to the joyful crowd. The clowns cry out in fright at the Raingods' cacophony but soon recover and run forward to welcome them, crying:

Yes, yes, may it be so!
Our Great Ones
Wise gods and revered goddesses,
Come here
And warm yourselves
In our hearts
You have come to see us,
You are bestowing honor upon us
By coming to see your Children.
We rejoice seeing you.
Yes, yes, our Great ones,
Come here and feel welcome![21]

Meanwhile all the wild, diverse noises of the Raingods continue, along with the nature sounds they bring—thunder, wind, birds, bugs, and crickets.

21. I have substituted the word "you" for the term "ye," which Laski uses, in the hope of avoiding a stilted, archaic impression. Suffice it to say that in these speeches and prayers the Tewa were using the formal or more reverent form of the pronoun "you."

A storm west of the White Bluffs.

Finally the Chief Raingod emerges from behind the blanket screen. Masked and decorated with bells, colored yarn, feathers, turquoise, and evergreen, he moves forward majestically, roaring, stomping, and swaying, his yucca whips in both hands. The first clown reverently guides him without touching him, leading him toward the Winter and Summer Chiefs while the people pray, breathing on cornmeal and throwing it forward to "feed" the god.[22] *The Chief Raingod gives a watermelon to the First Clown, who puts it down in front of the Pueblo chiefs.*

One by one, each Kachina makes his entrance until all eight or ten are moving in a counterclockwise oval around the kiva. Some walk in a somber, stately way, others dance and hop; all make their own peculiar noises as they travel around the circle. Soon the other nature sounds stop. (The Winter men who were holding the blanket screen and making these noises fold their blankets and turn around to be part of what follows.)

Now the First Clown comes toward the gods with open arms, saying: "Yes, Great Ones! Let us be friends!" The Chief Raingod lashes out, hitting the clown with his yucca whip. "Ouch, goddamn, that hurts!" cries the clown, jumping back.[23] *But he reaches out*

22. Small bits of food, such as cornmeal, represent the Pueblo principle of much coming from little. "Scant or diminutive offerings among Pueblos are not, as is often said, symbolic, rather they are supposed to increase to the recipient; they are a kind of magical seed."

23. Laski explains that there are no Tewa cursing words. Swearing in Spanish or English, as here, "implies a ridiculing of the white man."

and tries again to approach the Chief Raingod and this time is accepted. The two clowns then approach each Kachina in turn and are first rejected, then accepted by each.

Then the Chief Raingod gestures that he wants to speak to the Summer and Winter Chiefs, for these two are qualified to interpret the supernatural Kachina language. The Chief Raingod gestures and the Winter Chief translates: "We have come from far, as we were concerned about you, and we wanted to see how our Children are getting along. It has reached my ear that you people have not listened to your gods, and we came to punish you."

The Winter Chief then protests that the people actually have not been disobedient, and have tried to live in peace and harmony: "We have been good people, haven't we, Children of the Great Ones?" The people all answer: "Yes, Yes!" Then the Winter Chief says, "We are glad and thankful that you Great Ones came to honor us humble people with your presence, and that you came to look after your Children. We humble people shall continue to be good and try to live in peace and harmony with one another. We were happy that you came, and now, to your loved ones, you may return."

The clowns agree, thanking the Chief Raingod for coming and considerately pointing out that "this climate is too warm for you." The Clowns then lead all the Kachinas slowly to the blanket screen, which the Winter Men have recreated.

The Raingods begin to leave, but as each one reaches the exit, he stops and gives his blessing to the attentive onlookers. He reaches up, down, and to the four directions, gathering in all the powers of abundance and fertility. He passes his hands over his body, then stretches his arms out to the people, bestowing this "Great Goodness" on them. The people all reach out as if catching something, then breathe in the Goodness deeply, saying, "May it be so."

Finally the last Raingod disappears behind the blanket screen. The people sit spellbound in the silent kiva. Then one of the clowns exclaims loudly, "Thank goodness, they are gone, these troublemakers!"

The Raingod Ceremony then continues with another long comic/dramatic ritual focusing specially on fertility. After its solemn and dramatic climax the clowns disappear behind the blanket screen. They reemerge pretending to be Kachinas, mimicking the gods' dancing and sounds as everyone laughs. They also give their blessing to the people: "May you be loved and liked . . . and may you die immediately!" Then they finally leave for good.

Now an extended prayer is spoken by both the Winter Chief and the people. The prayer ends this way:

People (catching and breathing in the Great Goodness which the Winter Chief has quietly thrown from himself to them):

*Cholla (*Opuntia *sp.), native to New Mexico. Pueblos collected the fruit and buds of this cactus for food.*

May it be so!
May we be loved and liked
And through the supreme goodness
Of the Great Motherly One,
O yi ka,[24]
Catch up with that
For which we are always yearning,
And gain
Life of Abundance.

Winter Chief (referring to the kiva entrance):

It is open!
Now go to your homes
Without worry
Without weeping
Without sadness.

People (as they go out quietly):

May it be so.

Later all those who helped to create the Raingod Ceremony hold a great feast in another kiva. Early next morning Winter Men ceremonially "feed" the sacred Kachina masks with cornmeal, remove their decorations, return evergreen sprigs to the earth, and store the masks away.

Now comes the deer up to our house
He brings the needed food of life,
While we give needed food to him.
Old women deer, old men deer,
We love you! So come now hither,
On the road that we have laid!
Come hither to our house where we
May love you! Eat now this little!

–Song of the Hunter's Wife[25]

For the Tewa, and all Pueblos, the spoken word carries great weight. Chattering or small talk as we know it is not part of traditional Tewa behavior. Instead, silence is highly valued. Frank Waters describes a meeting of Pueblo elders: "A Council meeting is one-half talk and one-half silence. The silence has more weight, more meanings, more intonations than the talk."

24. *O yi ka* is the goddess who gives the Winter Chief his strength and powers. The name translates literally as "ice." With a masculine suffix (*O yi ke*) her name is extended to the Winter Chief himself.

25. While her husband hunts, the Tewa wife helps by making a path with a cotton thread leading to her house. Then she sits inside, singing this magical song.

Deer or elk petroglyphs near San Cristóbal Pueblo, probably created before A.D. 1350. These show a stylistic similarity to some Plains art. The animals' unusually large horns may have been intended to give the design greater power.

The spoken word is often elevated to ritual song and prayer, and as such, it accompanies almost every occasion or task in life, from planting corn to grinding it, from naming a baby to burying the dead.

Traditional Tewa songs came into being in different ways. Many are so ancient that their origin is unknown; some, in fact, like those of the Medicine Society, were even handed down in a foreign language, Keresan. Some songs were created during visions or trances. Some were given to people by nature powers, as in the story told by P-o p-oe, a Tewa Medicine Man. P-o p-oe's father told him about a beautiful day in his youth when he sat with his grandmother by a spring. He kept hearing a lovely song over and over. Finally he discovered, to his astonishment, that the song was coming from the spring itself. When he sang the wonderful song for the elders of the village later, they liked it so much that "they gave a dance which lasted four days in honor of the new song that had come to the people."[26]

Tewas pass on all their history and traditions through such songs, and

26. Ahlee James heard and translated this story in the 1920s. Since the storyteller's father was a young boy when the event occurred, it probably took place in the 1870s or earlier.

through oratory, ritual dance, and drama. Thus in the past there was no need for a written language; instead Tewas needed powerful memories and attention.

Each of the *Patowa* societies has its own secret prayers, chants, and songs which novices learn during a rigorous initiation period lasting a year or more. The body of sacred lore often amounts to hundreds of songs and prayers. Since the Made People are responsible for the continuance of Tewa life, all the words and corresponding actions must be learned with absolute precision—otherwise they will not be effective. And, in addition, all songs and prayers must be sung with an impeccable "good heart"—without worry, fear, anger, or sadness. As H. J. Spinden explains, in many Native American cultures, "'to sing' often means 'to make magic' and back of it all lies the idea that the song has been ordained." Thus the song must be performed exactly as it was "given" by the sacred source.[27]

Tewa history naturally expanded as time went on, so now Spanish and Anglo characters appear in certain narratives. Often the clowns lampoon whites in ritual drama or dance; the "Anglo" may, for example, appear as a harried figure carrying an alarm clock. At one Pueblo Corn Dance in 1992, a clown wore a dollar bill attached to a cord around his neck.

A Tewa woman named Blue Flower told this story in the early 1900s:[28]

Once upon a time there was a girl who was very lazy. No matter what her parents tried, she either refused to work or else did the work so badly they had to redo it themselves.

One day her mother firmly demanded that she help with the washing. The lazy girl grudgingly started, but soon began complaining to herself, and decided to run off to her favorite place, the lake, to dream. When she got there and began to wander about, to her dismay she happened upon a large washtub. Looking inside, she saw some lovely decorated dresses in need of washing. Then suddenly a beautiful woman rose out of the lake and came toward the tub. The woman started washing one of the dresses, singing as she rubbed:

I wash the dress, I wash the dress,
I hang it out to dry

The lazy girl watched, entranced by the beauty of the singer and the happiness in her voice. She made the work seem pleasant, almost not like work at all. The lazy girl edged

27. Pueblo music in general is considered to be "the most complex music of North American Indians" as well as "exceedingly exuberant."

28. This tale was related to Ahlee James by Blue Flower, who heard it from her grandfather, probably in the late 1800s; condensed and simplified, with exact quotations by the main characters.

closer.

"Who are you?" she asked the woman.

The woman replied that she was the Spirit of the Lake. The lazy girl said shyly that she hadn't known the lake held such a lovely Spirit. Then the Spirit told the lazy girl that she would also be lovely if only she weren't so lazy. Looking at the lazy girl, she said,

"Your continued slothfulness is beginning to show in your face and you are growing ugly."'

The lazy girl cried out in horror that she did not want to be ugly.

"But you will be, unless you become useful, help your parents, and take your proper place in the pueblo," said the Spirit of the Lake. "Some play is good, but if you become interested in work you will find that it is pleasant also, and makes play more delightful than when you play all the time. Try it and see."

Tewa girls at Hano Pueblo in 1900 (Edward S. Curtis, photographer).

Tewa Deer Dancer from San Juan Pueblo; illustration by Virginia M. Roediger.

So the lazy girl determined to change her ways. The Spirit of the Lake taught her the happy song, and promised her the beautiful dresses if she would finish washing them. Then she disappeared into the lake again. When the lazy girl's parents came looking for her they were astonished to find their daughter smiling and singing as she worked. The lazy girl told her story, saying that henceforth she would be known as Busy Girl, for she had learned to love work. And her grateful parents gave many thanks to the Spirit who had brought them this blessing.

For the people of fifteenth-century Yam-p'-ham-ba, their pueblo was the root and flower of life. They worked almost continuously, and the work was always first of all for the community.

A Tewa named Crow Wing explained the reason for the emphasis on community and cooperation as being "because at any time anyone may need help, therefore all help one another." So, although work was generally shared by extended families who farmed their own plots of land, the land was still understood to be owned communally. If one family's crops failed, various customs insured that others would share their food. Thus there were no classes in this society, no clear economic distinctions. (Prehistoric graves confirm this, as well as equal-sized pueblo rooms.)

Tewa society today is loosely patrilineal with the Winter and Summer Chiefs (also called *caciques*) acting the role of stern but benevolent fathers. But Alfonso Ortiz, the noted Tewa scholar, believes that this situation was influenced by both the Spanish and Americans, and that below its surface is a strong matriarchal leaning. "Women," Ortiz says, "have always been deferred to as knowing the most about the things of home, family, and society."

Now as in the past Tewa women and men each have their areas of expertise. In prehistoric times the men of San Cristóbal hunted and gathered food, herbs, and wood; planted and harvested crops; built dams and reservoirs; wove cloth; carved ceremonial and household objects; and made leather goods. The women took care of their children and homes, embroidered clothes, ground corn, hunted and gathered on occasion, repaired and replastered the pueblo exteriors, and made pottery, much of which was traded to other towns. They also helped with the planting and harvesting.

In addition to these everyday tasks the constant round of ceremonial activities required time, effort, and unflagging commitment. But these were essential, for Tewas were not born, but gradually "made" by participating in these duties. As Pueblo elders still say, "It is hard work being a Tewa."

Except in the case of some healing rituals, all Tewa ceremonies sought blessings for the whole pueblo, rather than for individuals. Laski describes her strong impression from watching Pueblo dances that "each participant gives up his personal identity to become part of a larger group through which, and for which, he is reaching out for the supernatural . . . 'seeking life'." As the elders say, "We are all in one nest. No Indian is an individual. He is a piece of the pueblo, the tribe."

> Be a man and be a woman!
>
> –*A form of hearty encouragement used in many Tewa rituals*[29]

In the Tewa world every form of matter has a spirit either male or female. This spirit may or may not inhabit the matter at any given time. A rock, for example, is on one level simply a rock. But on another level it also has a spirit presence which can come and go. This spirit is similar to the human spirit because everything in the universe is animated by the same eternal "breath." Also, the Pueblos assume that just as they sometimes don masks or costumes, everything in the universe is also in a temporary guise of "reality" (similar to the Platonian concept of ordinary reality as a mere shadow world) while underneath is a human spirit.

Thus the Tewa have two words for sky. One is the literal *makowa*, or sky, and the other, *Makawasendo*, is Sky Old Man. Sky Old Man is the spirit of the sky, a humanlike force that is abstract yet real simultaneously. Still, Sky Old Man is never considered a literal being, like you or me, and is rarely given a visual form.

Sky Old Man is considered the husband of Earth Old Woman. (For the Tewa, "Old Woman" and "Old Man" are terms of great reverence.) Sun Old Man is the divine force of the sun. He is said to live in a house in the east, sometimes with a wife, though many stories exist of the sun becoming enamored with earthly women. Though tremendously brilliant and powerful, Sun Old Man is also fallible and must periodically be assisted in his travels by human beings.[30]

Moon Old Man rules that body. The Evening Star is Old Woman with the Yellowish Hoary Hair, and Wind Old Woman lives on top of Sandia Mountain. Morning Star, or Dark Star Man, is the messenger of the sun, and the Tewa pray to him for help with hunting and war. A myriad of other spirits, such as the Cloud Boys, the Dawn Youths, and Yucca Old Man, do their part to sustain life on earth, and may intercede to help humans. All these dieties populate the rich body of Tewa folklore and fables.

Tewa women's costume from the Buffalo Dance at San Ildefonso Pueblo; illustration by Virginia M. Roediger.

29. Among these rituals are the Summer or Winter Initiation for young boys and the preparation of the Medicine Man who is going into a healing trance. Its general meaning is: "Be as brave as a warrior and as strong as a woman giving birth."

30. The traditional Tewa relay race between Summer and Winter People began "to help or control the progress of Sun and Moon, Morning Star and Evening Star."

Tombay ("Drum"), from the Tewa pueblo of Santa Clara (Edward S. Curtis, photographer, 1905).

Ocoowa Tsay ("Yellow Cloud"), from the Tewa pueblo of San Ildefonso (Edward S. Curtis, photographer, 1905).

Ana-Ah-Pobe ("Flower Beads"), from the Tewa pueblo of Nambe (Edward S. Curtis, photographer, 1905).

Pose Anyi ("Raining"), Nambe Pueblo (Edward S. Curtis, photographer, 1905).

*Blazing star (*Mentzelia *sp.), native to New Mexico. Archaeologists have found storage jars full of these seeds at prehistoric sites such as those in Chaco Canyon. They were used as a sweet meal, and to prevent constipation.*

The Pueblo character is unique and strikingly different from the typical Spanish or American personality. In fact, the very qualities that both America and Spain have traditionally valued are those which most Pueblos dislike.

Ruth Bunzel describes the ideal Pueblo type in this way:

> In all social relations, whether within the family group or outside, the most honored personality traits are a pleasing address, a yielding disposition, and a generous heart. All the sterner virtues—initiative, ambition, an uncompromising sense of honor and justice, intense personal loyalties—not only are not admired but are heartily deplored. The woman who cleaves to her husband through misfortune and family quarrels, the man who speaks his mind where flattery would be much more comfortable, the man, above all, who thirsts for power or knowledge, who wishes to be, as they scornfully phrase it, "a leader of his people," receives nothing but censure and will very likely be persecuted for sorcery.

Naturally certain Tewas, such as village chiefs, must wield power, and their abilities are sometimes even considered to be supernatural. But their knowledge is used solely for the benefit of the pueblo, and after leaving office they return to being simply another member of the group.

Pueblos value hospitality and generosity as part of a pragmatic approach to life. "An Indian treats the stranger kindly and makes him presents from the same feeling that he plants his seeds in the soil, that is, in the hope of a return, sooner or later, at least tenfold."

The Pueblo personality does not come about by accident. On the contrary, every piece of the social structure helps to mold it. And that whole social structure rests on the belief that human beings have a definite role to play in maintaining the balance and harmony of the universe. If one keeps one's own internal world in order, with a "good heart" and peaceful thoughts, this will help support the cosmic balance. From this understanding and ideal come the many customs and rituals which train Pueblo children and restrict Pueblo adults.

Early childhood, when almost anything is permitted, is the only time of real outer freedom.[31] When a child turns two, Pueblo parents become more stern and vigorously attempt to teach the virtues of hard work, stoicism, and thriftiness. Parents almost never hit children; instead they use fear to enforce behavior. They warn the children about horrible ogres who will carry them off if they disobey, and sure enough, masked monsters do periodically appear in the village, brandishing whips and searching for unruly children. Sometimes these ogres even make "the child or children dance while they crack whips at their heels."

31. The exception to this rule was the use of cradleboards. Dozier says, "the child was put into the cradleboard when it cried and when it became difficult to manage. The cradleboard became, in fact, a device which meant discomfort and confinement rather than an object of warmth and comfort." This description of childhood is paraphrased from Dozier's *Pueblo Indians*.

Later, when a Tewa child is ten or older, the "finishing" rite is held. This ritual "finishes" making children into men and women, and also into either Summer or Winter people. As part of this ceremony, girls are lightly and symbolically whipped, but boys are hit hard, and "huge red welts appear on either side of the boy's naked rib cage; some are even cut." After the boys have all been hit the whipping god removes his mask, revealing himself as one of the boys' relatives or neighbors, and "the mood of the occasion passes quickly from solemnity to mirth," as the boys now try on the mask. Still, the welts and cuts remain. These whippings are thought to be very beneficial to the child; at Zuni, the people explain that children are whipped "to save their lives." The idea seems to be that if children do not learn to honor and submit to the great forces around them, either these forces will eventually kill them, or their lives will become worthless.

Sometimes dietary restrictions are part of this initiation too. Later inductions into Made People societies also impose discipline and make many demands on the novices.

Everyday customs also sculpt the Tewa personality. One is the lack of privacy within the Pueblo household. Family members, for example, all sleep together in the same room, except in the case of newly married couples. This practice may have helped to create the Pueblos' reticence.

Children are not the only ones to feel fear and anxiety. Adults dread the barbs of the sacred clowns, whose weapon is ridicule. During many ceremonies and dances the clowns are at full liberty to point out any foibles or deviant behavior in very public and embarrassing ways. (The clowns themselves indulge freely in deviant and comic behavior, but this serves as a kind of vicarious safety valve for the Pueblos, and an example of how not to behave.) In such a conformist society people also tend to fear gossip, especially since it can lead to being branded a witch. "Witch" is "the most abusive and insulting term in Pueblo vocabularies." Anyone who is "envious, jealous, retaliatory or revengeful, quarrelsome, self-assertive, and noncooperative, entirely too unconventional or . . . too much of an individualist" is suspect, and in much danger. Because witches are thought to be a cause of disease, drought, and many other misfortunes, they are always ostracized, and sometimes even banished or killed.

Hopi Whipper and Runner kachinas; painting by LeRoy Kewanyema.

Parsons describes the underlying motivation behind much of Pueblo behavior:

> [It is the desire] to keep clear of pernicious influences, whether from witch or spirit. It enters into Pueblo ideas or feelings of discretion, prudence, and caution, producing a code of live and let live, of taking no responsibility apart from what is conventional, of suppressing or ignoring grief or distress, and of remaining indifferent to the strange or unknown—indifferent if not afraid.

Pueblo personality traits form a kind of blueprint for a self-enclosed society capable of surviving indefinitely. And that is exactly what has happened for almost 1,000 years.

But this stereotypical personality—"modest . . . polite, well-behaved, and noted for mildness of manner"—is not universal. From prehistoric times there have been rebels in every pueblo, in every generation, despite the overwhelming push toward conformity. Also, the popular misconception of a totally placid and passive people has been refuted by well-documented evidence of the courage and fighting spirit of Pueblo auxiliaries in Spanish times.

The Southern Tewa of San Cristóbal and the other Pueblos of the Galisteo Basin were probably the most aggressive Pueblos of all. Many references in Spanish documents note their "warlike" nature, and their leading role in battles from the Pueblo Revolt of 1680 to uprisings in the late 1690s.[32]

Perhaps the Southern Tewa developed this quality because they lived so close to the plains. Plains tribes attacked them with regularity (in what is now known as a trading/raiding relationship) so the Southern Tewa were constantly forced to defend themselves. Over time they may have absorbed some of the attitudes and culture of the fierce nomadic tribes, possibly even intermarrying. Rock art experts support this theory, stating that certain Southern Tewa petroglyphs reveal a "highly developed ceremonial war cult or warrior society."[33]

The Southern Tewa at San Cristóbal built their homes from sheets of sandstone, covering eleven-inch-thick walls with adobe. Their finished town contained eight or nine apartmentlike room blocks arranged around five ceremonial plazas. Early Spanish chroniclers reported that the pueblo was four to five stories high, but this has not been confirmed archaeologically. If we assume only a ground floor and partial second story, there would have been at least 800 rooms; if the pueblo had five stories there would have been many more. In the middle of the largest plaza was the kiva, a round, partly underground ceremonial center. (This kiva may originally have been a pithouse of even earlier people.) Just north of the creek were two more kivas, which may have been for the Summer and Winter groups. By the year 1400, anywhere from 500 to 1,000 or more people were living here, at what is now called the "old pueblo" south of San Cristóbal Creek.[34]

Later the tribe would build a new kiva and ten to eleven new room blocks north of the creek, with at least 1,000 rooms. Gradually they would abandon their old pueblo, letting it fall into disrepair.

32. After the 1680 rebellion, the Keres and Pecos began fighting the Southern Tewa of San Cristóbal and San Lázaro. Richard Lang has suggested that perhaps some periodic hostility may have also been present prehistorically.

33. Anthropologist Polly Schaafsma refers to the rock art of Comanche Gap, a volcanic dike "bristling with protective powers" about 6 miles from San Cristóbal Pueblo.

34. Scholars determine population figures by a means of a formula that takes into account the total number of rooms in a pueblo and assumes that anywhere from 40 to 90 percent of the town was occupied at any given time. This information, and rough population estimates, was obtained from anthropologist Winifred Creamer of the Field Museum of Natural History in 1989.

Canyon Ceta and the White Bluffs.

Fourteenth-century pottery from the Galisteo Basin. (Clockwise from top right) Largo Glaze Polychrome jar; Abiquiu Black-on-gray bowl from Pueblo Largo; Galisteo Black-on-white bowl; Espinosa Glaze Polychrome jar from north of San Marcos Pueblo; Cundiyo Smeared Indented jar (center) from San Marcos Pueblo.

In 1582 the Spanish explorer Antonio de Espejo gave an account of a nearby Pueblo people which serves as a fairly accurate picture of the Southern Tewas too. (He was describing the Piros, who lived to the south of San Cristóbal and also spoke a variety of Tanoan.)

> As we were going through this province, from each pueblo the people came out to receive us, taking us to their pueblos and giving us a great quantity of turkeys, maize, beans, tortillas, and other kinds of bread. . . . They grind on very large stones. Five or six women together grind raw corn . . . and from this flour they make many different kinds of bread. They have houses of two, three, and four stories, with many rooms in each house . . . in each plaza of the town they have two *estufas* [kivas], which are houses built underground, very well sheltered and closed, with seats of stone against the walls to sit on. Likewise, they have at the door of each *estufa* a ladder on which to descend, and a great quantity of community wood, so that strangers may gather there.
>
> In this province some of the natives wear cotton, cow hides [buffalo], and dressed deerskin. . . . The women wear cotton skirts, many of them being embroidered with colored thread, and on top a *manta* like those worn by the Mexican Indians, tied around the waist with a cloth like an embroidered towel with a tassel . . . and all, men as well as women, dress their feet in shoes and boots, the soles being of cowhide and the uppers of dressed deerskin. The women wear their hair carefully combed and nicely kept in place by the moulds that they wear on their heads, one on each side, on which the hair is arranged very neatly. . . . In each pueblo they have their *caciques*. . . . These *caciques* have under them . . . *tequitatos,* who are like [policemen], and who execute in the pueblo the *caciques's* orders. . . . And when the Spaniards ask the *caciques* of the pueblos for anything, they call the *tequitatos,* who cry it through the pueblo in a loud voice . . .
>
> They have fields of maize, beans, gourds, and [tobacco] in large quantities. . . . Each one has in his field a canopy with four stakes . . . where he takes his siesta, for ordinarily they are in their fields from morning until night . . .

If Espejo had been describing the people of San Cristóbal, this account would differ in one major respect. As previously mentioned, the Southern Tewa were a wary people, and they did not welcome Espejo's party with the warmth and generosity their southern neighbors showed. On the contrary, when Espejo arrived, they pulled up their ladders, rebuffed his requests for food, and watched from the rooftops until the Spaniards were gone.

The uncompromising stance of many Southern Tewas persisted into the seventeenth century. Late in the 1600s many of the people of San Cristóbal refused to submit to the Spanish invaders and left the Galisteo Basin. In time they aban-

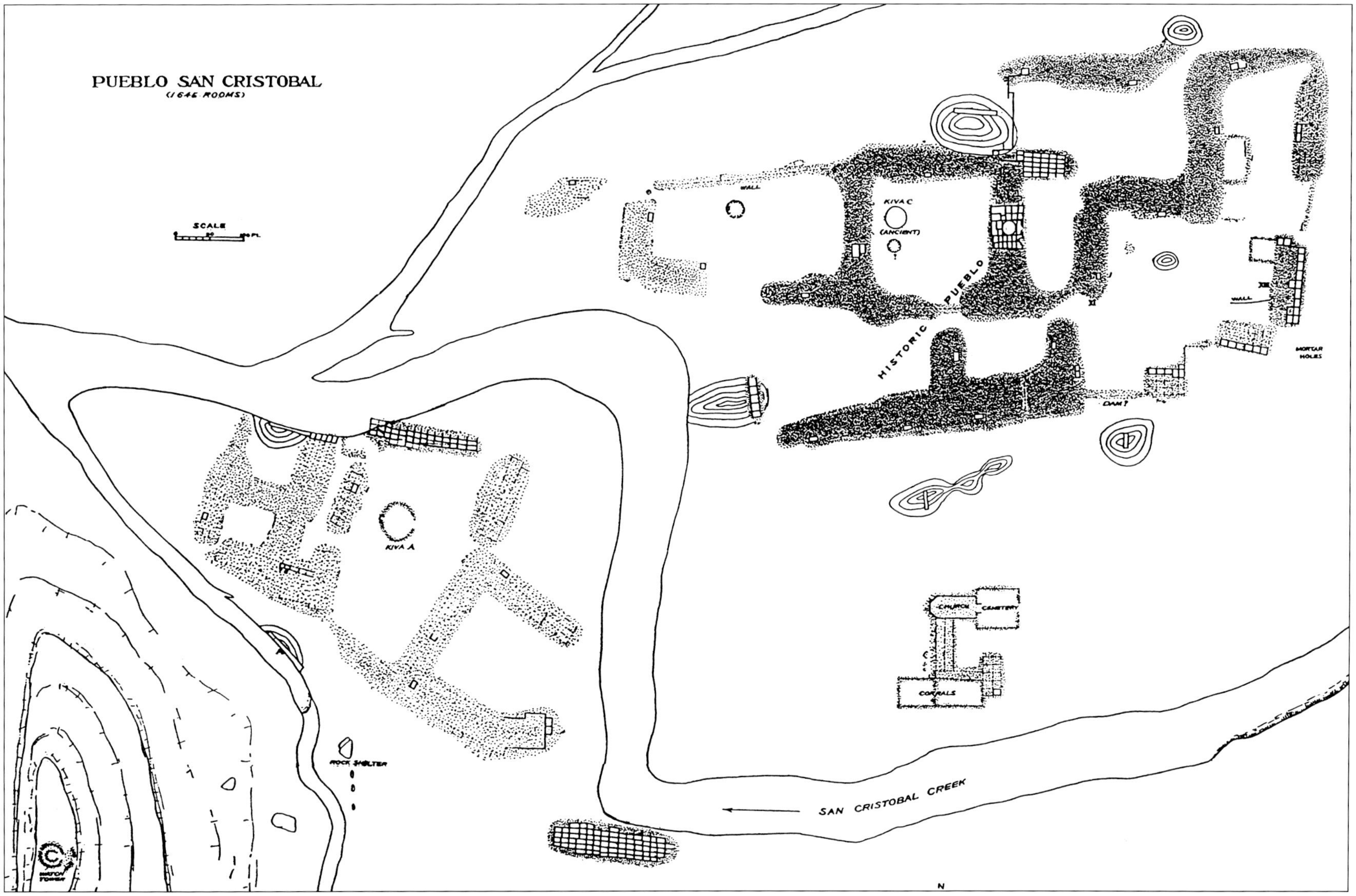

Map of the San Cristóbal Pueblo ruins, by N. C. Nelson, made in 1914. The old pueblo is at left; the later one, built after 1400, is to the right.

doned the Rio Grande area entirely, migrating with other Southern Tewas to Hopi First Mesa, where they created the town of Hano. Even today these Hano Tewa show distinct personality differences from their relatives, the Northern Tewa and the Hopi. The Hano people are generally less reticent, more aggressive, and more individualistic than most Pueblos. According to Polly Schaafsma, "Hano songs and dances exalt warrior prowess," and Hano people are more comfortable with individualistic Anglos than are most Hopis.

But the Tewa fighters who escaped to Hano were just a tiny remnant of the thousands who once lived in the Galisteo Basin. A great number of these Pueblos

Hano Pueblo on Hopi First Mesa, ca. 1882 (John K. Hillers, photographer).

The chiefs of Walpi, Hano, Sichumovi pueblos, Hopi Mesas, Arizona, ca. 1880–1882 (John K. Hillers, photographer).

died in uprisings against the Spanish invaders. The few who survived made a place for themselves on Hano, withstood being outsiders for many generations, and still live as traditional Tewas there today.

Yam-p'-ham-ba was only one of several pueblos on what is now the San Cristóbal Ranch. Southern Tewa built at least five other villages here; three of these flourished for centuries but were probably abandoned by the time the Spanish arrived.

Hish-í, or as we know it now, Pueblo Largo, was a long, narrow village of 489 ground-floor rooms set in open grassland. People lived there from the late 1200s until about 1500. Not far from the pueblo were at least fifteen pithouses and two kivas even more ancient than Largo.

Tze-man-Tu-o, or Pueblo Colorado, had eleven room blocks made of striking red sandstone, which surrounded six or seven plazas. Many of the apartments were multistoried. The pueblo was just southeast of a towering sandstone bluff which could be seen throughout the southern Galisteo Basin. Tewas lived here for three centuries, from the late 1200s or early 1300s to about 1600.

Pueblo Shé was occupied at about the same period as Pueblo Colorado. It had 1,543 ground-floor rooms, eleven plazas, and several kivas, both above and below ground. Just south of the town was a shrine or watchtower on a high cliff. Though the surrounding land was somewhat bleak, there was a spring within the village.

Colina Verde was a tiny settlement, probably a pueblo in its first stages. Its room blocks (one of which contains two kivas) were scattered on both sides of a juniper and piñon-covered arroyo. People lived here only a short time, from the late 1200s through the mid-1300s, abandoning it for unknown reasons.

Archaeologists have recently discovered another pueblo ruin, as yet unnamed, about 3 miles south of San Cristóbal Pueblo. Prehistoric people lived here at approximately the same time as the Colina Verde occupation. The dirt-covered town appears now only as a gentle mound, almost indistinguishable from the rest of the broken terrain.

San Cristóbal Pueblo room block.

CHAPTER 3

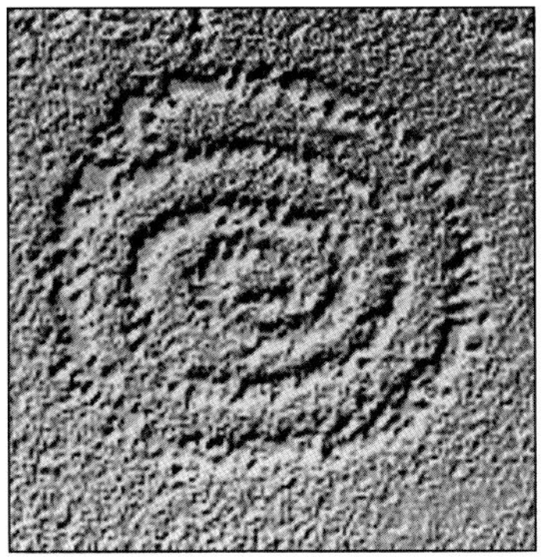

THE PETROGLYPHS

Storm Serpent Old Man
Come hither now
For here we are dancing.

Laden with rain
Now you arrive!
–Song of Avanyu, *the Storm Serpent*[1]

THE SOUTHERN TEWAS HAVE LEFT THEIR RECORD at San Cristóbal but it is a cryptic and mysterious one. Increasing numbers of scholars are recognizing this site for its abundant petroglyphs, and many come to visit the sandstone outcropping adjacent to the now-buried pueblo. All have theories or speculations, but no one can say with absolute certainty what the images mean.

We do know that most of the rock art at San Cristóbal was created between 1325 and 1680, the era of "Rio Grande Style."[2] Thus, many of the images here are kachina masks, ceremonial figures, horned serpents, stars, shields, corn plants, cloud terraces, and animals with ritual meaning. But some of the art is much older. Certain petroglyphs date from A.D. 1100 to 1300 and show a Western Anasazi influence which was still widespread then. Images from this period include deer and other four-legged animals, birds, stick figures, lizards, flute players, tracks, and handprints. A few San Cristóbal petroglyphs are even more ancient, dating to around A.D. 1 or perhaps even earlier. According to Polly Schaafsma, these are usually very simple geometric designs or wavy lines in the "Abstract Style" of the hunter-gatherers who first lived here.

Rock art appears (or hides) all over San Cristóbal Ranch, often in places that require effort to reach. But two sites are especially abundant in images: one is a

1. *Avanyu* can be dangerous; this is one unusual instance in which his name is spoken.

2. Polly Schaafsma, research associate at the Museum of Indian Arts and Culture/Laboratory of Anthropology, Museum of New Mexico, in Santa Fe, contributed greatly to this chapter, through her publications and through personal communication between 1990 and 1994.

"Unidentified man carving pictographs" at Hopi, Arizona, ca. 1911 (H. F. Robinson, photographer).

rocky outcrop near San Cristóbal Pueblo; the other, a volcanic dyke at Comanche Gap, a warrior shrine on the western side of the ranch.

All these rock art images, from the simplest to the most sophisticated, seem clearly designed to communicate *something*. What could the Tewa have intended in creating them? The large amount of time required to chisel even a small or simple design, coupled with the fact that the ancient Pueblos were almost continuously working or else involved in ceremonial activity, leads one to conclude that this art was not created idly or as an exercise in representation for its own sake. As the late Pueblo scholar E. C. Parsons pointed out, all the Pueblo arts, from poetry to embroidery, have a purpose beyond themselves; they are "measures to invoke or coerce, to gratify or pay, the Spirits." Parsons also told the story of Crow Wing, a Tewa who in drawing a picture for her "of the Tewa winter solstice altar . . . left out Water Serpent, whose clay image belongs on the altar, as being 'too dangerous to draw'." So most authorities agree that Native American rock art in general had magical and ritual significance, and therefore was often sacred in nature.

Clearly for the Tewa, and all Pueblos, designs in themselves often have great power. And since the Tewa regard rocks as "stone people" (or as having a living spirit), surely the inscription of potent designs into the greatest or weightiest of these rocks was a special statement or sacred request of some sort. Sometimes designs were pecked in a certain area because the spot was known to have power; sometimes the images themselves impart power to the location.

Many rock art areas probably functioned as shrines. Some designs were simply "beneficial imagery" that attracted positive influences to the lands around the pueblo. Some may even have been territorial markers. And Tewas apparently created many as part of ritual activities undertaken to bring about successful hunting, warfare, or weather.

Rock art scholar Jane Young points out that the Pueblos were not trying to *control* nature by means of such magic, as some writers have implied; rather, their rituals acknowledge that humans "are relatively weak beings who must consequently depend on the aid" of higher forces. Traditional Pueblos believe that humans and gods need each other; that if we serve and feed the eternal beings, they will respond in kind.

Mexican culture seems to have had considerable influence in the Pueblo region after 1300. In fact, Polly Schaafsma has found petroglyphs from Casas Grandes, the powerful Mexican center thriving in the 1300s, which are strikingly similar to those of the Rio Grande. Much of the iconography of the two areas, such as masks and horned snakes, is also the same. Many scholars now believe that the Kachina cult began as a variation on the cult of Tlaloc, the ancient god of rain and fertility in Mesoamerica and Mexico. And much of the war imagery at San Cristóbal and other nearby sites also appears to have parallels in Mexico. Early Spanish accounts reveal the extent of this Mexican influence. Espejo, speaking of the Piros in 1583, said that "the paintings of their houses, and the things which they have for balls and dancing, both as regards the music and the rest, are all very much like those of the Mexicans." He also describes Zia, just 50 miles west of San Cristóbal, as a pueblo whose houses were "white washed and painted with colors and pictures after the Mexican custom."

Mexican and Mesoamerican themes are apparent at San Cristóbal in the predominance of petroglyphs created after 1300. This "Rio Grande Style" commenced as small pueblos coalesced into larger villages, population grew, and society became more complex. The new style clearly reflected the ideology of the Jornada Mogollon peoples just south of the Pueblos, who were also influenced by Mexico.

But for all our progress in classifying styles of rock art, real understanding of the images remains a tricky and baffling enterprise. Sometimes information gleaned from other ancient media can help us interpret the petroglyphs, since rock artists often created the same symbols, figures, and designs that we see on pottery, clay pipes, and kiva murals. In fact, Schaafsma believes that "rock drawings are but an echo" of the beautiful and colorful paintings discovered on kiva walls. Unfortunately the meaning of many of these designs and figures was lost centuries ago. And even those images that are still identifiable often have many layers of symbolism. Some meanings may be active while others are dormant, depending on factors such as the location of the image, the direction it faces, or other designs placed near it.[3]

Despite this "involutedness," Schaafsma believes that the more one studies Pueblo iconography, the more one begins to see order and unity emerging from the crowded rock art panels.

Of all the Pueblos, modern Hopis and Zunis clearly have the most complex ceremonies and extensive pantheon of gods; from this fact many scholars have assumed that they were the center of the "Classic" Pueblo culture during the fourteenth to seventeenth centuries, disseminating their ideas eastward to the Rio Grande. But Schaafsma believes the opposite. She says archaeological evidence points to the Rio Grande area (including the Galisteo Basin) as a culturally vibrant center from which many new ideas spread. The Rio Grande Tewas and Tanos, she thinks, once practiced many of the ceremonies and rituals now surviving only at Hopi and Zuni. (Hopi and Zuni country were relatively isolated from European influences and repression, whereas the Spanish prohibited or destroyed a great deal of the Rio Grande religion.) Today many Hopis readily

Stylized parrot near San Cristóbal Pueblo.

3. Jane Young calls this phenomenon of symbolic layering "multivocality."

Many of the animals in this panel are very old, predating A.D. 1350. Note the small animal standing on another's back (near top) and the earless animal biting another's tail (center). Schaafsma believes the figure with bow and arrow and ax was added later, after 1350.

Martineau's theory about such generic quadruped creatures is that most often they do not represent animals at all but rather human actions. In his view, the direction and number of the animals, as well as any appendages or missing features, would all convey a story.

acknowledge that some of their Kachinas and other symbols were brought to them by Galisteo Basin Tewas in the seventeenth century.

Essentially, scholars see Pueblo rock images like those at San Cristóbal as a form of art that communicated values, world views, and beliefs about the supernatural. This approach is widely held and respected, but as it often cannot illuminate meaning, other investigators have put forth theories as well. LaVan Martineau, for example, has advanced a theory that the petroglyphs are literally a form of writing. His thesis is that the symbols are a kind of code, in many cases based upon the Indian sign language, which Native Americans used for centuries as a continentwide linguistic bridge. He believes that many petroglyphs relate myths or histories of important events, both tribal and individual, while others give directions to places like springs and shrines.[4] (It is interesting that Zunis translate the name of one rock art site, *Atsinakwi,* as 'the place of the writing.' The Hopis also have a rock shrine they call *Tuteveni,* or 'writing.') A few rock art experts have adopted Martineau's approach, but most remain skeptical, and find his case untenable. Schaafsma, for example, says Native American cultures never intended rock images to be functional in the literal way that Martineau often suggests; she sees his theories as an example of linear thinking applied to a nonlinear culture.

In facing the mystery of these images, it is good to remember that in the Native American world, art, work, religion, and daily life all merged into a whole. Much as we would like to separate these aspects in order to study them in our habitual Western way, we cannot. They are really all one. So in looking at these petroglyphs and pictographs from San Cristóbal we are once again led back into the heart of the Tewa world.[5]

4. See Carol Patterson-Rudolph's 1991 book for examples of research based on Martineau's theories.

5. Petroglyphs are images chiseled, pecked, or carved into rock; pictographs are rock paintings.

These twin one-horned serpents convey boldness, power, energy, and movement. They depict Avanyu, *the horned or plumed water serpent of the Pueblos.* Avanyu *is the deity of rain, clouds, fertility, and irrigation; he is also the god of rivers and springs, where he lives. At the same time he may be a variant on* Quetzalcoatl, *the ancient feathered serpent of Mexico, "god of life . . . fertility, and agriculture, and the patron of twins and monsters."* Quetzalcoatl *is sometimes "seen combined with his twin brother . . . the Death God, thus symbolizing the duality of life and death."* Quetzalcoatl *sometimes appears as the Morning Star, thus star designs may be related to him. (The left serpent's tail may be a star design, although cloud symbolism is also possible. Both connote the celestial realm.) Schaafsma believes the serpent's necklace is similar to the checkerboards in kiva murals, which symbolize corn (and by extension, fertility). Between the two serpents is a clown face.*

Climbing to the petroglyphs above San Cristóbal Pueblo.

These intriguing figures clearly seem to contain some lost message. The two top figures are probably ducks, birds that played a part in Native American rituals all over ancient Mexico and the Southwest. Pueblos believe that deities may take on the form of ducks, or that ducks can act as messengers of the gods, bear seeds, and carry prayers to the rain clouds. Sometimes ducks are associated with healing.

Human figures holding staffs, such as the one-horned being at right, are usually priests or shamans, and are often symbolically linked to the animals depicted nearby.

The two stepped pyramids are often called "cloud terraces." Note the tiny joined figures at center.

The central figure on this huge boulder between pueblos Colorado and Largo conveys a sense of power and mystery. On the left are two bear paws; possibly they hold some clue to the main figure's identity. Schaafsma says that "in the Pueblo world the bear track stands for the curing power of the bear, and the paw is equal in power to the mask of other dieties." Bear paws are among the sacred objects used in the Bear Society ceremony for inducting a new "Bear" or Medicine Man. Toward the end of this long ritual, to which the whole village is invited, the new Bear becomes magical and cures several sick people by pulling or sucking rags or stones out of their bodies.

Native Americans created "handprints," such as the two on this boulder, at holy places all over the Southwest. Pueblos still leave their handprints when they pray at a particular shrine, believing that the deity of the shrine will be able to identify them in this way. Perhaps the central figure here represents such a deity.

These two humanlike beings seem to be dancing. One has a radiating sun attached to his hand.

A buffalo, perhaps of the historic era, rarely depicted in the Galisteo Basin. Pueblos of the historic period traveled regularly to the Plains for buffalo hunts. Martineau describes the odd-looking symbol almost attached to the buffalo's tail as a quadruped-head abstraction meaning "a good journey." Interestingly, this latter symbol points east-southeast, the direction of the Plains.

This design is almost hidden in a narrow gorge leading up to the major petroglyph panels (following the direction the arrow is pointing—which may or may not be intentional.) It seems to combine an earthy substantiality with an alert, somewhat masculine head. It may represent one of the Arrow Swallowers, a Warrior Society whose members performed magical feats. Carol Patterson-Rudolph has suggested that the figure may be the Corn-Mother-Sky-Father, pointing out similarities to a well-known Hopi and Zuni deity seen in kiva mural art. At right is a female fertility symbol.

A warrior shield between pueblos Colorado and Largo. The decoration shows an eagle head and tail, representing the fierce power of this bird. "At Zuni the eagle is known as the Beast God of the Zenith, and also as Knifewing, a war power with feathers made of knives. Knifewing is said to help scalpers." The bullet holes may indicate something more than simple vandalism. Zunis in the late nineteenth century, and perhaps other tribes as well, shot arrows at petroglyphs of game animals as part of their ritual preparation for hunting. Jane Young believes that Zunis in the recent past may have shot at rock art as part of the same tradition.

This scene seems to show a turkey hunt. Schaafsma believes that the turkey and the two figures, as well as the arrow design at right, are older than the curving arc, which appears to have been added much later.

This four-horned creature may be an upright bear or bear shaman. The paws are clearly typical bear paws. Since it is not possible to reach this design from the lower boulder, creating it must have been a challenging feat. Note the smaller, echoing figure on the same rock face partially hidden by brush. The insectlike figure at left has three horns. Schaafsma says, "Insects depicted may have shamanic power or participate in certain myths and rituals." The Zunis carved insect petroglyphs to help them in war, believing that the depicted insects would sting and poison their enemies. Warriors also appealed to insects with protective coloring to help make them invisible to their foes.

Hopi priests playing flutes at Mishongnovi Pueblo in 1907 (Frederick Monsen, photographer).

Masks, flute players, stars, snakes, profile heads, handprints, birds, and abstract designs combine and overlap here. The jug-eared mask at right is probably a Mudhead Clown. There are two humpbacked flute players, the small one playing, the larger one holding his flute. Known as Kokopelli *among Pueblos today, this figure originated among the Anasazi sometime during the first millennium* A.D. *The humpback is a sign of supernatural attributes, and insectlike antennae may symbolize locust qualities. Among the Pueblos, locust is an important creature who "plays his flute to melt the snow when appealed to by the sun-loving snakes." Nowadays* Kokopelli *is known as a kind of trickster who specializes in courting and seducing maidens, giving them presents which he carries in his hump. Thus he is associated with fertility. Some also consider him a kind of rain priest, able to call rainclouds with his flute.*

This faded painting (pictograph) in red and yellow may represent a mask with feathers.

Horned mask with falling lines of dots, which may indicate water or rain.

This warrior and shield figure is decorated with eagle feathers, white with black tips; note the spear at left. All these elements are powerful war symbols. This petroglyph is not at the San Cristóbal Pueblo site, but on a large boulder outcrop approximately midway between pueblos Colorado and Largo. It appears to be of finer quality than many other images because of this rock's softer material, which makes a different technique—incising—possible. On harder stone, Pueblos chipped away rock with either a hammerstone alone, or a hammerstone and chisel tool.

Bear, stars, masks, animals, birds, and horned beings combine in this powerful panel. Created sometime after A.D. *1350, the images seem ferocious and full of warning. The large animal is probably a bear, as the feet and tail appear particularly bearlike. Bears are patrons of both the Medicine and War (or Scalp) societies, and traditional Pueblos believe that shamans may turn themselves into bears, just as bears may remove their skins and become people. In this case the bear has star designs which, like all sky symbols, signify war. Five other stars, including the tiny star face at top, reinforce the warlike theme. Parsons pointed out that "the stars . . . have more supernatural significance or weight for the Tanoans than for other tribes." And among modern descendants of the Southern Tewa, the morning star connotes war and scalping, as well as hunting. Star faces may symbolize the warrior Star Kachina or the Heart of the Sky God (a variation on* Quetzalcoatl*). The one-horned serpent profiles probably signify a* Quetzalcoatl*-like figure with his myriad attributes, one of which is power in fighting. (Perhaps this link explains why star faces and one-horned serpents appear together here and in many kiva murals.) The small figure at left appears to be an eagle. Some of the faces may be sacred clowns; note the small round ears similar to Hopi Mudheads. The horned masks are probably Kachinas. The cornstalk, chiseled in the same period but by a different artist, is a Pueblo symbol of life, fertility, and abundance. The small bird and "lizard men" at right were pecked earlier, probably in the late 1200s.*

This painted wall is protected by a rock overhang. The faces may be kachinas with masks and feathers. Kachinas are not actually gods, per se, but rather powerful archetypal figures who embody the essence of things such as rain and corn. The two black masks may be related to war, as Pueblo warriors often painted their faces black.

The star face at center could symbolize war, or possibly the Heart of the Sky God, and thus fertility. In a link that seems strange to the Western mind, war and scalping were related to rain and fertility in the Pueblo world. Any Tewa who wanted to become a War Society member had to take an enemy scalp. The captured scalps were often insulted and abused, but later they were ceremonially adopted into the tribe as rain-bringers and fetishes. At Zuni, for example, one scalp prayer goes, "Though in his life the enemy was a worthless lot, now through the Corn Priests' rain prayers and seed prayers, [his spirit] has become a rain person." Among the Tewa, the Women's Society cared for the scalps, ritually feeding and cleansing them.

The overhang with its many crosslike stars is called a "star ceiling"; these are often seen on Navajo land and were probably derived from the Pueblos. More small stars cover the rock faces below the "cave" (just out of sight).

The Pueblos considered painted masks like these especially potent because of the paint itself. The pigment was often gathered from sacred places, and prepared in a special way; thus it was considered full of power. The long lasting colors used here are the colors of the directions: red, yellow, blue (very faded now), white, and black. At Zuni, only certain high-ranking kiva men were allowed to paint such masks.

These boulders seem to be bursting with life and magic. Snakes traverse the different rocks, linking the separate panels, where masks, handprints, animals, anthropomorphs, humans, and more serpents all crowd together. Two-horned snakes like these began to appear around 1300. No one knows for certain what they signify, but snakes in general are associated with the underworld and its immense reservoirs that connect to all bodies of water on earth. (According to Schaafsma, such two-horned serpents are probably "iconographically distinct from the one-horned serpent with ideological relationships to the Mexican Quetzalcoatl.*") Schaafsma says that several of these faces may be clown masks, commenting that snakes and clowns are often seen together in the Galisteo Basin. At Hopi, clowns ritually wrestle snakes coming out of pots, and Schaafsma believes that similar ceremonies probably existed at one time among the Southern Tewa. (It is even possible that Tewas brought this ritual with them when they migrated to Hopi country.)*

As in many rock art panels, symbols are repeated over and over. There is clearly a dominant serpent/mask theme, which may relate to rituals performed here. The Tewas may have repeated images as a way of magnifying their power. Young, speaking of the Zuni, says that repetition can also be an attempt to make the village environment "echo" the vital ideas and beliefs of the pueblo.

The lower central mask may represent Hehea, *an ancient and widely depicted Kachina with fertility and clownish characteristics;* Hehea *always has a crooked mouth.*

An oddly distorted animal figure. Tewas pecked the face at right on a rock corner, as did Pueblos and Mogollon people all over the region.

Dr. Edward Krupp of Los Angeles's Griffith Observatory with a large shield design made sometime after 1350. At left is a star, often associated with war. At right is a partial one-horned serpent with checkerboard collar.

This may be a female birthing figure, whose face also symbolizes the female.

This panel is full of eyes gazing intently at us. The figure in the pointed cap is possibly a variation on Quetzalcoatl. *There is evidence that among the Jornada Mogollon people to the south, such caps became part of the attire of* Quetzalcoatl*-like figures. Some scholars think this deity eventually metamorphosed into* Sotuqnang-u, *the Hopi Sky God, who also wears a conical cap or horn, and has* Quetzalcoatl *attributes. The one-horned serpents of the Pueblos have been related to* Quetzalcoatl *as well, and both had some warlike characteristics.* Quetzalcoatl *was also associated with Morning Star, thought to be a warrior who protects and heralds the sun. Schaafsma says the shield with star design to the far left supports this warlike connotation. At left are two masks. Curved-in horns denote kachinas, while straight lines usually indicate the cornhusk headgear of the sacred clowns. Note the eyes and mouth with no encircling face.*

Comanche Gap is a break in this volcanic dyke. Comanche bands used it as a gateway to the northern Galisteo Basin. Petroglyphs cover many of the south-facing rocks.

Warrior images at Comanche Gap. At far left is a female figure pregnant with a baby warrior, ready for battle with spear and horned headdress. In the center is another warrior with a spear and an eagle feather headdress. The two shield-bearers carrying axes at right may be the war gods. Schaafsma believes that the two circles on the upper shield "probably represent the sun, as do the triangular points around the edge of the shield"; the lower shield is decorated with bear claws.

Stars, a snake, and a spiral (which may also be a snake) at Comanche Gap. All are part of the war symbology on this volcanic dyke.

CHAPTER 4

THE SPANISH *ENTRADAS*

THE SPANISH DOMINATED THE AREA now called San Cristóbal Ranch for nearly 150 years. We do not know if any Spanish actually called the land home, though they sent their priests to San Cristóbal Pueblo to build a chapel and convert the Tewas. Spanish families may well have built *ranchos* or *estancias* (family homesteads) on the land, as part of the community surrounding the mission center of Galisteo, which was nearby, large, and active. (At present, no direct evidence confirms this possibility; more research needs to be done.)[1] Still, Spanish policies drastically altered the lives of the San Cristóbal Indians, and played a part in their decision to abandon the pueblo forever.

The story of Pueblo-Spanish encounters actually began in 1527. In that year a large expedition of Spanish ships set sail from their base in Cuba, intent on continuing Spain's conquest and colonization of the New World. The voyage from Cuba was a series of adventures and catastrophes, culminating in a shipwreck off an island near Texas. Most of the 600 crew members died, a few disappeared into the mainland, and finally only four survivors remained on the island. These were Alvar Núñez Cabeza de Vaca (an aristocrat who was the

1. Many seventeenth-century Spanish records were destroyed in the Pueblo Revolt of 1680, severely truncating archival material from the pre-Revolt period. Future archaeological research may uncover more about this era.

A map of the New World, 1548. At this time the Americas were generally believed to be extensions of Asia.

ship's treasurer), the ship's captain, a sailor, and a Moorish black man named Estévan. Enslaved by Indian captors, the four survivors eventually escaped, wandering the Southwest for seven years in search of Mexico, where they knew they would find their countrymen.

The travelers followed Indian trails, often suffering intense privations. Here is one example from Cabeza de Vaca's journal on their sojourn in the Texas hill country:

> I have already said that we went naked through all this country; not being accustomed to going so, we shed our skins twice a year like snakes. The sun and air raised great, painful sores on our chests and shoulders, and our heavy loads caused the cords to cut our arms . . . . often, when we gathered wood, blood flowed from us in many places where the thorns and shrubs tore our flesh. . . . My only solace in these labors was to think of the sufferings of our Redeemer, Jesus Christ, and the blood He shed for me . . .

Sometimes they traveled with escorts of whole tribes:

> We traveled in that region [the Plains] through so many different villages of such diverse tongues that my memory gets confused. They ever plundered each other, and those who lost were as content as those who gained. We attracted more followers than we could employ or manage.

Cabeza de Vaca came to have great respect and admiration for most of the Native Americans he encountered, and he learned six of their languages. Likewise, most tribes treated him and his companions with kindness and great generosity. They were deeply impressed by the Spaniards' healing abilities, which, according to the pious Cabeza de Vaca, had miraculously developed as a result of their long ordeal.

When Cabeza de Vaca, his companions, and a large protective contingent of Indians finally reached northern Mexico, the first Spaniards they met were slave hunters scouting for victims. Upon hearing that the slave hunters and Cabeza de Vaca were of the same nation and religion, the Indians refused to believe it, for, as they said:

> . . . we [Cabeza de Vaca and his companions] had come from the sunrise, they from the sunset; we healed the sick, they killed the sound; we came naked and barefoot, they clothed, horsed, and lanced; we coveted nothing but gave whatever we were given, while they robbed whomever they found and bestowed nothing on anyone.

These comments are revealing, as they illustrate the complex and contradictory nature of many Spaniards of these times. Deeply religious, committed to ideals of courage, loyalty, and generosity, Spaniards, like many other contemporary Europeans, were often proud to the point of arrogance and sometimes prone to brutality.

Cabeza de Vaca's great adventure came to a close in 1537 when he at last sailed home to Spain. He tried to obtain permission to lead a colonizing expedition back to the Southwest; he longed to help bring Christianity, better health, and peace to the Indians he had come to know. But he was only offered a second-in-command position, and fearing the possibility of another inept captain and another shipwreck, he refused.

His lengthy report of his journeys, however, became our first written record of the land and peoples of the Southwest. A fascinating epic, it also reveals much about the depth of religious spirit of many sixteenth-century Spaniards.

It appears that Cabeza de Vaca came within 300 miles of San Cristóbal, but never actually saw any pueblos. He heard many stories of "towns of great population and great houses," and also of lands to the north where there was copper, malachite, and turquoise. Once in Mexico, his stories were just the spark needed to rekindle the popular legend of the Seven Cities of Cíbola, mythical northern cities where gold and silver were supposedly plentiful. As Cabeza de Vaca's account passed from person to person it became wildly exaggerated.

As it turned out, the Spanish authorities took Cabeza de Vaca's second-hand reports quite seriously, and the organization of *entradas* began. And with these expeditions, the European version of the history of the Pueblo Indians also began.

"Animal Feo y Fiero": the American buffalo, drawn by a Spanish artist in 1554 from the accounts of explorers. The creature was described as "a wonderful composition of divers animals; it has crooked shoulders, with a hunch on its back like a camel; its flanks dry, its tail large, and its neck covered with hair like a lion, it is cloven footed, its head armed like that of a bull, which it resembles in fierceness, with no less strength and agility."

The people of Yam-p'ham-ba doubtless heard about the four foreign travelers who visited their southeastern neighbors in the 1530s. News spread quickly among native peoples—partially by means of smoke signals and swift runners, and also through extensive trading and long-distance hunting trips.

But when the San Cristóbal Indians heard this news they may not have even been in their pueblo. According to Tewa legend, a large nomadic tribe swept down from the north between 1525 and 1535, destroying many Southern Tewa villages.[2] The pueblos of Shé, Colorado, Largo, and Colina Verde may all have been casualties of this or other attacks, although drought probably played a part in their ruin as well.[3] The San Cristóbal people may have survived by temporarily retreating to a fortified mesa about 1 mile northeast of their town. (The ruined

2. The Pueblos called these fierce invaders "Teyas." Schaafsma describes the Teyas as "Caddoan–related dog nomads" who lived on the southern Plains.

3. Schaafsma, following a theory proposed by Bandelier, believes that nomadic incursions probably caused these three pueblos' abandonment; Richard Lang believes that "drought was probably the major factor, not a temporary incursion."

Ruined sandstone walls of the fortified mesa, once a haven for embattled Southern Tewas. The mesa overlooks Yellowhouse Pasture and the distant Ortiz Mountains.

A section of the ruined fortress wall.

walls of this fortress are still visible.)

An oral tradition from Santo Domingo Pueblo provides an interesting version of this invasion story. The tale relates that long ago, before the Europeans came, a "wild tribe" from the Plains invaded Rio Grande country. The raiders were threatening Santo Domingo, and witches within the pueblo were plotting betrayal. One night the village men followed a witch outside the town, where they heard him signaling to the nomads. They set a trap and succeeded in capturing a strange wolf, which they brought back to the kiva. When they untied the wolf,

> he sat up, dog-fashion, and gazed stolidly into the fire. Only when the incantations began for breaking the charm by means of which men can change themselves into animals did he show signs of uneasiness. A roll of mountain tobacco was forced between his teeth, and at the first puffs the wolf vanished and a warrior of the [nomads] stood in its place.

Thus, the story continues, the witches' conspiracy was exposed and the traitors were routed from the village. The frustrated nomads then attacked a neighboring town but failed to take it. They rode off angrily toward the Plains, but the Southern Tewa pueblos lay in their path, and the raiders surprised and destroyed nearly all the towns. (The nomads in the Santo Domingo story are called *Kirauash*, which Bandelier points out sounds quite similar to the early name for the Apaches, which was *Querechos*.)

By the late 1520s and 1530s, drought was also adding to the difficulty of life in the Galisteo Basin, and inter-pueblo warfare may even have occurred. (Scholars at one time thought that peaceful interaction, trade, and mutual hospitality were the unbroken rule among the Pueblos, but evidence now shows that war between villages was common.)

So we cannot know for sure where the San Cristóbal people were during the 1530s as the stories of the four strange travelers circulated among the pueblos. Possibly the people were too overwhelmed by catastrophic circumstances to pay much attention to this news from the southeast. Or perhaps they were curious, hoping the wanderers might embody some form of spiritual aid. They might even have been suspicious, wondering if the foreigners might be witches. Hard pressed as the San Cristóbal villagers must have been at this time, it probably never occurred to them that the strangers were forerunners of others who would one day arrive in great numbers to change their history forever and disperse them to the four directions.

Life's a dream, the future but a lying vision,
As for friendship and for love mere lies are they;
And but lies as well are all the fond illusions
The misguided heart is conjuring up alway.
–La Mentira *(The Lie)*[4]

In New Spain, the stories of prosperous Indian cities had caught the imagination of the authorities, and soon they chose a twenty-seven-year-old nobleman named Francisco Vásquez de Coronado to oversee the plans for exploration. The preliminary scouting party was led by a fearless Franciscan friar, Marcos de Niza. Cabeza de Vaca's Moorish companion, Estévan, who had learned many native languages and customs, went along as guide. The strange story of this journey has been told (and perhaps exaggerated) many times: how the charismatic Estévan acquired a following of over 300 Indians along the way and eventually was sent on ahead by the friar; how Estévan sent back a huge cross, symbolizing the discovery of a town of immense wealth, to the friar's excited party; how on reaching the famed Cíbola (actually one of the Zuni villages) Estévan somehow aroused the suspicions of the village elders, and he and his followers were killed, with only a few survivors escaping to tell the tale.[5] When Marcos de Niza heard the story, he decided to view the town from a distant hill. Hurriedly claiming it for Spain, he headed back to Mexico. Apparently he trusted Estévan's inaccurate report and let his imagination embellish the distant town he had seen, for he gave a very exaggerated account of Cíbola, saying that the natives used large amounts of gold, silver, and turquoise.

These reports created great excitement in New Spain, and Vásquez de Coronado began organizing a major expedition with himself as leader. In the spring of 1541 he set off with between 300 and 400 men.[6] Scholar C. Douglas Inglis describes the recruits:

> Recent arrivals in Mexico for the most part, they possessed little more than their arms, clothes, and a horse, so they offered their all to the venture hoping for a return that would establish them for life as *hidalgos*[7] of Mexico. Only the leaders showed any wealth prior to the expedition.

At least 600 Indian servants and allies and 5 Franciscan missionaries, including Marcos de Niza, accompanied the soldiers. Clearly the Spaniards were hoping to

Don Francisco Vásquez de Coronado; illustration by José Cisneros.

4. This New Mexican song was imported from Spain; only the first verse is here.

5. Conjecture about Estévan's death abounds, and includes one theory that he actually escaped death and went into hiding. Another legend holds that the Zunis found his claim of representing white men, while he was black, suspicious. Yet another says that during his travels with Cabeza de Vaca, Estévan had been given a sacred gourd, symbol of the Medicine Man. The story goes on to relate that he decided to send this talisman ahead to Cíbola in an attempt to impress the Zunis, but unfortunately the elders recognized the gourd as being from an enemy tribe.

6. Not all of Coronado's company were Spanish. Among his party were also a German, five Portuguese, two Italians, a Frenchman, and a Scot.

7. The *hidalgo,* or lowest class of Spanish nobility, included professional soldiers, clergy, and administrators. Some were wealthy and others poor, but all were extemely proud of their position. Their ruling ideal was honor, with loyalty, courage, and generosity corollary virtues.

Charles V, King of Spain and Holy Roman Emperor, anonymous portrait in the manner of Jan C. Vermeyen. Rijksmuseum, Amsterdam.

find "another Mexico," a promised land where they could pursue their twin aims: to serve their God by saving souls and to serve their king by acquiring land. The third aim, not often stated, but clearly paramount, was to find wealth and attain glory.

The Spanish in 1540 were extremely nationalistic, reveling in their "golden era" as they warred on and colonized countries all over the world.[8] They had expanded into the Netherlands, parts of France and Italy, Sardinia, and many distant countries such as Borneo and the Phillipines. And they had created a huge empire in the New World by conquering the Aztecs, Incas, and their millions of subjects. The monarch who presided over this epoch was the indomitable Charles V, King and Holy Roman Emperor. As both spiritual and national leader, he inspired intense loyalty in his vassals, who followed a feudal code of behavior, idealizing chivalry, honor, and pride. As church and state merged, Spain came to see itself as the propagator and defender of the true faith against a host of infidels. Perhaps the long conflict with the "heathen" Moors began this theme. In any case, devotion to Catholicism became deeply intertwined with militarism, and all Spain's wars became holy wars. (By 1540, new Spanish laws had begun to discourage the forced conversion of New World natives, but an unquestioning belief in the superiority of Spanish civilization and religion was still customary.)

Back in the wilderness north of New Spain, months passed as Vásquez de Coronado and his huge party trekked on. At one point on the long route Vásquez de Coronado received a message from some northern Indians, warning that any white men who entered their lands would be killed. Ignoring this threat, he went on, first to the towns of the famed Cíbola, attacking and entering one of them. It was immediately apparent that the Zuni town was only a modest pueblo with no gold or silver at all, and the chagrined Marcos de Niza, feeling the anger of his disappointed countrymen, soon returned to Mexico.

Undeterred, Vásquez de Coronado began a thorough exploration of the whole region, which then included between 75 and 134 inhabited pueblos. It is very likely that he visited San Cristóbal but difficult to prove conclusively. The names that Vásquez de Coronado's chronicler had given the towns were different from the names later historians chose. However, Pedro de Castañeda, the chronicler, described two or possibly three inhabited towns in the Galisteo Basin. Every archaeologist who has studied these old records has his or her own theory as to which towns they describe. But San Cristóbal, Galisteo, San Lázaro, and San Marcos were the only villages that could have been occupied during this time, though there were many other ruined and abandoned pueblos in the area. Vásquez de Coronado's expedition crossed the Galisteo Basin at least nine sep-

8. The British, French, and Dutch were also successful colonizers during this era.

arate times, so it seems very unlikely that he would have missed San Cristóbal. However, it is possible that San Cristóbal may have been temporarily abandoned at this time, as previously mentioned, due to Apache or Caddoan attacks or drought.

Castañeda made another remark that has mystified historians; he said that the Galisteo area had three towns, all "under the jurisdiction of Cicuye [Pecos]." Perhaps this referred to their trade relationship, as Pecos was certainly a large and powerful trading center.[9]

As winter set in, Vásquez de Coronado headquartered his army near a cluster of pueblos he called Tiguex, in the lands of the Southern Tiwa (about 50 miles southwest of San Cristóbal). The natives welcomed his army with generous gifts of food, in customary Pueblo fashion. But when the snows began, the army ousted the inhabitants of one whole town, Puaray, and began to demand extra food and clothing. Unused to this type of behavior from guests, the Tiwas became alarmed. The last straw came when a Spaniard raped an Indian woman. The next day the Tiwas "staged a minor rebellion" trying to get the Spanish to leave. Vásquez de Coronado squelched their resistance and then, as a warning against further revolt, executed 200 villagers, "mainly by burning at the stake." At this atrocity all the Tiwas banded together against the Spaniards, and fierce fighting continued all winter. By the time Vásquez de Coronado finally left, hundreds more Tiwas were dead and ten of their twelve villages were abandoned.

Before he returned to Mexico, Vásquez de Coronado and a large group of soldiers went in search of another mythical town of fabulous wealth called Quivira. A Plains Indian captive had described it to them in glowing terms and then volunteered to guide them to it. The Spanish searched for almost three months, as far as Kansas, before they realized that they were being purposely led astray by the Indian. He had been leading them back to his original homeland, and confessed that he had undertaken the mission on the orders of the Pecos chiefs, who hoped the Spaniards would die on the Plains. The infuriated soldiers choked the Indian to death, then turned back.

Apparently it was clear to the Pecos people, as well as the Southern Tiwas, that these initially impressive visitors were arrogant and ruthless. Thus, customary Pueblo hospitality turned to mistrust and a tendency toward guile which was not easily overcome. The Southern Tewa of the Galisteo Basin, located precisely between these two groups (Pecos and Tiwa country), certainly heard all this news.

Finally Vásquez de Coronado returned to Mexico. He wrote an honest report that disillusioned many and discouraged further expeditions for almost forty years.

By 1556 Charles V's son, Philip II, had ascended the Spanish throne. Firmly

Philip II, portrait by an unknown artist in 1580. National Portrait Gallery, London.

9. Dr. Frances Levine, a Southwestern ethnohistorian, points out that "the relationship may have been more than economic. We really don't know what the ideological or political organization of the pueblos was."

committed to Spain's role as the champion of Catholicism, he expanded Spain's power and boundaries even farther than his father had. As an indirect result, in 1581 a small but zealous religious party, determined to honor their king and God, decided to try once again to spread Christianity north from New Spain. Three priests, eight soldiers, their Indian servants, and a large herd of livestock traveled up the Rio Grande visiting many pueblos, among them Galisteo and San Cristóbal. They described San Cristóbal as being on the edge of the buffalo country and named it *Piedra Quita*.[10] The trip's historian, Hernán Gallegos, says:

> "Four pueblos were discovered here [in the Galisteo Basin] the first of which had three hundred houses five stories high. It was named Piedra Quita. It was given this name because all of it is of rock."

The Spanish asked the San Cristóbal people for food, but the Indians refused them. The Spaniards and Pueblos began to argue, and the village chief "threatened to gather three thousand men within an hour to destroy the Spaniards." Eventually the travelers managed to intimidate the San Cristóbal natives into supplying them.

But the eight Spanish soldiers were becoming fearful. They sensed the general hostility, and sometime after the San Cristóbal incident, they decided to return to Mexico, leaving two determined missionaries to fend for themselves. (Fray Juan de Santa María had earlier tried to return alone to Mexico, departing from the Galisteo Basin on September 7, 1581. A few days later, while he slept, "local natives dropped a big rock on him, crushing him in the manner they reserved for evil witches." Tanos were thus responsible for the first Franciscan martyr of the Southwest.) Only days after the soldiers left, the remaining friars, Fray Agustín Rodríguez and Fray Francisco López, were killed by the Tiwa of Puaray, the same town that Vásquez de Coronado had devastated forty years earlier.

The next year Antonio de Espejo, a wealthy and energetic Spaniard in the cattle business, organized another small party: fifteen soldiers, one priest, and fifteen or more Indian servants.[11] Ostensibly they were looking for the three lost missionaries, but they were also scouting the area for minerals and possible colonization sites.

Espejo's party traveled all over Pueblo country and beyond, visiting Acoma, Hopi, Zuni, and Jémez, and most of the Rio Grande towns. Many pueblos received them with friendliness, gifts, and provisions; like Vásquez de Coronado's men, Espejo's group survived on food given by the Indians. It is impossible to know whether the Pueblos' memories of Vásquez de Coronado's visit had faded over time or whether they were simply hoping that the Spanish,

"San Antonio de Padua and Ruego del Nos" carved by Jorge Sánchez. St. Anthony of Padua is always portrayed holding the Christ Child. Trained by San Francisco (St. Francis), San Antonio performed many miracles, supported by visions of the infant Jesus. In New Spain he became the patron of cattle and burros, a saint who could be invoked to help locate lost articles, find girls good husbands, and help women who wish for children.

10. Most modern scholars agree that the town these Spaniards called *Piedra Quita* was San Cristóbal. This particular *entrada* is referred to as the Rodríguez–Chamuscado expedition.

11. Descriptions of the early explorers vary considerably. Kessell makes the following comments about Espejo: "Lay officer of the Inquisition, cattle rancher and buyer, convicted accomplice in a murder case, Don Antonio had removed to the frontier [of New Spain] to avoid his sentence, a considerable fine." Espejo may have undertaken his northern expedition to try to redeem himself in the eyes of the authorities.

if well-treated, would depart without damage. It seems that some Pueblos were friendlier than others. Espejo's chronicler, Pérez de Luxán, reports one incident that occurred at a village he calls "Puala," which is probably the same Tiwa pueblo of Puaray mentioned earlier. Pérez de Luxán says that when the soldiers asked the "Pualans" for food, the people "mocked them," so,

> as the pueblo was large and some had hidden themselves there, we set fire to the big pueblo of Puala, where we thought some were burned to death because of the cries they uttered. We at once took out the prisoners two at a time and lined them up against some poplars . . . and they were garroted and shot many times until they died. Sixteen were executed, not counting those who burned to death.

Pérez de Luxán continues that "the news of what had happened at Puala spread throughout all the provinces and they were so afraid that all served and regaled us." Thus Espejo's visit reestablished the Spaniards' reputation for violence.

One week after the burning of Puala, Espejo visited the nearby Galisteo Basin. Pérez de Luxán describes the towns of San Cristóbal (Pocos) and San Lázaro (Jumea), which were very close to each other and whose Tano people had much in common. Clearly they had heard the news of the calamity in Puaray.

> . . . marching three leagues we came to the pueblo of Jumea [San Lázaro], in the province of the Atamues [Tanos], a people more bellicose than those of the other provinces. They possess well-built houses, as the most astute people in war, and the flat roofs have drainage troughs. They are three and four stories high, with movable ladders so that when raised they cannot go up to them. They wear their hair like the Pataragueyes [a Caddoan group], with a sort of scull cap made of it. The women are more comely than those of the other provinces; they dress like the others. They gave us turkeys, pinole, and of other things which they had . . .
>
> From this pueblo we went two leagues farther for provisions, to the pueblo of Pocos [San Cristóbal] of this province, which is a very large pueblo. It must have over fifteen hundred warriors with bow and arrow. The houses are of four and five terraces, with wooden palisades before their houses as a war measure. They did not wish to give any provisions to four men who went to ask for them. They said they did not have any; that there was a lack of rain and they were not certain they would gather any maize. They raised their ladders and no one would come down. Thus they [the Spaniards] turned back, not wishing to disturb the land.

Espejo's party then went on to Pecos, one of the largest pueblos and a great trade center. These Indians also refused to give the Spaniards food and "acted in the

Canyon Ceta reservoir.

Blooming salt cedar trees near Pueblo Colorado.

same manner as the people of [San Cristóbal]." Desperate, six soldiers forced their way into the pueblo, intending to burn it. Pérez de Luxán reports that "the people were so frightened that they gave it [pinole] to us against their will." The Spanish stayed two days at Pecos then forced two men to guide them to the Plains to hunt buffalo. Soon after, they returned to New Spain.

The increasingly wary attitude of the Pueblos helped to convince the Spanish that a larger army would be needed for any real colonization. But would-be explorers of the sixteenth century had many obstacles to overcome before their journeys could begin. Any *entrada* required royal permission, and letters traveled exceedingly slowly between Europe and the New World. King Philip II was preoccupied with Spain's endless war against the Dutch, and after 1588, with the stunning defeat of the Spanish Armada by England. One impatient colonial governor, thinking he had found a loophole in Spanish law that might allow a northern journey, decided not to wait for the monarch's formal approval, but set out on his own in 1590 to colonize Pueblo country.

When Gaspar Castaño de Sosa arrived at Pecos Pueblo with his 170 settlers, the Indians seemed to welcome them. But during the first night, the Pecos people launched a surprise attack. The Spanish fought back, and eventually forced the Pueblos to flee to a nearby mesa top. Castaño de Sosa then traveled all over the Rio Grande area from Taos down to the Tiwa country. He gave new names to many pueblos, one of which was San Cristóbal.[12]

Unfortunately for Castaño de Sosa, a party of Spanish soldiers arrived unexpectedly to arrest him for acting without royal permission. His entire party was driven back to Mexico in disgrace, and Castaño de Sosa was exiled to China.

Back in Spain, the defeat of the armada had proved to be a turning point, and the country entered a long period of decline. As Philip II continued to pour all his country's resources into military battles, the treasury drained dry. By 1600, Spain's colonies were still largely intact, but its economy was crumbling, and famine raged as thousands became homeless. Philip III, "a complete weakling who lived for pomp and ceremony alone," now ascended the throne, and he and his court retreated to a world of dreams where Spain still reigned supreme.

But the colonizing mechanism that had been operating for a century continued, partially on its own momentum. Even though the promise of great riches in the New World had faded, the Spanish still needed to colonize. For one thing, they needed to protect their borders and empire from other European powers who were beginning to explore America. And the residents of New Spain clearly needed new cheap labor, or slaves, now more than ever, since almost half the Mesoamerican indigenous population had been slaughtered or decimated by European diseases. From the missionary point of view, the souls of the heathen

Philip III, equestrian portrait by Velásquez, 1634–1635. Museo del Prado, Madrid.

12. Most Southwestern authorities, including Adolph Bandelier, believe that this designation was given to the same pueblo we know as San Cristóbal today.

Juan de Oñate de Salazar; illustration by José Cisneros.

Pueblos still needed to be saved as well.

Juan de Oñate de Salazar, a wealthy miner and general, led the next effort at colonization. Thousands of Spaniards were arriving in the New World, desperate to escape chaotic conditions in Spain; from these, Oñate was able to gather a group of 400 would-be settlers.[13] Oñate's effort was the most successful one to date. Like his predecessors, he was aided by New Mexican Pueblos many times: once so fortuitously that he renamed the helping town Socorro, or succor, and once by Northern Tewas so hospitable that he christened their village San Juan de los Caballeros ('of the gentlemen'). (Oñate passed through San Cristóbal, but his historian recorded no details of the visit.) Oñate settled his party at San Juan, deciding to make it his capital, and began building houses and the colony's first Christian chapel.

The Spaniards dedicated their chapel on September 8, 1598, with great celebration and ceremony. The climax of the festivities was a performance called "Los Moros y los Christianos," a dramatic re-enactment of a battle between Christians and Moors. Indians came from all directions for this event, in many cases to assess the Spaniards' military capabilities, so Oñate decided to invite representatives of all the pueblos to a great meeting. At this gathering, the Spanish explained that they had come to bring the Pueblos salvation and the opportunity to submit to the "two magesties" (the Pope and Philip II) and thus become obedient vassals. In return, the Spaniards said, they would commit themselves to "defending them [the Pueblos] against their enemies and prospering them in many ways and in matters pertaining to their political and economic welfare . . . ." The Pueblos "submitted" readily, falling on their knees and kissing Oñate's hand as instructed. The promise of a powerful new ally against their nomadic enemies surely played a large part in this decision. Pueblo leaders also took care to inform the head priest that "so far as the Holy Catholic faith was concerned they would adopt it, provided, after they had received proper instruction, they found it desirable." Oñate then divided the Pueblo country into seven districts, and assigned priests to each; the missionaries left for their areas with Indian escorts. Fray Juan de Rozas was sent to minister to San Cristóbal, as well as to eleven other pueblos.

As the Spanish traveled Pueblo country, the scenes of acceptance were repeated, though often in lukewarm fashion. Whether the acceptance was sincere or feigned we cannot now know, although it is likely that splits of opinion and varying reactions occurred among many tribes. As time went on relations between Spaniards and Pueblos deteriorated, as one of Oñate's priests explained to his superiors in 1601:

13. For fascinating studies of the participation of crypto-Jews in this and other colonizing efforts, see Tobias 1990, Steiner 1989, and *El Palacio* 98(3). Due to the Inquisition, Jewish immigration to the New World was massive. Steiner says "by 1545 . . . one-quarter of the Spaniards in Mexico City were Jewish." Judaic beliefs and customs went underground in New Mexico, but likely contributed to the evolving Catholic Hispanic culture, as traces still survive today. Scholars Stanley Hordes and Tomás Atencio are leading current research on this subject.

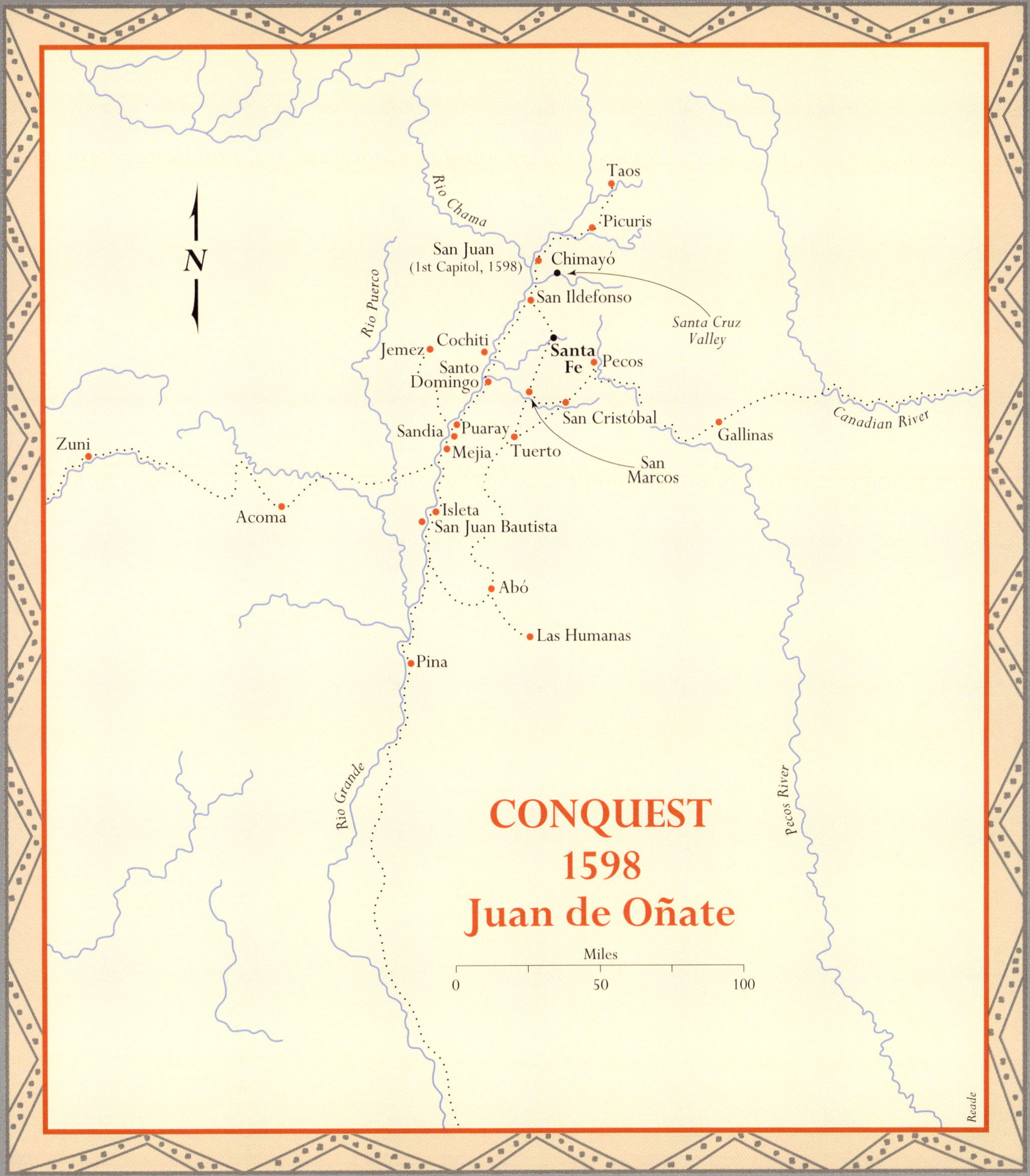
Taos
Rio Chama
Picuris
San Juan
(1st Capitol, 1598)
Chimayó
N
Rio Puerco
San Ildefonso
Santa Cruz
Valley
Jemez
Cochiti
Santa
Fe
Pecos
Santo
Domingo
San Cristóbal
Gallinas
Canadian River
Sandia
Puaray
Zuni
Mejia
Tuerto
San
Marcos
Acoma
Isleta
San Juan Bautista
Abó
Las Humanas
Pina
Rio Grande
Pecos River
CONQUEST
1598
Juan de Oñate
Miles
0
50
100
Reade

Acoma Pueblo, about 100 miles southwest of San Cristóbal Pueblo (photographer unknown).

> . . . now the Indians have to provide everything. As a result, all the corn they had saved for years past has been consumed, and not a kernel is left over for them. . . . they eat dirt and charcoal ground up with some seeds in order to sustain life. . . . Your lordship must not believe that the Indians part willingly with their corn, or the blankets with which they cover themselves; on the contrary, this extortion is done by threats and force of arms, the soldiers burning some of the houses and killing the Indians. This was the cause of the Acoma war . . .

When Oñate's nephew, Vicente de Zaldivar, went to the fortresslike mesa of Acoma to obtain blankets and provisions for an expedition, the Acomans killed him and twelve of his men. Fearing that all the pueblos might now revolt, Oñate mounted a fierce assault on the Acomans, storming the heretofore impregnable mesa. Eventually the Spaniards shot or burned to death the majority of the population. Of those taken captive, all the men over twenty-five years of age "were sentenced to have one foot chopped off and to twenty years hard labor" and all the women over twelve were given twenty years of slavery. This brutal defeat of a town that Pueblos had always considered unconquerable caused the surrounding villages to lose all hope of expelling the invaders.

Meanwhile the Spanish colonists were becoming thoroughly disillusioned with wilderness life and with Oñate, who drained the colony's resources with his constant expeditions in search of treasure. By 1601 almost all the settlers deserted, heading back to Mexico. By 1608 the viceroy in New Spain was considering abandoning the tiny northern colony (even though Oñate had persuaded some settlers to return) and he recommended this step to the king. But the king responded that the colony should continue for the sake of christianizing the Indians, even if there were no riches to reap. He ordered all treasure hunting to cease immediately and recalled Oñate, who was tried and convicted in Mexico for his harsh treatment of the Acomans, among other things.

In 1610 the capital was relocated to Santa Fe with a new governor at its head, Pedro de Peralta. Colonization finally took hold and the Spanish way of life began to flower in Pueblo country.

CHAPTER 5

A REMOTE COLONY

". . . another ten leagues to the north we come upon the first and principal pueblo of the Tanos nation, called Galisteo. It [the Tano nation] extends for another ten leagues, with five pueblos, where there must be more than 4000 baptised souls. It has one convent, and a fine church with three naves, and all use it for their service. They are very well instructed and ministered to, with their schools of reading, writing, singing, playing musical instruments, and praying, just like all the others."

—Alonso de Benavides, first "guardian" of the Franciscans in New Mexico

FROM THE BEGINNING, SPANISH COLONIZATION in the New World had two clear goals: to convert the Indians and to create wealth. By 1630, the date of Benavides's report, Spain's need for wealth was desperate. The nation had continued to decline under Philip III, and corruption, inflation, and disillusionment were widespread. The Royal Armada, once the envy of all Europe, now had only seven galleons. But Spain still saw itself as the defender of Catholicism and medieval ideals, and, as the Reformation wrought upheaval all over the continent, Spain fought the changes on every front. When sixteen-year-old Philip IV became King in 1621, many hoped he would somehow restore Spain's glory. But the huge challenge overwhelmed the young man, and he spent his days in fantasy and frivolous diversions as the country disintegrated around him.

The situation in Spain's colonies inevitably mirrored all this. In Pueblo country, Spaniards were dividing into two camps: on one side were Franciscan priests still committed to spreading the faith, and on the other were soldiers, settlers,

Philip IV with the dwarf Soplillo, by Rodrigo de Villandrano, 1615–1620. Museo del Prado, Madrid.

and officials committed to making profits as the funds from Spain dwindled. Clearly these two were destined to clash. Their conflict intensified with every year, creating first tension, then tragedy.

At first the missionaries seemed quite successful. In 1630, for example, Alonso de Benavides, a Franciscan "who had had considerable experience as an official of the Inquisition," claimed that 60,000 Puebloans had been baptized. This figure is obviously exaggerated, and it is true that baptism may have been a meaningless ritual for many Indians. But clearly the missionaries made great strides in their first thirty years in New Mexico.

Most of the friars who came to the new colony were sincere men who risked their lives to spread the Catholic faith. They saw the Pueblo people as fully human beings (in contrast to many settlers, who did not share this view). But the priests believed the Indian deities and Kachinas were "idols" or "devils"; their mission was to save these "devil-worshippers" from the eternal fires of hell.

The people of the Galisteo Basin must have felt some respect for the bravery of the first priest to visit them, Juan de Rozas. We have no record of his work, but probably he kept his conversions simple, partly since he knew very little Tewa, stressing veneration of the cross and recitation of simple prayers. He may have told the Indians Biblical stories; these intrigued many Pueblo people, who were great storytellers themselves. Perhaps they responded to his tales of the compassionate St. Francis who, like them, felt a kinship with all living beings. Some may have wondered if perhaps the potent gods of these white strangers could help improve their own lives. No doubt they had heard the story of the apparent power of two of Oñate's priests. These priests, on arriving at San Juan with Oñate's army, heard that the Northern Tewas were in the midst of a serious drought. The Indians had been dancing for rain for weeks, and they pointed out their drooping crops to the priests, who kindly promised to pray for rain. The next day thunderclouds appeared and a huge storm began.

Many Southern Tewas may have thought this new religion worth a try; of course, only in addition to their ancient ways. Like all Pueblos, they had always borrowed and added elements from neighboring tribes' rituals and beliefs. This kind of exchange had been part of life for centuries.

But most tribal elders, including the *caciques*,[1] remained skeptical and adopted only the most minimal forms of Catholicism for the sake of peace with the Spaniards.

The building of churches went on, carried out in all cases by Pueblos. In fact, Benavides states that all the early churches' walls were built by Indian women with help from older children. By 1621 Fray Pedro de Vergara had become San Cristóbal's first permanent priest, and the first to take up residence there. But by

1. In Tewa society, *caciques* are a combination of priest and leader; they are the chiefs of the Summer and Winter societies.

1626 the Spaniards had established a larger mission with a church and a *convento* for priests at nearby Galisteo Pueblo, and San Cristóbal and its small chapel soon became merely a *visita*, or outlying, dependent branch of the Galisteo parish. Fray Alonso de Estremara was the last Franciscan to live at San Cristóbal, in 1628. After this, Galisteo priests journeyed to San Cristóbal and other *visitas* on a rotating basis.

Until the 1630s the Pueblos were relatively peaceful, though there were sporadic instances of resistance. Many Pueblos outwardly accepted the new order; Indians and Spaniards intermarried, and friendships and other close bonds were formed. Perhaps the natives welcomed the abundance of new crops: wheat, oats, onions, chile, peas, melons, and fruit trees. New livestock—goats, cattle, and sheep—were flourishing, too. But these positive signs only partly softened the drastic change Spain had brought to the Pueblo world.

The whole economic system of the Pueblos had been turned upside down. The Spanish instituted an *encomienda* system as a reward to certain colonists, who were allowed, as *encomenderos,* to collect annual tribute, mainly in the form of corn and blankets, from a certain pueblo or number of Indians. Another system, *repartimiento,* guaranteed colonists the forced labor of Indians who lived nearby. Well-intentioned Spanish laws, such as the Pope's 1537 edict prohibiting abuse, enslavement, and forced conversion of Native Americans, and even King Philip's orders to the same effect, were bypassed at every opportunity. Far from the "civilized" world, the remote colonists of New Spain simply went their own way.

Sister María de Jesús, spiritual guide to Philip IV. Many stories circulated in early seventeenth-century Spain about Sister María's adventures, including the one illustrated here, in which Sister María instructs the Indians of New Spain after having been carried there by angels. Sister María herself tended to downplay such stories, saying, in this case, that "perhaps an angel had impersonated her."

Both the church and the secular government demanded frequent Pueblo tithes and tribute in the form of grain, produce, and handicrafts. At first the Pueblos did not object, as they were used to donating food to their own leaders and sharing crops with neighbors. But soon it became apparent that Spanish demands on their time and energy were going to be very heavy indeed.

Many governors of the new colony used their position as an opportunity to build businesses in weavings, salt, piñon, and hides. Forcing the Pueblos to work for nothing, or next to nothing, each governor quickly produced the yearly tribute to the Spanish crown then continued to amass profits for himself and his officials.

The missionaries, on the other hand, were intent on creating bustling agricultural compounds at every mission. They also needed free labor—to build churches, till the fields, herd flocks, assist at mass, and personally serve and aid the friars. They, too, started businesses, such as exporting livestock to Mexico, then spent the profits on richer chapel furnishings, vestments, and organs.

The Pueblos were becoming virtual slaves in a feudal system, with two mas-

Ruins of the Spanish chapel built about 1620 at San Cristóbal Pueblo. A cemetery adjoined it.

The mission at Isleta Pueblo in 1867 (William A. Bell, photographer).

ters warring over their services. In addition to the labor demands, the priests expected the Indians to attend frequent religious services and conform to a strict Catholic moral code.

From the Spanish point of view, none of this was excessive. After all, they reasoned, they were bringing the Pueblos not only civilization, but salvation, too. Why shouldn't the Indians serve and obey their "superiors," if only out of gratitude?

From the Pueblo point of view, the situation was verging on disaster. They had accepted these strangers from a mixture of fear, caution, and hope for protection from the nomadic raiders. Because of their rivalry and independence, and because there had never been any reason to unite, the Pueblos had never coalesced into one force, and the divisions of opinion in the first years of the Spanish colony had created the effect of paralysis. But they had always been a patient people, and even now some among them took a "wait and see" attitude.

One unspoken but crucial fact of the new order was that in spite of all the Catholic "conversions," most of the converts continued to practice their native

Feathered prayer sticks.

religion. For most Pueblos it would have been unthinkable to stop, since their ceremonies were the core of their entire way of life. Besides, they believed the new religion could simply be added on. The priests tried to be patient with this attitude, which seemed to them a sort of stubborn incorrigibility, and some looked the other way. But by the 1630s it was evident that the old Pueblo ways were as strong as ever. So the clergy began trying to prevent the native dances and rituals, harassing native religious leaders and severely punishing minor infractions of church attendance. Resentment grew all over Pueblo country, and between 1644 and 1670 at least five attempted revolts occurred, one of which was led by Clemente, governor of all the Tano pueblos. Literate in Spanish and respected by both Pueblos and Spaniards, Clemente succeeded in uniting all the Pueblos in the conspiracy, but the plan was discovered and he was hanged. Time after time rebel leaders were found out and either executed or sold into slavery before any damage could be done.

All this unrest only exacerbated the conflicts and division among the Spaniards, and by the 1640s the clergy and the governors were at each others' throats. The clergy accused the governors of exploiting and corrupting the Indians, taking them away from their mission duties to toil without recompense. Helped by the Inquisition, they proved many cases. The civil authorities, for their part, accused the missionaries of whipping and abusing the Indians, and of sexual misconduct, and also proved many cases. In 1661, for example, a San Cristóbal woman accused Fray Diego Parraga, a priest from another pueblo, of sexual abuse. (He was similarly accused at his own pueblo.) This period in New Mexican history was one of frustration and anger on all sides, with colonists, clergy, soldiers, and Indians all sharing in the general discontent. The governors probably suffered the least, although they were constantly harassed and besieged by complaints because of their corruption.

Governor Bernardo López de Mendizábal, who took office in 1659, so outraged both colonists and clergy that after only one year numerous petitions were filed against him. Among the thirty-four complaints filed on behalf of the Pueblos were allegations that "twenty-two Indians from Galisteo were sent to the house of Captain [Nicolás de] Aguilar in the Salinas area for maize to be transported to Santa Fe [without pay]" and that the Tano Pueblos had manufactured 165 pairs of stockings for the governor's account with no recompense. The list of Indian activities noted in other petitions gives a good idea of both the extent of the governor's businesses and the demand on the Pueblos. These included cutting and hauling timber for wagon parts; constructing wagons for hauling; gathering and transporting piñon, salt, and corn; "washing of hides, tanning leather, painting leather door-hangings, manufacturing shoes and leather doublets."

Governor López de Mendizábal further alienated the clergy by demanding that they pay for Indian services rather than receive them free, and the friars soon responded with a long list of grievances, saying that various missions had suffered heavy losses in sheep, cattle, oxen, and maize because they didn't have funds to employ the Pueblos. At the *convento* of Galisteo alone, they said, 100 head of livestock were lost.

Though the governor objected to the missions' exploitation of the Indians, he was hardly a sincere Pueblo ally. Rather, he wished the Pueblos to be free for *him* to exploit. Galisteo's friar Nicolás de Villar, for example, complained that "the Pueblo [mission] interpreter was removed and sent to herd livestock for the governor."

Hopi ceremonial mask.

A more telling example, and one that led to tragedy, was López de Mendizábal's encouragement of native dances and rituals. The missionaries, of course, had long felt that the purpose of the dances was "to invoke the powers of the devil." But the governor watched the people of Tesuque dancing and was reported to have said, "These scoundrel friars say that this is evil; it is not evil, but very good; and but for the fact that I am the governor I would go out and dance myself." López de Mendizábal later claimed he was misquoted, saying only that he viewed the dances as Indian nonsense. But he had given the Tesuque natives permission to dance as a means of honoring his presence, and at any other time they wished. The priests were shocked and enraged.

Partly in retaliation, the Franciscan custodian, Alonso Martinez (the leader of all New Mexico's clergy), in 1661 decreed a complete ban on all Pueblo dances. He gave orders to priests to raid all the kivas for Kachina masks, prayer feathers, and other sacred objects, and soon over 1,600 masks were destroyed. This began a religious reign of terror—the most devastating blow to the Pueblos yet.

At about this same time a severe drought began. Crops failed and many people died as the rains nearly ceased for ten years. The Pueblos must have seen a clear connection between the destruction of their sacred Raingod masks and the environmental devastation around them.

As the drought worsened, the Plains Indians, who had periodically raided the Pueblos for centuries, began to attack with even more ferocity. They hit Tano towns like San Cristóbal and Galisteo, close to the eastern Plains, especially hard. The Apaches had been raiding San Cristóbal long before the Spanish arrived, but in those prehistoric times there had been a "trading-raiding" relationship. This meant that the people of San Cristóbal and other Tano towns would sometimes trade with the Apaches and sometimes suffer their raids, but they managed to maintain a respectful, though circumspect, relationship.

Castañeda, Oñate's chronicler, describes the Galisteo Basin peoples' attitude toward the "Teyas," Plains raiders who destroyed prehistoric basin pueblos in the 1500s and who "before leaving the land made friends with all." He said,

> [These nomads] often go to the latter's pueblos to spend the winter . . . the inhabitants do not dare to allow them inside. Evidently they do not trust them, although they accept them as friends and have dealings with them. At night the visitors do not stay in the pueblo, but outside under the eaves.

Al–Che–Say, Chief of the White Mountain Apaches, and his warriors, in 1889.

The Pueblos acknowledged the Apaches as a powerful people, having great medicine men who followed a warrior religion. Therefore a sense of mutual respect had colored the pre-Spanish relationship. (Remains of Apache tipi rings are still visible near San Cristóbal Pueblo.) Still, one reason the Pueblos had originally allowed the Spaniards to stay was the promise of protection from these raiders. The Spanish tried to fulfill this promise but could barely manage to protect themselves from the Apaches and the Navajos (the latter began raiding in Pueblo country around 1629).

The Spaniards also greatly exacerbated the situation with their slave-trading. There had always been a few slaves in Pueblo country even before the *entradas,* usually Plains Indians captured by the Apaches. At the large town of Pecos overlooking the plains, Apaches and other nomadic tribes would come and set up their tipis several times a year, and great trading fairs would go on for days. Pueblos came from all over the Rio Grande, and in pre-Spanish times the main items of trade were buffalo hides and dried meat in exchange for turquoise, salt, piñon, and woven goods. But when the Spanish colonists arrived with their great need for laborers, from farm hands to household servants (since almost all respectable Spaniards disdained manual labor), the slave trade at the Pecos fairs boomed. Apaches, and later Comanches, traded their Plains captives to Spaniards for horses, knives, and guns, and the result of this short-sighted commerce was that soon these warriors became expert horsemen and even deadlier enemies. Although the trade fairs were a major source of slaves, the Spanish were not satisfied. Under the guise of retaliatory action they began attacking Apache camps, taking large numbers of captives, often women and children. Sometimes they kept them for their own use; more often they sold them to slave traders for work in mines to the south. Thus, the Apaches, who Castañeda in 1542 described as "gentle people, not cruel, and faithful in their friendship"[2] soon became terrifying and implacable foes of the Spanish, and of the Pueblos, whom they saw as Spanish allies.

By the 1670s many southern pueblos had to be abandoned because of inces-

2. Oñate's chronicler describes the early Apaches in positive terms: "Here we were met by some Indians of the nation called Apache, who welcomed us with demonstrations of peace. The governor and the men treated them generously, so that, although at first only a few came to meet us, within a short time, men, women, and children flocked to our camp and confirmed their peaceful disposition by raising their hands to the sun, which is their sign of friendship. They brought us some small fruit, black and yellow . . ."

Olun Tsan, Tewa Cacique of Santa Clara Pueblo, by Edward S. Curtis, around 1904.

sant nomadic attacks.[3] San Cristóbal and Galisteo fought off the invaders but suffered terribly. For years they struggled to raise their crops on the drought-plagued land only to have their meager harvests carried off by either Apaches or Navajos.

By 1675 the situation in New Mexico was desperate. A few rainstorms had eased the drought, but famine and suffering had brought everyone near the breaking point. Many christianized Pueblos felt the new religion had failed them, and attempting to heal the disruption in nature, they went back to their traditional dances and ceremonies. For the Spaniards, the crisis finally forced the warring priests and civil authorities to reconcile. Unfortunately, the result of their alliance was a decision to suppress the troublesome Pueblo religion once and for all. In 1675, Governor Juan Francisco Treviño raided and burned many kivas, arresting forty-seven Indian leaders and *caciques* (all of whom were Tewa) on charges of bewitching some priests. After a trial, three were hanged and a fourth committed suicide. The court ordered that the remaining leaders be publicly lashed in the plaza of Santa Fe, then imprisoned.

Soon after, a group of seventy Tewas descended on Governor Treviño's office, demanding the release of their leaders. Luckily the governor decided to let them go, for the Indians had planned to kill both the governor and all the citizens of Santa Fe had he refused.[4] But as it turned out, this episode, with its combination of persecution, humiliation, and execution of their holy men, proved to be the last straw for the Pueblos.

Now Tewa and Northern Tiwa war chiefs and other leaders began to meet secretly.[5] At first their talks focused on giving the Spaniards some sort of ultimatum, but soon men who knew the Spaniards well were drawn in, and these men, many of mixed blood, said that such halfway measures would fail—that instead the Europeans must be totally driven out. Gradually the original leaders accepted this view and began to map out strategy. More and more chiefs joined the plotters: the famous Popé from San Juan, who was one of the Tewas whipped and imprisoned by Treviño, was an early organizer, but there were many others. Among them were several prominent Tano leaders, including Antonio Bolsas, Juan of Galisteo, and Cristóbal Yope of San Lázaro. The conspirators usually met on fiesta days to avoid suspicion, waited until after midnight to begin talking, then left before dawn, running home through the dark.

In August of 1680, the spirits who advised Popé told him to make ropes with knots signifying the number of days until the uprising. Two Tewa runners carried these through all the participating pueblos, and the men who received them sent up smoke signals to indicate their agreement. But some Pueblos refused to go along with the plan and began to warn their Spanish friends. As the appoint-

3. An epidemic of European disease in 1671 also contributed to pueblo abandonments.

4. This information was related by a Spaniard who claimed to have spoken to the Indians after their meeting with the governor. However, the Pueblo author Joe Sando makes a relevant point: he says that the Spanish tended to exaggerate Pueblo bloodthirstiness, and that the Pueblos' main emphasis was always on compromise or forcing the Spanish to leave, rather than bloodshed.

5. According to some sources they had already been meeting prior to this event and just stepped up their meetings at this point.

ed date, August 13, approached, tensions became explosive, and rather than risk another aborted revolt, Popé killed his own son-in-law for threatening to betray the plan.

On the warm evening of August 12 the women and children of San Cristóbal watched as the last of their men, some on horseback and others on foot, left to make war on the Spanish. The past two days had seemed like a storm, as if the world were turning upside down. Warriors had come tearing into the village on Spanish horses, whooping victoriously with the news: their husbands and brothers, along with other Tanos, had killed the priests at Galisteo, then all the Spanish settlers who had gathered there seeking protection. They had caught two priests from Pecos who were hurrying toward Galisteo, surrounding them in a field and killing them, too. Then the warriors had ransacked the mission church on the outskirts of the pueblo. Now the warpainted men said they were joining others from Galisteo, San Marcos, La Cienega, San Lázaro, and Pecos; that together they would soon attack Santa Fe and force the hated Spanish to leave or die. The women quickly prepared food for their journey, praying and singing for victory as they worked.

Galisteo Pueblo, too, was a scene of chaos and tense preparations. By nightfall a great force of hundreds of men was making its way northward, out of the Galisteo Basin and up through the foothills and plains that led to the villa of Santa Fe. The warriors were elated. They had finally smashed the Spanish yoke, killed their oppressors, and ransacked the churches. Now, they felt, they were unstoppable. Normally self-controlled and measured in speech and action, they could hardly contain their exultation. Some did war dances as they went, some blew on captured Spanish trumpets. Riding at their head was a Tano known as Juan, wearing a Spanish leather jacket. He was fully armed with dagger, sword, and harquebus, and draped like a banner across his chest was the red taffeta sash from the convento *of Galisteo.*

How exactly had all this come about? After so many aborted attempts over the previous decades, the Pueblo people, who in all likelihood had never before united, somehow came together and were able to rout the Spanish as no other natives on either continent had done.

The story of the Pueblo Revolt has been told and retold, but probably will never be fully understood. All we have now are the official letters and records of Spanish officials of the time, the statements they took from captured or allied Indians, and the oral traditions of the Pueblos themselves. In each case the

authors are hardly unbiased. So we must piece it all together like a giant puzzle, and see what kind of picture it makes.

If we look at San Cristóbal's part in the uprising, the pieces of the puzzle fit very awkwardly, and the picture becomes a true enigma. For this town played a pivotal but mysterious role in the Pueblo Revolt.

Being close to Santa Fe, the Tanos of San Cristóbal had come into close contact with the Spaniards for years. As mentioned previously, the thriving mission in Galisteo had sent priests to visit San Cristóbal's chapel regularly, and there were groups of settlers in *ranchos* nearby. There may even have been a few Spaniards living at or near the pueblo.

So it is very likely that San Cristóbal had borne its share of taxation, tithing, forced labor, and religious repression. The Tanos' general reputation as the most warlike of all the Pueblos should be remembered, too. One document quotes an Indian from Galisteo saying that "the captains of the Tagnos [Tanos] told him before the revolt that they had desired and discussed it in these parts for more than twelve years."

Yet according to the records, the revolt was nearly sabotaged by the leaders of San Cristóbal, who went to Santa Fe and revealed the date of the uprising to the Spanish governor.

This in itself seems strange, but even stranger is the fact that after the leaders' trip to Santa Fe, the Tano people from every village, including San Cristóbal, rose as one to kill the Spaniards and march on the villa. How can this be explained?

Luckily the Spaniards kept fairly extensive records of all their activities. Francisco Xavier, Secretary of Government and War, a notorious figure among the Indians for his persecuting zeal, documented the days that led to the revolt. Most of the information that follows is from his journals, which were usually signed by Governor Antonio de Otermín as well.

The records begin on August 9. On that day, three messages arrived at the governor's palace: one from a priest at Galisteo, Fray Juan Bernal; one from the Pecos padre, and one from an official in Taos. All three messages contained the same news: that the Pueblos were planning a major revolt for August 13.

Xavier recorded that the Indian "governors and captains of the pueblos of Tagnos [Tanos], San Marcos, and La Cienega" were "responsible" for this information reaching Fray Bernal and that these Tano leaders came in person to Santa Fe. There they revealed that two young Tesuque messengers had run to San Cristóbal to inform them of the uprising. The messengers had said that all the pueblos were involved and that even the Apaches were allies, and that the revolt would begin August 13. On hearing this, Governor Otermín immediately ordered the arrest of the messengers. Brought to his office that same day, they confessed that they had been sent on a secret mission carrying "a deerskin thong with two knots in it, which signified the two days intervening between the execution of their treason." (This would make the planned date August 11.) They claimed they had not been privy to the meetings of the elders; all that the Indians knew was that an order had come from "very far away toward the north," from "an Indian lieutenant of Po-he-yemu" saying that the pueblos must all rebel, and whichever one did not would be destroyed. The messengers reported that the "Indians of San Cristóbal were unwilling to receive the message they brought, and reported it to the rest of their nation [the other Tanos]." Otermín gave no more orders that day, perhaps thinking he had one to three days to plan his strategy.[6]

But the next morning, very early, a soldier and interpreter named Pedro Hidalgo galloped into Santa Fe with the news that warpainted Tewas of Tesuque Pueblo, north of Santa Fe, had killed their priest and fled with their arms into the mountains.

Otermín immediately sent riders to warn Spaniards in the outlying settlements, but it was too late. He soon received word that all the Tewas and Northern Tiwas had likewise killed their priests and gone on the warpath. Then, on either that same day or the twelfth, Otermín heard that the Tanos, Keres, and Pecos Indians were at war, and had killed Father Juan Bernal of Galisteo along with three other priests. (Oddly, Otermín's own record varies by two days from Xavier's account.) The Tanos had massacred all the settlers from the surrounding *ranchos* except three women whom they took captive.

This means that despite the San Cristóbal and Pecos governors' warning to the Spanish on the ninth, a violent onslaught began either the next morning or very soon thereafter. At nine in the morning of August 13,[7] the Spaniards saw the men of San Cristóbal, San Lázaro, Galisteo, Pecos, San Marcos, and La Cienega "armed and giving war whoops" as they advanced through the fields near Santa Fe. The Indians cried out that now, "God and Santa María were dead . . . and that their own God whom they worshipped never died."

The Spanish were astonished to see Juan of Galisteo as one of the leaders of the Indian army. As a longtime Christian and trusted servant of Spaniards, Otermín had sent him several days earlier to notify Galisteo officials of the impending revolt. Now Juan entered the villa as the rebel emissary. He told Otermín that other Indians were bringing two crosses, one red and one white, for the governor to choose between. The white one meant that the Spanish

San Francisco de Asís (St. Francis of Assisi) was the founder of the Franciscans. As a young man he experienced several visions, which led him to leave his wealthy family and devote himself to poverty, self-mortification, and preaching; he eventually became marked by the stigmata; carved by Rafael Aragón (1796-1862), New Mexico.

6. The two knots in the deerskin thong could have signified either one or two days left before the uprising, depending on when the messengers arrived at San Cristóbal, or, if Otermín chose to believe the three earlier messages, he would have had three days until August 13.

7. Charles W. Hackett gives the date as August 15 according to one document of Xavier's, which is somewhat vague. Governor Otermín, in a later statement summarizing the seige, states that the Pueblo army was seen approaching on August 13.

would leave their "kingdom" forever and the red one meant war.

Otermín never even considered the white cross. To him, this Indian demand probably seemed the height of presumption. He told Juan that the Pueblos would always be Christians and Spanish subjects, that they must immediately repent their deeds and ask for pardon. When the Tanos heard this message they shouted in derision and began setting fire to the outlying buildings.

A bloody battle ensued and many Tanos and Pecos men died. From Galisteo alone six warriors were killed and many more were wounded. (In revenge, the furious Galisteo Tanos killed the three Spanish women they had taken captive.) The fighting raged all day, and the Spanish, clearly better armed and trained militarily, were beginning to get the upper hand on the Indians. Just as the Tanos were about to give way, warriors of Taos, Picuris, and all the Northern Tewa pueblos came charging in on captured Spanish horses. They made a furious attack from the north side of the villa and took several houses and the church, which they burned. Overwhelmed, the Spanish retreated.

Now the colonists were surrounded. They held on for six to nine days while more and more Indians arrived.[8] Soon the Pueblos cut off their water.

Finally, desperate and half-starved, the Spaniards decided to make one last stab at victory. On the evening of August 19, Otermín exhorted the women to redouble their prayers and told the priests to be ready to say a mass before dawn. At sunrise, Spanish soldiers sprang on the surprised Pueblos, and, of the 1,500 or more in the vicinity, killed 300.[9]

By 11 o'clock in the morning, the remaining Indians had fled the city, leaving behind forty-seven captives. Otermín restored water to the villa, then interrogated the prisoners. The captives told him that:

> they had the mandate of an Indian who lives a very long way from this kingdom, toward the north . . . and who is the lieutenant of Po-he-yemu; and that this person ordered all the Indians to take part in the treason and rebellion, saying that they would kill immediately anyone who refused to agree to it.

This declaration made no effect on the governor, who executed the prisoners.

Of the Spaniards, only five had died, though many were wounded; the survivors seemed "to have been miraculously protected by the most serene Virgin Mary," according to Xavier.

Still, Otermín now knew that the end was inevitable. The Spanish had no food left and their water could easily be cut off again. He decided to abandon

8. Whether the colonists actually lasted six or nine days is unclear. The confusion ensues from the two different dates given for the beginning of the conflict.

9. The figures for the total number of Pueblo warriors present is also unclear. At one point, Otermín says that more that 2,500 Indians surrounded the villa, and Donald Worchester describes the revolt as "a movement in which both Apaches and Navajos took an active part."

Santa Fe. The next morning he and his weary countrymen, about 1,000 in all, emerged from the villa in ragged military formation and began the long march south. The Pueblos watched from the hills, making no attack. By this time, fewer than 100 Spaniards had weapons, so it would have been relatively easy to fall upon the settlers and kill many, if not all of them. That the Indians let them go is testimony to the sincerity of their original stated aim: to drive the Spanish out, and not, as many Spanish claimed, to simply massacre them all.

In Xavier's journals there are many references to the Indians' plan to kill all the Spaniards, but what is usually omitted is that this plan went into effect only if the Spanish refused to leave. From the Indians' point of view, giving their oppressors such a choice seemed generous and reasonable; to the Spaniards it seemed merely a declaration of war. The concept of their own expulsion was alien, even absurd, to them; thus, they heard only the latter alternative.

Once the Spaniards were gone, jubilation and destruction reigned. The Pueblos burned almost everything associated with the Spanish, including their histories and records.[10] Many Indians tried to eradicate every trace of Christianity, and practiced their dances and rituals without fear for the first time in eighty years. According to some accounts, Popé tried to assert pan-pueblo authority, but soon failed. The antagonisms and rivalries that had existed for generations before the revolt resurfaced, and before long many villages were at war. The Pecos and the Keres, for reasons now unknown, began to make war on the Tano towns, including San Cristóbal. Simultaneously, the Apaches resumed their ferocious attacks on all the Galisteo Basin pueblos. Overwhelmed, the Galisteo Tanos moved into the Governor's Palace in Santa Fe. The people of San Cristóbal, who now numbered about 800, soon decided to abandon their village, too. Along with the Indians of San Lázaro (6 miles west of Galisteo), they moved first to San Juan, then north to the Santa Cruz River, rebuilding their pueblos on the site of an old Spanish settlement, and giving their new homes the same Spanish names—San Cristóbal and San Lázaro.

Tanos resettled Galisteo several times over the next century but never lived in the old San Cristóbal Pueblo, or its environs, again. The abandoned village slowly fell into decay, its roofs collapsing and its walls crumbling as wind-blown dirt and scrubby piñons covered them.

10. Frances Levine comments: "No doubt some of the crops remained as did the livestock. Some scholars even believe that Hispanic people who married into the Pueblos remained."

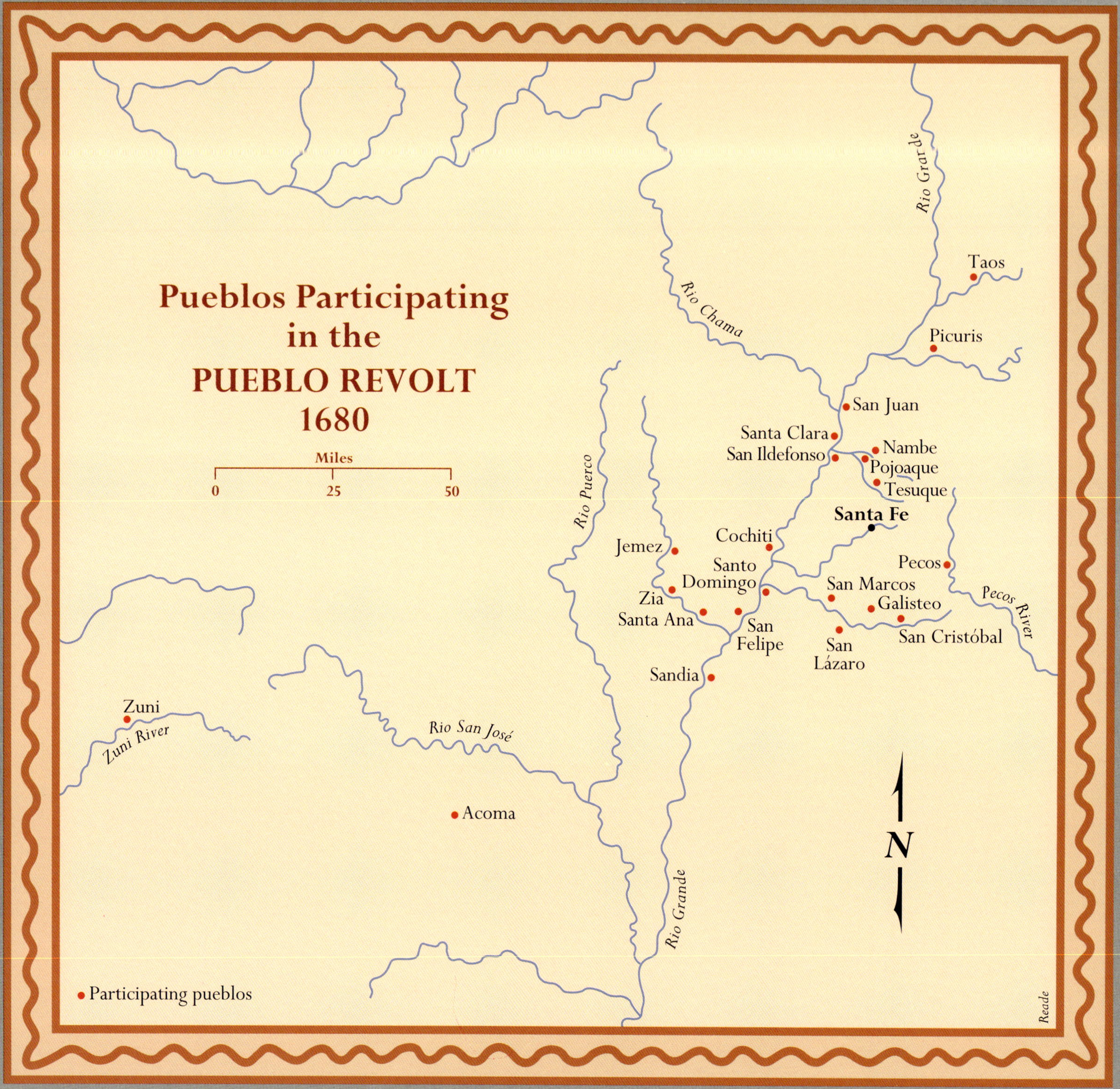

Pueblos Participating in the PUEBLO REVOLT 1680
Miles
0
25
50
Rio Grande
Taos
Rio Chama
Picuris
San Juan
Santa Clara
San Ildefonso
Nambe
Pojoaque
Tesuque
Santa Fe
Rio Puerco
Jemez
Cochiti
Santo Domingo
Pecos
San Marcos
Galisteo
Zia
Santa Ana
San Felipe
San Lázaro
San Cristóbal
Pecos River
Sandia
Zuni
Zuni River
Rio San José
Acoma
N
Rio Grande
Participating pueblos
Reade

The Pueblo Revolt

In keeping with their warlike reputation, the Tanos were the first to arrive at Santa Fe (along with the Pecos men) and the first to attack. Xavier describes their mood as they arrived as one of "audacity, boldness, impudence . . . and fury."

So it seems incongruous that they and their leaders would have opposed the revolt only a few days earlier, especially given Pedro Garcia's testimony that their leaders had been discussing revolt for twelve years. (Pedro Garcia was a Galisteo christianized Indian who joined the retreating Spaniards after the revolt; he gave them his sworn testimony on the journey south.) There are several intriguing explanations for this mystery but none is entirely satisfactory.

One possibility is that the Tano governors were part of a conspiracy to advise Otermín of the wrong date. Countless uprisings in the past had been sabotaged, so the leaders of this one surely must have prepared for such a possibility. According to Pedro Garcia's account of the two Tesuque messengers' visit to San Cristóbal, when the Tanos there learned of the revolt they passed the word on to the neighboring pueblos, Galisteo's "father custodian also learning of it." He does not mention *how* the priest came to hear of it, or that any Pueblos opposed the plan. In fact, he reports that the Tanos wanted "to kill the custodian, the fathers, and the Spaniards, and have said that the Indian who shall kill a Spaniard will get an Indian woman for a wife . . . and . . . that they are going to kill all the servants of the Spaniards and those who know how to speak Castilian, and they have also ordered that rosaries be taken away from everyone and burned."

It is possible that the Galisteo priest learned the news inadvertently and that perhaps the Tano governors, on discovering this, journeyed to Santa Fe to at least make sure Otermín prepared for the wrong date. Perhaps August 13 had been prearranged as the date which would be generally known, with the real date of August 10 or 11 known only to an inner circle of planners. It also seems odd that prominent Spaniards in Taos, Pecos, and Galisteo would all simultaneously, on August 9, learn of the date of the planned revolt, but somehow this is what happened.

Another intriguing fact is that the powerful pueblo of Pecos, which historically had some influence over the Tano pueblos, took a leading role in the organization of the revolt, and then accompanied the Tanos up to Santa Fe.

Otermín himself, in commenting later on the revolt's beginnings, said that he had tried to notify outlying officials of the Indians' plans, but that "the cunning and cleverness of the rebels was such, and so great, that my efforts were of little avail." (The Pueblos had planned their strategy so that all Spanish messengers were intercepted.)

Unfortunately, the statements of the two Tesuque messengers do not fit into this picture at all. The messengers implied that the date for the revolt was the eleventh or twelfth (by the deerskin thong with only two knots in it.) Thus, *they* were clearly not a part of any conspiracy. And, if not part of a plot, their statement that the "Indians" of San Cristóbal were hostile to the revolt must have had some truth to it. Unless we disregard their testimony altogether the conspiracy theory finds itself at a dead end here.

A second possibility is that the Tanos were against the uprising but were intimidated into fighting by rumors about the mysterious lieutenant of *Po-he-yemu* and his death threats against all traitors. Captured Indians mentioned *Po-he-yemu* several times in Spanish documents. But this theory doesn't hold up well. The stories of the twelve years' discussion of revolt, along with the enthusiasm and early arrival of the Tanos makes this an unlikely explanation. Also, Joe Sando, the Jemez historian, explains that this story is still a "legendary joke" among the Pueblos. When Spaniards captured Indians after the revolt and demanded to know who the leader was, the Indians would always point to the north and say it was *Po-he-yemu*. (This is a Tewa word. Keresans would reply *Payastiamo* and Towas would say *Payatiabo*.) But all three names refer not to a living person, but to a deity "whom the Pueblos address in their prayers to intercede for them with the One above beyond the Clouds." And Edward Dozier, the famous Pueblo scholar, says that *Po-he-yemu* is another name for Montezuma, a god who could "perform miracles and foretell the future." He says that for the secretive Pueblos, Montezuma became "a 'god' that might be mentioned conveniently to white people."

Perhaps the most credible explanation is simply that there was division among the Tanos. The revolt was not unanimous; Otermín never describes more than 2,500 warriors outside Santa Fe, when there were at least twice as many able-bodied men in Pueblo country. Xavier's reports state that the "governors and captains" of the Tanos revealed the plot to Otermín. Who exactly the "captains" were is unknown, but the governors in that period were Indians (originally chosen by Spaniards) who acted as liaisons between the Spanish and the Pueblos. Even in recent times the governors are primarily tribal representatives for the outside world; the real leaders and decision-makers are the *caciques,* or chiefs, who are also the spiritual leaders. When the governors visited Otermín they explained that "they were unwilling to participate in such wickedness and treason, saying that they now regarded the Spaniards as their brothers."

Clearly there was some division among the Pueblos. Among those who had long served the Spanish, intermarried with them, or otherwise become close, many were loyal. Pedro Garcia describes the Indian Bartolomé, a mission assistant at Galisteo, coming up to him "weeping" to warn him of the revolt. Perhaps the San Cristóbal "governors and captains" were simply Spanish allies.

In this case the San Cristóbal governors would have warned Otermín in all sincerity. The prearranged date was probably August 13, and perhaps, as Hackett suggests, when the Tesuque runners arrived with news of the new date (August 11) they perceived opposition and did not divulge it (or only divulged it to the *caciques,* and not the governors). In this way the majority of the San Cristóbal Indians would have been obeying and supporting their real leaders, rather than the governors, when they began to carry out the uprising.

This scenario seems plausible, even likely. But there are so many small discrepancies in the Spanish reports, so many odd inconsistencies, that the evidence finally begins to seem more like shifting sand than concrete fact. And since all our sources refer only to the Spanish interpretation of Pueblo actions, the picture is even further clouded. We may never know for certain what really took place in the village of San Cristóbal in the days that led up to the Pueblo Revolt.

Oyaygeh-o-Onyeh ("Moving Frost"), governor of Santa Clara Pueblo, ca. 1905. The governor holds two original silver-headed canes of office, symbols both of his authority and his pueblos's autonomy. One cane is Spanish and engraved with a cross; the other, more elaborate, is a "Lincoln Cane," that is, one of the canes President Abraham Lincoln presented to all Pueblo governors in 1863 (Edward S. Curtis, photographer).

Don Diego de Vargas Zapata y Lujan Ponce de Leon (1643-1704), Palace of the Governors, Museum of New Mexico, Santa Fe.

For the Spaniards, the Pueblo Revolt was a "lamentable tragedy, such as has never before happened in the world." Governor Otermín told the king that God had only permitted such an event to occur in "this miserable kingdom" because of "my grievous sins," which remained unnamed.

The Spanish had never been routed by Indians before, and though they were humiliated, they would not tolerate defeat for long. They made several attempts to reconquer New Mexico, but all failed until Diego de Vargas took command. An aristocrat from a long line of commanders and conquerors, Vargas at forty-seven was determined, proud, and decisive. His plan was to make a preliminary expedition to "subdue" the Pueblos by diplomacy rather than force whenever possible. Then he would return to New Spain to assemble his colonists and guide them north to the outpost he called "remote beyond compare."

When he and his soldiers reached Santa Fe in September of 1692, it was night, and the Tanos thought the horsemen outside their walls were Pecos or Apaches masquerading as Spaniards. The Indians asked them to play their Spanish clarion as proof, and when the soldiers did, the Tanos cried out that they would kill them all and, according to Vargas's journal, "commenced to shout furiously. This lasted well over an hour." Finally Vargas was able to parlay with the Tanos' spokesman, Antonio Bolsas, whom he described as "very clever," and eventually the Spanish were received into the villa without a battle. The warriors of the new San Cristóbal and several other pueblos, hearing of the Spanish arrival, came south to help their Tano kin, but ended up meeting with Vargas peaceably. Soon after, Luis Tupatú, leader of all the Tewas, Tanos, and Picuris, arrived with 200 to 300 warriors. Vargas describes him dismounting a splendid horse and advancing on foot with his retinue, wearing the "pelts of animals and in front at the crown of his head a band of palm fibers tied with a cord, and in the middle of that . . . was placed a shell in the form of a heart which seemed a crown at twenty paces from my tent." Tupatú made peace with Vargas, then suggested that the Spanish join forces with his people against their enemies, the Pecos, Keres, and Faron Apaches; Vargas agreed to this.

In October, Vargas visited the people of the new San Cristóbal village in the Santa Cruz Valley, baptizing many and telling them through his interpreter that he was reclaiming the pueblo and themselves "for the royal crown and our holy faith." Vargas's journal says that "they were received joyously" by the San Cristóbal people. All in all, Vargas's first expedition seemed to be a great success.

The reconqueror headed south to Mexico for his colonists, having won back the Pueblo country by means of his own, as he put it, "craft, skill, and sagacity." But while he was gone, rumors spread that he planned to kill all those who had participated in the Pueblo Revolt. The tribes had never been unanimous about

The ascent to the White Bluffs, west of Pueblo Largo.

the wisdom of readmitting the Spanish, and now even more division arose.

When Vargas returned to Santa Fe with his colonists in the winter of 1693 he found some of his old allies loyal, but a coalition of Tanos, Tewas, Northern Tiwas, Apaches, and Navajos had united to resist him. Now his negotiating skills were truly tested. The 800 settlers who had trekked north with him were freezing, hungry, and angry that Vargas had prepared no place for them to stay. Meanwhile, the Tewas and Tanos hunkered into their warm Santa Fe quarters, giving no intention of moving out. Resentment grew on both sides. After two weeks of covert war preparation by the Indians, who claimed to be preparing for a deer hunt, and much counter-manuevering by Vargas, the Spanish attacked and won the villa.

Vargas then executed eighty-one Tanos and Tewas, including Antonio Bolsas. Several other Indian leaders committed suicide. Vargas gave as his reason for the executions the "blasphemous declarations" of the Indians during the battle and their destruction of a large cross and other sacred objects he had left on his previous trip. He gave orders that the remaining Tanos and Tewas of Santa Fe be enslaved, but not unduly abused.

From 1693 to 1695 Vargas worked tirelessly to pacify the Pueblos and establish his colony. He rode from village to village, sometimes overcoming the people's initial wariness with his friendly words, sometimes encountering warriors who "wanted only to wage open battle and die like men." Some villagers fled their pueblos at his approach, hurriedly painting large crosses on their homes in hopes that the Spanish would not burn them.

Interpueblo warfare continued, and the San Cristóbal people fled their new village in 1694 because of raids by the Cochití and the Utes. (During their absence the Spanish came in and carried off their remaining stores of corn.) They managed to return to the village later, but in 1695 Vargas told them that new Spanish settlers were coming and that they (and the nearby people of San Lázaro) must move out. From Vargas's point of view this demand was entirely justified since the village was on an old Spanish site; further, he was allowing the Tanos to stay until after their harvest. But from the Pueblo point of view it was an arbitrary and arrogant order. Why should they give the homes, irrigation ditches, dams, and drains they had built to the Spanish, especially after they had defended them for fifteen years? But they had little choice, and after gathering their crops, they left.

Most of them went to the vicinity of Chimayó, where Vargas had promised them land, but they were very bitter about the situation and moved up into the mountains, perhaps to plan revolt. (It was said that planning for revolts had started as early as August 1695, and that the San Cristóbal people had participated.) Soon after, they were persuaded to return to their village in the Santa Cruz Valley; as it turned out, only San Lázaro had been taken over by the sixty-six families of colonists, who renamed it the Villa of Santa Cruz.

By the spring of 1696, tensions along the Rio Grande were again becoming unbearable. Another drought had struck, followed by a plague of worms that ruined the remaining crops. The ragged, disease-ravaged Spaniards nearly starved, selling their clothes to the Indians for food and eating dogs, cats, and leather hides to survive. Some went to work for the Pueblos to earn enough to eat; about 200 died.[11]

Fray José Arbizu had been stationed in the Santa Cruz Valley, and his letters to Governor Vargas in 1696 are anxious and despairing. He reports in one that he has done everything he can to assure the Tanos that Vargas means them no harm, but to no avail. The San Cristóbal people told him that Vargas had not only taken their lands and sent them to the "sierra of Chimayó, where there is no place to live, but only open land," but that now he wanted them to move to Galisteo where they would be under almost constant attack. From all this they concluded that his real plan was to eliminate them, probably because of their fighting nature. So they gathered their belongings and went into the mountains of Chimayó again, making horse traps at the entrances.

At this point Fray Arbizu feared for his life and worried that if the San Cristóbal Indians were not dealt with in some way, more trouble would follow, for "it is known they are instigating the others."

On March 17, Fray Arbizu wrote an angry letter to the father custodian saying that he had abandoned San Cristóbal, as Vargas could provide no guard for him and many Tanos clearly wished to kill him. He was deeply concerned that if he were killed, his death might not be a "true martyrdom," for his mission work was now only an exercise in futility, creating "irritation and obstinacy" among the Indians. Although in an earlier letter he had said he would give his soul for any of the San Cristóbal Tanos, by April 18 he was calling them "the senseless ones who are tolerated, although their purposes are known with their wicked and depraved customs, rooted in fifteen years apostasy, and now more apostates than then."

For all his bitterness, he soon relented and returned to San Cristóbal. But his fears were justified, for on June 4, 1696, a group of Tanos attacked and killed him. The Indians then set on Antonio Carboneli, a visiting priest from Taos, and the revolt began. Tanos united with groups of Keres, Tewas, Apaches, Hopis, and Pecos people, massacring settlers and missionaries. As fire and fighting spread over Pueblo country again, the Tanos apparently retreated into the hills near Chimayó.

Retablo of San Cristóbal (St. Christopher), a legendary giant of Canaan once named "Offero" who carried the Christ Child across a river, almost collapsing from His weight. He then took a new name, "Christ-bearer," and soon after became a martyr. The patron saint of travelers, he also helps believers to prepare for death; painted by Rafael Aragón (1796-1862), New Mexico.

11. These descriptions are from a report written later, in 1697, called the *Acusación del Cabildo,* which denounced Vargas and his governorship. Espinosa believes they may possibly be slightly exaggerated on this account.

Bulto of La Familia Sagrada (The Holy Family). The three figures also symbolize the Trinity, and together, they are the patrons of refugees and families.

From this point on, chaos engulfed the Tanos. Vargas forged into the mountains of Chimayó in early July to look for them, but they were already gone. They moved continuously now, and the group disintegrated more and more as families split off to join other pueblos. Some moved to Zuni, some to Taos, Picuris, Santa Clara, Tesuque, and Acoma; some still hid in the mountains. Some fled to the Plains, where they joined or were enslaved by the Apaches. Although they were widely feared because of their bravery, the Tanos had been prime instigators of the revolt, and now they were clearly on the run.

As Vargas pursued all the rebels, other tribes split similarly, and alliances formed and dissolved in a crazy swirl as families left their villages and fled in different directions. Many villages were permanently abandoned at this time, and others were left with only a few inhabitants.

By the time Vargas finally brought the Pueblo country under nominal control, most of the Tanos were gone. A sizable number had gone to Hopi country in Arizona and settled on First Mesa, founding the village known as Hano.

(The tradition among the people of Hano is that their Tano ancestors were invited there by the Hopis, who were having trouble fighting off Utes. According to this legend the Hopis had heard of the Tanos' reputation as great fighters and had begged them for help. The Tanos routed the Utes and were given part of First Mesa and farmland in return.[12] The legends also say that other later groups came to Hano because of trouble with the Spanish. Many elements of Hopi religion and culture have blended into Hano ways, but the Tanos kept their native tongue, Tewa, and still speak it today.)

Back in their original homeland in the Galisteo Basin, the Tano pueblos were ruined and the land was empty. In 1706 Vargas moved eighteen families of Tanos who had been living at Tesuque back to Galisteo, probably to create a buffer against nomadic raiders, and renamed the pueblo Nuestra Señora de los Remedios. The people were quickly decimated by Comanche attacks and disease, and by 1776 Fray Francisco Atanasio Domínguez described their lives this way:

> They are enduring even more deplorable poverty . . . [for they] no longer have anything to sell in order to live. . . . Most of the year they are away from home, now the men alone, now the women alone . . . [the Comanche threat] drives many of them to depart, as has been said. And those who remain eat the hides of cows, oxen, horses, etc., in a sort of fried cracklings, and when they do not find this quickly, they strip the vellum from the saddletrees or toast old shoes. . . . In short, they are so discouraged that they have thought of abandoning the pueblo and dividing themselves as best they might among the pueblos with

12. Albert Yava, a Tewa-Hopi, tells this story in more detail. He uses the name 'Tewas' instead of 'Tanos' throughout. The name 'Tano' was discarded in the early 1700s and 'Southern Tewa' began to be used instead.

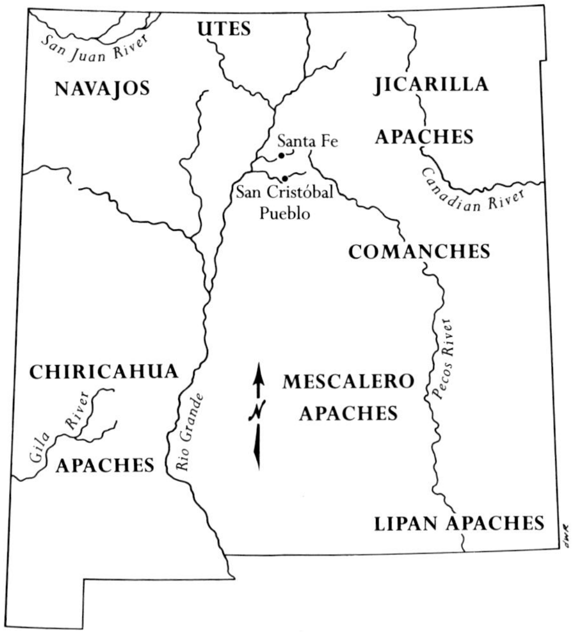

Eighteenth-century nomadic tribes in New Mexico.

> good supplies, but they have not done so for fear of the government.

A smallpox epidemic in 1780–1781 was the final blow, and the Galisteo burial book of that era ends in 1782. Most of the fifty-two remaining Tanos moved to Santo Domingo. Years later the people of San Ildefonso gave this metaphorical account of the abandonment:

> The ancient people of Galisteo had a snake, a big one and a black one, which they kept in the estufa [kiva]. When they went hunting and got game of any kind, they fed it to him. Mule-deer, buffalo, white-tailed deer, antelope, elk, rabbit, jackrabbit, birds—all these they fed to him. In return he gave them anything they wanted. Corn, squashes, chokecherries, berries, yucca fruit, cactus fruit, Tewa berries, moccasins, leggings, deerskin shirts he gave them.
>
> One morning they went out to look at him and did not find him. At midnight he had gone out. Nobody had seen him issue, nobody knew in which direction he had gone. They found tracks leading to the arroyo—big tracks, and they followed them. They followed his track along Galisteo Creek, where he went along the bed. They followed them to the mouth, where the tracks went into the waters of the Rio Grande. They went back to their pueblo and they held a meeting that next night. And the old men said to the old men: "The snake has gone. What are we going to have of those things which he gave us? He has gone away. Now we also must be going away." And they all went down to Santo Domingo Pueblo, where they settled.

Life went on all around San Cristóbal, on the harsh frontier still known as northern New Spain. The Spaniards had learned some lessons from the revolt of 1680 and neither the missionaries nor the governor made quite as many demands on the Pueblos as before. Colonists and Indians competed over land and water use but Pueblo rights were generally more respected in the 1700s and court records show many instances of Pueblos winning land battles against Spaniards. Pueblo soldiers or "auxiliaries" united with the settlers against their common foes, who had multiplied and now included Utes to the north, Navajos to the west and northwest, Comanches to the east, and Apaches from many directions. For many villages, life continued to be very dangerous except during the time of the annual trade fairs—at Pecos, Abiquiu, or Taos—when hostilities temporarily ceased.

Frontier society became a melting pot, though Spanish-born colonists tried to keep a semblance of European order. To this end, they formulated a complex system of castes that included twenty-two possible racial combinations. *Españoles,* those of pure Spanish blood, represented the top strata, with those born in Spain at the very pinnacle. Below them were those of *color quebrado* or

Wildhorse Mesa and the Ortiz Mountains.

"broken color," including those of Spanish-Indian blood *(mestizos)*, christianized Indians brought up as servants in Spanish households *(genízaros)*, full-blooded Indians, blacks (who were brought to the New World as slaves from the sixteenth century onward), and others of mixed heritage. Despite this pecking order, the Indian and Spanish cultures were merging in many ways, and the people were coming to terms with each other.

For a few years the only stirrings of activity in the Galisteo Basin were Spanish trade caravans on their way to Chihuahua and traveling bands of Comanches, who first appeared in the early 1700s. But Santa Fe badly needed a buffer against the nomads, so it looked to Galisteo, which in the past had traditionally served this purpose. Between 1790 and 1795, a detachment of Hispanic troops built a house near the abandoned Galisteo Pueblo and moved in. (They remained stationed at their lonely post until 1814.) Then in 1799, Galisteo's first civilian Hispanic settler, Juan Aragon, received a grant of grazing land.[13] In 1816 the village itself was born, as nineteen families built homes around a plaza and began to farm their individual grants. Over the next few decades more Hispanics settled in and around Galisteo, some scavenging rock from the pueblo ruins to build their new homes. Slowly the northwestern lands of the future San Cristóbal Ranch became grazing, pasture, and timber lands for many families.[14]

13. Aragon was the first settler to be given an official grant; there may have been earlier settlers who lived there unofficially. The validity of Aragon's grant was later disputed.

14. The grazing of Galisteo residents' sheep on what is now known as the San Cristóbal Grant was largely unofficial, according to repeated decisions made by the United States courts. Many Galisteoans, however, disputed these decisions for decades. The earliest Galisteo grants were made very close to what later became San Cristóbal's northeastern border. The land was open and unfenced in those times so Galisteoans were free to use any adjacent land as pasture or timberland. According to José Ortiz y Pino III, Galisteo author, *curandero*, and former state senator, several families also built rock homes on the interior of the grant, though without official sanction.

CHAPTER 6

A MEXICAN GRANT

Todos dicen que soy un viejo— Yo no sé en que se pueden fundar. Yo me encuentro tan gordo y robusto Que tres veces me puedo casar.	They all say I'm a useless old fellow, But I know not by what they can score; For I find myself merry and mellow And quite fit for three marriages more
Coro: En el morro paseaba el joven Combatiendo contra el invasor. Tanto sangre en los campos regaba, No te causa verguenza, traidor?	*Chorus*: How the lad held his own in the castle, Fighting off the invader amain! Blush ye not, ye invaders and traitors, Thus with blood to be watering Spain?
Todos dicen! "hipócrito viejo!" Paque en misa me gusta rezar, Y en el baile me gusta tener Una novia á quien apretar.	"You old hypocrite!" everyone tells me, Just because at the ball and the mass I am faithful alike—I love praying, And stepping the dance with a lass.

—"El Viejo" *(The Old Man)*[1]

1. A popular New Mexican folk song, only partally reproduced here, whose chorus dates from the Moorish wars. Lummis comments, "one of the most popular folksongs in New Mexico is the rollicking 'Viejo,' which has a tinge of humor in its words, as well as a taking swing in its measure. . . . In English it is difficult to render this as cleverly."

THE RULE OF MEXICO BROUGHT MORE SETTLERS to the San Cristóbal area, especially the northwestern corner near Galisteo. Several generations of Hispanics raised families, grew crops, and pastured animals on what is now San Cristóbal Ranch. Mexicans were also the first to bound the land as a distinct area, calling it the Rancho del Pueblo de San Cristoval. They made it an official land grant, and bequeathed it to the first of its non-Pueblo owners.

The story of Hispanic life at San Cristóbal began far to the south in New Spain. When the Mexican Revolution ignited in September of 1821, the Mexicanos, as they now called themselves, overthrew their Spanish masters. After a few weeks the news filtered up to Santa Fe that the area now belonged to Mexico, not Spain. On hearing this, the happy citizens promptly staged a five-day-long celebration. One of the first Anglo traders ever to visit Santa Fe, Thomas James, reported his version of the festivities:

> All classes abandoned themselves to the most reckless dissipation and profligacy. No Italian carnival ever exceeded this celebration in thoughtlessness, vice, and licentiousness of every description. Men, women, and children crowded every part of the city, and the carousal was kept up equally by night and day. There seemed to be no time for sleep. Tables for gaming surrounded the square, and continually occupied the attention of the crowds. . . . I never saw any people so infatuated with the passion of gaming. Women of rank were seen betting at the faro bank and dice tables . . .

After five days of revelry, he writes,

> the crowds then dispersed to their homes, with all the punishment of excess with which pleasure visits her votaries. . . . The Indians acted with more moderation than the Spaniards.

In defense of the Santa Feans, it should be noted that James had just gambled and lost all his assets on a catastrophic trade expedition to Santa Fe, so he was not in a friendly state of mind.

It quickly became apparent that the new government of Mexico was unstable and prone to coups; soon monetary support to the remote northern colony dwindled to almost nothing. Nomadic raiding, temporarily diminished in the early 1800s due to Spain's initiation of a "bartering for peace" policy, also resumed.[2] Still the tenacious settlers and Pueblos hung on.

The same year Santa Feans heard about the Mexican Revolution, soldiers discovered another Anglo trader, Captain William Becknell, on the plains east of the city.[3] Like many other merchants, Becknell had heard about the scarcity of

2. Frances Levine notes that "bartering for peace" was a Spanish concept that reflected the importance of trade and exchange as the basis of seventeenth- and eighteenth-century diplomacy.

3. The term "Anglo" or "Anglo-American," when used in the Southwestern United States, has come to mean a person of European heritage (any part of Europe, not just the British Isles), rather than an Indian or a Hispanic.

A Hispanic farm family of northern New Mexico, autumn, 1895 (photographer unknown).

"La Baile": dancing in old Santa Fe, ca. 1873.

A Santa Fe Trail trade caravan arrives at the outskirts of the city, ca. 1844.

goods in Santa Fe from the report of Zebulon Pike, the U.S. Army lieutenant captured outside the city in 1806. (Governor Joaquín del Real Alencaster had arrested Pike and his exploratory party as foreign trespassers and sent them south to Mexico. Mexico later returned them to the U.S., where Pike published his story.) This time Governor Facundo Melgares invited the foreign trader into Santa Fe, and Becknell sold his few goods for a small fortune. He then hurried back to his home state of Missouri, where word of his profits spread like wildfire. Soon caravans of traders in Conestoga wagons were rolling down the Santa Fe Trail.[4]

Just as this new era was beginning, Santa Fe's prosecuting attorney, Domingo Fernández, a self–described "descendant of the conquerors and pacifiers of this kingdom," decided to petition the governor for a certain piece of land. He had fallen in love with the mesas, canyons, and meadows surrounding the ruined San Cristóbal Pueblo, and on April 26, 1822, he asked Governor Melgares to make him a grant.

He explained that he did not "solicit said land through avarice" but primarily because he wished to repair the "sacred temple" (the small, ruined chapel near the pueblo), which he said was "suffering under the disgrace of being a habitation for beasts, stable for sheep and a manger for cows and calves, and in a word a lodging for brutes." He also planned to farm the land with his son and

4. The famous Santa Fe Trail was actually several routes, not just one.

Cliffs above San Cristóbal Canyon.

some other companions. Fernández took care to say that the people of Galisteo could continue to water their livestock and gather wood on the land, and that "in time of war" (the nomadic raids) he hoped that he, in turn, could count on their assistance. Such comments were expected in a grant petition, since communally shared pasture and timber land was often the rule for both Spaniards and Mexicans.

Governor Melgares turned the matter over to the "illustrious Corporation," Santa Fe's ruling body, which requested more information from Fernández regarding water sources on the land and the settlers' identities. (The Mexican government, like its predecessor, was interested in permanently colonizing the land, so they always tried to verify the existence of adequate resources for farming and grazing, and provide enough settlers to fend off Indian attacks.) Fernández found a guide from Galisteo who showed him all the springs and ponds, then he reported back to the corporation. This time he made an indignant appeal on behalf of the landless poor of New Mexico, saying that in view of "the immense amount of public land existing in this province," he hoped the corporation would grant each settler a decent plot. Otherwise, he said, "it may result in driving them to a strange country for lands. The indigence that is suffered in this city cannot be hidden," he continued, and on behalf of "so many poor servants of both their Magesties" he again made his request for the grant, listing the names of thirteen would-be homesteaders.

The corporation then made their own investigation. Don Fernández had reported twelve springs on the land, but they found only two small ones. Still, they concluded, "if the petitioners labor with as much perseverance as it is seen [the Tanos] did, they will be rewarded for their labor if they are aided by God our Father, with water from heaven to fill their tank, as in truth from the existing springs they will reap very little benefit."

In 1824, after two years of delays, the corporation granted the land to Fernández. Unfortunately something went awry, and three long years later Fernández was still petitioning. Somehow the corporation members had never forwarded the grant approval to the governor, and now they were stalling. Caught in red tape, Fernández contacted them over and over about sending the document, but was put off, as he said, "under the pretext that they are looking for it."

In June of 1827 he made one last request, this time to the Provincial Deputation of New Mexico, for firm title to the grant once and for all, on behalf of himself and thirty others. He reported to them that he had gone with two Indians, "Francisco the white-eyed" and "Ramon of the Pueblo of Pojoaque," to the San Cristóbal lands, and been told by these natives that there was abundant water under the land and also "sacred vessels and ornaments buried, which they promised to show me."

The new governor, Manuel Armijo, finally granted Fernández the land, providing that he use it only for agriculture, and that "the rest of the public [be allowed] to pasture their animals in the vicinity thereof." The grant was officially made under the aegis of the Mexican government, but it was also written according to the provisions of Spain's Royal Edict of 1813, which was still in effect. So, in a sense, it was both a Mexican and a Spanish land grant.

The boundaries were set in the usual relaxed fashion that served well during both Spanish and Mexican times, but caused plenty of disputes later. (Many Anglos have been mystified by the "vagueness" of Hispanic boundary lines, but when seen in their own cultural context, the boundary markers were quite serviceable. Eighteenth-century Hispanics were concerned only with subsistence use of the land; selling it was forbidden. They assumed that any interested parties would know the local geography well, therefore it was perfectly adequate to use physical features, irrigation ditches, and other people's tracts as boundaries.)

A frozen reservoir in Canyon Ceta.

The Pueblo de San Cristoval Grant's boundaries were:

> on the north, by the summit of the crestón; on the east, by the Ojo de la Baca; on the south, by the Bajada de los Comanches; and on the west, a point opposite the middle crestón.

On August 21, 1827, the constitutional justice of Santa Fe accompanied Fernández and his compatriots to San Cristóbal, and delivered the grant in the customary fashion. The justice pointed out the boundaries, and then Domingo Fernández:

> pulled up weeds, scattered handfuls of earth, broke off branches from the trees, and uttered loud exclamations of joy and pleasure, and [his compatriots] answered, 'Long life to our actual president, Don Guadalupe Victoria! Long life to the Mexican nation!'

All this was traditional behavior on receiving Spanish and Mexican land grants. Fernández received a document that recorded the ceremony in detail, but the ceremony itself counted much more than the piece of paper.

The official conveyed about half of the land to Fernández, decreeing that the rest was to be communal land shared by all the settlers for pasturage, wood, and water. The tradition of shared land was transplanted from Spain to the New

World, and ensured that the largest portion of every community grant in New Mexico was communal.[5]

Two years after this happy event, Fernández came before the new governor, José Antonio Chávez, with bad news. The other grantees had promised to help him clean springs and build ponds, but on the appointed day no one had appeared. So Fernández asked the governor to order the settlers to either work on the grant or resign. The governor agreed, decreeing that if the settlers did not work, "industrious individuals will be substituted in their place."

After this event there is little mention of San Cristóbal in the archives. We do not know if Fernández ever built a home on his grant. Witnesses later testified that his compatriots had all built houses, opened springs, and started farming, though they were driven off, perhaps periodically, by nomadic Indians. Ruins of stone walls, which may have been sheep corrals, are scattered over the grant; remains of stone dwellings can also be seen. Fernández never did repair the "sacred temple" near the pueblo ruins, so it probably continued to shelter sheep, goats, and cattle for the next twenty-four years.

An altar screen or reredo, *used in a morada. (Clockwise from top) God the Father; San Rafael, Archangel and guardian angel of all human souls; San Antonio (St. Anthony of Padua) holding the Christ child and a quill, symbol of his great scholarship; bulto of Nuestra Señora de Guadalupe (Our Lady of Guadalupe), the patron saint of New Mexico, who stands on the moon, held up by an angel, with rays of the sun surrounding her (and whose appearance in 1531 in Mexico City was the first apparition of the Virgin Mary to a native of the New World); Santa Gertrudis (St. Gertrude), a Benedictine nun who devoted her life to the worship of the sacred heart of Christ; San Miguel (St. Michael), the Archangel who carries scales to weigh souls; the Franciscan emblem: the hand of St. Francis in his blue cassock crossed with the hand of Christ.*

> From the time I was three years old . . . I never went to bed without praying for rain . . . I could always tell anyone exactly to the day and hour since the last rain, and I knew how many snowfalls we had in winter and how many rains in spring. We would remember an unusually wet year for a lifetime; we enjoyed recalling it during dry spells . . . My mind still holds memories of torrential rains. Papa would walk from room to room in the house watching the rain from every window and open door. I would follow like a shadow . . . only those ever watching and waiting for rain can feel the rapture it brings.
>
> —*Fabiola Cabeza de Baca, describing her nineteenth–century New Mexican childhood*

Like the Tanos, the Hispanics of Galisteo Basin were utterly dependent on rain. They dealt with this great need much as their predecessors had, by relying on prayer and ritual. Though Tano beliefs and Catholicism were worlds apart in terms of both particular tenets and flavor, Pueblos and Hispanics often approached the spiritual realm in similar ways. Both groups had great faith in ritual activity, both believed in spirits (or saints), which could intercede on their behalf, and both recognized the need for a sincere attitude when addressing the higher powers: a "good heart" as the Indians put it. Spanish settlers and Pueblos began to merge early in the 1700s, and the Pueblos and their traditions clearly colored the Hispanic way of life. To this day most Hispanics "feel"

Spanish, but the truth is that they are not. They are not Spanish, not Mexican, and not Indian, but rather a unique people, "an indigenous Hispanic culture that rooted itself in New Mexico."[6]

The Hispanics of San Cristóbal faced a precarious existence. Their land had great beauty but limited resources, and nature was stubbornly unpredictable. Water was scarce even in good years, with wind and sun always working to dry out the land. And when rain finally came, it often arrived as a torrential downpour that flooded arroyos and washed away crops.

But nineteenth-century Hispanics adapted to the isolation of their remote homes, creating tightly knit communities based on mutual support, deep religious faith, and strong ties to the land. Both Mexico City and the Catholic Church usually ignored them, and small settlements like those at San Cristóbal and Galisteo became self-protective, largely self–sufficient islands. The San Cristóbal settlers were mostly a people in transition, moving frequently, always looking for greener and safer pastures. Traces of what likely were their ruined buildings or lambing pens are found scattered over wide areas. Probably they were dependent on nearby Galisteo in many ways.

For most Hispanics, life was a group effort, from plowing to harvesting, from lambing to shearing. Almost no one built fences, except around fields, and goats and sheep with different brands ranged freely over common pasture land.

In autumn men from neighboring villages would come together with their oxen, mules, and wagons, and a caravan would set out for the buffalo plains. The men would travel for weeks, hunting for winter meat. Armed with six-foot metal lances,

> the hunters formed a group before dashing into the herd, bowed their heads in prayer and invoked Santiago, the patron saint of Spain, to help them and guide them in the hunt. After making the sign of the cross, into the herd they rode.[7]

The villagers used every part of the buffalo, drying the meat for jerky, melting down the fat for cooking or candle-making, cutting the hides into ropes, robes, and rugs, and saving the wool for spinning into yarn or filling mattresses.

Our picture of early Hispanic life comes largely from the accounts of early American and European travelers, whose impressions varied greatly.[8] Some Americans commented on the devotion and piety of the Hispanics, while others seemed to imply that fandangos and gambling were the main activities. But most agreed that the great majority of the people were poor and that their lives were very simple.

An American traveler named M. M. Marmaduke described Hispanic vil-

Threshing with sheep in northern New Mexico, ca. 1935 (T. Harmon Parkhurst, photographer).

5. This tradition of "usufruct," or the use of land that is not one's own, grew out of the Castilian belief that no one person was entitled to monopolize resources provided by nature, and that an individual could truly own land only by interacting with it, usually by farming or grazing animals for several years.

6. Orlando Romero, writer, sculptor, *santero*, and librarian of the History Library, Palace of the Governors, Museum of New Mexico, made this comment in 1992.

7. The Indians showed the Hispanics how to use these long metal lances. They had originally captured them from the early Spanish, then adapted them to buffalo hunting.

8. Recent scholars such as Janet Lecompte have also been using New Mexican archival records extensively. And some of the traditional elements of modern Hispanic life were doubtless part of nineteenth-century culture as well.

Colonel and Mrs. Venseslao Jaramillo of New Mexico on their wedding day in 1898 (Schumacher, photographer).

The Catholic church at Galisteo, built in 1882.

Ancestors of Eliseo Rodriguez husking corn, New Mexico, ca. 1905 (Edward Andrews, photographer).

lagers of 1824 this way: "The inhabitants appear to me to be a miserably poor people, but perfectly happy and contented." He went on to criticize their lack of moral principles, but added, "In justice to them, however, I cannot forbear to remark that there does exist among them one single virtue, and that virtue is hospitality." Like the Pueblos, Hispanics received strangers warmly, offering whatever food or comfort they had.

Marmaduke was not the only American visitor offended by what he saw as deplorable morals. Many Americans found it shocking that Hispanic women wore only comfortable chemises and ankle-revealing petticoats, items which served as underwear in America. And court records indicate that New Mexicans' sexual mores were also freer, in general, than those of Americans. Adultery, for example, was common, and though it was sometimes punished by the courts, it was not at all unexpected.

Explorer Zebulon Pike gave another point of view: scenes of people of all ages joining together "at the common labor . . . the cultivation of the fields was now commencing and everything appeared to give life and gaiety to the surrounding scenery." And an American woman recalled the Hispanic women she met as "decidedly polite, easy in their manners, perfectly free."

Galisteo was likely the meeting place for Hispanics of San Cristóbal, simply because it was the nearest town and had a church. An American soldier described his impressions of the village in 1846:

> Visited Galisteo, which contains about 200 inhabitants. The houses are built of adobe, or sun-dried bricks, whitewashed inside, and with flat roofs, as in Bible times. . . . The waters in the mountains converge into streams and fertilize a depression in the valley, so that corn can be raised sufficient for the scanty dish of *atole* (mush) and *tortillas* (thin cakes) used by the people. Some wheat is also raised; thrashed by hand, winnowed by the breath, or by throwing in the air, ground between two stones by the women, and baked into very tolerable bread—for hungry men. The cooking utensils are pots and bowls of earthenware, made by the Pueblo Indians. . . . A kind of incipient cheese, or curds compressed by hand, is made in profusion, and is no doubt wholesome. The inhabitants at this season rarely sleep in their houses, but spread their mats or blankets before their doors and sleep in the open air. In day time their beds are folded up and used for seats inside the rooms. The kitchens have neat chimneys in the corners . . . several looms are seen . . . also spinning wheels of rude construction. The village has a church, about thirty feet long by twenty feet wide, neatly whitewashed inside . . .
>
> Visited Galisteo this afternoon and had some further insight into the characters and habits of the villagers. The people are rather filthy in their cooking and

their persons . . . this is true of the lower orders, the great mass of people. The arrival of Señor Pino, the owner [sic] of the village, reported, and a fandango spoken of for the evening.[9]

Hispanic society of the nineteenth century was more egalitarian than that of the seventeenth century; the complex Spanish caste system had faded from use when Mexico became independent. *Ricos*, or wealthy men, such as Domingo Fernández, were treated with special deference, but there were no rigid class barriers, and poor individuals with exceptional abilities and luck could rise to wealth and high standing. For decades there were so few luxuries in New Mexico that the gap between *ricos* and *pobres* was small, and "rich and poor worshipped together, danced together, attended each other's family baptisms, weddings, and funerals."[10]

Like the Pueblos, Hispanic villagers had an ambivalent relationship with the Comanches, who still attacked and robbed them regularly. On one hand they feared the raiders, who traveled in bands of hundreds, but during peaceful interludes they also relied on the tribe for trade. After the Comanche Peace Treaty was signed in 1786, a new breed of Hispanic traders, called *Comancheros*, began to follow the wide-ranging nomads, making a business of exchanging "flour, biscuits, woven blankets, and hardware for Indian horses, hides, jerky, and an occasional captive." Still, the careful relationship between the two peoples continued. For example, the *Comanchero*s sometimes traded liquor to the Indians, but only in the most circumspect way. They would bury it near a Comanche camp and depart, leaving one of their men behind. The lone Hispanic guide would wait until his companions had made a good start, guide the Indian buyers to the hiding place, then immediately jump on his horse and ride off before the alcohol took effect. (Many years later when Anglos began to make serious inroads, the Comanches and *Comancheros* would again join forces to rustle cattle from the Texan invaders.)[11]

But even after the Comanche Peace Treaty, other nomadic groups remained, keeping life dangerous and unpredictable. When raiders attacked, anything could happen. Fabiola Cabeza de Baca recalled the story of an old man who fought in both the Mexican and Civil wars and lived to be 105:

> [W]hen he was a small child, Antonio lived in Taos [in the early 1800s]. A band of Arapahoes came down upon the village and, after raiding the town, they killed several persons—among them Antonio's parents. They took Antonio with them into Montana. He lived with the Indians until he was a grown man. While he was among the Arapahoes, he married a squaw. One night there was an Indian dance which his wife refused to attend. At a very late hour, after the

A Comanche Chief, ca. 1868 (photographer unknown).

9. Señor Pino, a wealthy miller, was a prominent citizen, but not the "owner" of Galisteo.

10. The widespread *patrón* system, in which one wealthy man rented breeding herds and land to tenants, and basically dominated their lives, for better or worse, only flourished after U.S. occupation and the growth of the livestock industry. Nearby Galisteo was run by such a patrón, the famed Don José Ortiz y Pino, in the early 1900s. His grandson, author José Ortiz y Pino III, writes that New Mexico *patróns* were largely benevolent and beloved men who organized society and provided a livelihood for all villagers, even in hard times. See his book *The Last Patrón*. For a fascinating autobiographical account of life among New Mexico's nineteenth-century *ricos*, see *Legacy of Honor*, edited by Jacqueline D. Maketa.

11. Toward the end of the nineteenth century, vengeful Comanche bands often rustled stock from the large Texan cattle ranchers who had usurped their territory, then traded it to the *Comancheros*. The Hispanics would drive the cattle off while the Indians stayed behind to fight any pursuing Texans. The *Comancheros* then sold the cows to Americans who specialized in hustling herds out of state for resale.

dance was over, Antonio returned to their tepee, where his wife was soundly sleeping. He saw his chance for escape [and knowing that the tribe had no suspicion but that he was one of them, he decided to take flight.] Cautiously, he pulled a reata [lariat] from under his wife's pillow and quietly went out to the enclosure where the horses were corralled. There he picked two of the best horses and started on his journey. He crossed many high sierras and although pursued, he finally succeeded in reaching a French trading post. The trappers were very kind to him and helped to hide him for several days while his pursuers were on the trail. The Frenchmen afforded protection for him in a secret room and when there seemed to be no more danger, Antonio continued to travel. After many months of hardship, he reached Taos, being guided all the way by trappers.

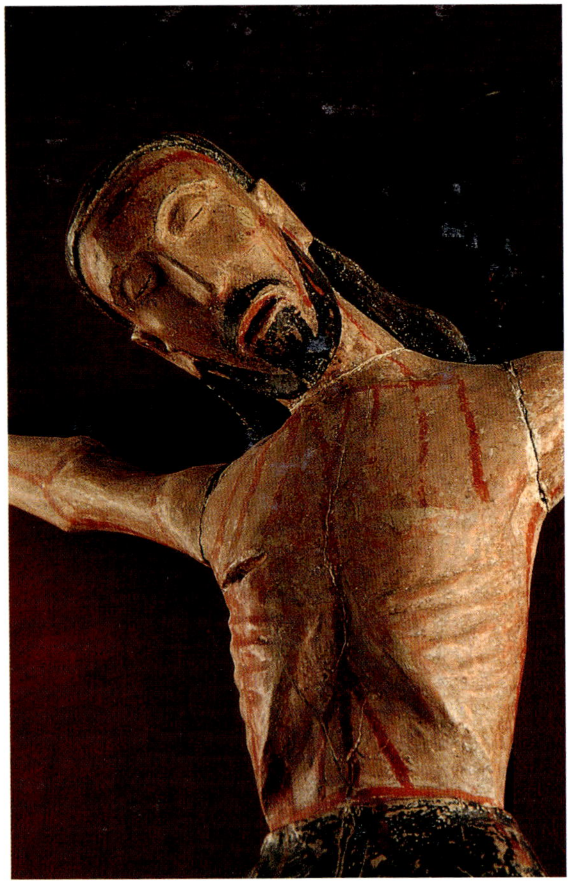

Carved and painted wooden Cristo from the late nineteenth century; by an unidentified artist.

En una columna atado Hallarás al Rey del Cielo, Herido y ensangrentado Y arrastrado por el suelo.	Upon a column bound You'll find the King of Heaven, Wounded and red with blood And dragged along the ground.
En agriesta disciplina, Si lo quieres aliviar, Llega, alma, á desagrabiar A la Paloma Divina.	In bitter discipline If you would ease his pain, Draw near, O soul, to give Peace to the dove divine.
Ay, Jesús! Ay, mi dulce dueño, Desagrabiar te queremos. Recibe, poder amoroso, Las flores de este misterio.	Alas, Jesus! Alas, my sweet master, We long to help You! Receive, O loving power, The flowers of this mystery.

—Las Columnas *(The Crosses) sung by the Penitente Brothers*

In 1849 there were only fourteen Catholic priests in all of New Mexico, serving a population of 65,000.[12] The priests spent most of their time ministering to the Indian pueblos, since that was their official job, and traveled from one Hispanic village to another when time permitted. Meanwhile, the Spanish-speaking population had been growing and migrating away from the pueblos for decades; by the 1850s settlers at San Cristóbal, or even Galisteo, might see a clergyman only one to four times a year. On these occasions all baptisms, marriages, and masses were performed at once, and the villagers celebrated with great fiestas. The men organized all kinds of contests, from bronco-riding to horse racing and "rooster pulls"; music, dancing, and feasting sometimes lasted all night and into the next day.

12. In 1850 Bishop Jean Baptiste Lamy arrived in Santa Fe and put more priests into the field. But the lack of clergy had been severe for about 150 years prior to this.

But the lack of priests was deeply frustrating to the Hispanic people, whose religion permeated every aspect of their lives. Daily prayer and ritual were crucial to them. Cleofas Jaramillo reports that even during a simple act like baking bread, if a woman "wanted it to come out specially good, the name of the Holy Trinity was invoked. A cross was marked on the bread dough before setting it away to rise."

In those communities that could afford a church, everyone would cooperate to build it, clean it, replaster the walls, and decorate the altar. At scattered settlements like San Cristóbal, the people would set aside a room in one of the larger homes as a chapel, ornamenting it with homemade *santos* (wood carvings of the saints) and *retablos* (religious paintings on wooden boards). Every village, no matter how small, dedicated itself to a patron saint; this way a priest might at least visit on the saint's holy day. But at sacred times like Holy Week and Easter, the villagers were on their own. Even worse, people died without receiving confession or the Last Rites, their bodies remaining unburied for days. "Spiritual administration in New Mexico," said one observer in 1832, "is in a truly doleful condition."

Thus it was in the late eighteenth or early nineteenth centuries that *La Hermandad de Nuestro Padre Jesús Nazareno* (the Brotherhood of our Father Jesus) evolved in the villages of northern New Mexico. Known as the Penitentes, the Brotherhood created their own Franciscan version of Catholicism centered around Christ's Passion.[13]

On holy days the members would form a slow procession, wearing black hoods to insure humility, and reenact Christ's journey to Calvary, reliving his scourging, suffering, and even crucifixion. The brother honored with Christ's role in this drama was not nailed to the cross, only tied; still, instances of death occurred. Much misunderstanding of the Penitentes arose from these simulated crucifixions. But the Brotherhood's aim was never death, or even pain for its own sake, but rather a oneness with Christ through suffering.

Penitentes began meeting in secular buildings they called *moradas*, where they created strict rules for initiation and life membership, often involving severe penances. Their rites demanded great devotion and discipline. Brothers dedicated their lives to ideals of forgiveness, prayer, reverence, and the striving to always place justice and charity above lower emotions. Penitentes and their wives provided a kind of welfare system for their villages, caring for the sick and poor, comforting the bereaved, and burying the dead. As there was no police system, Penitente men also enforced law and order, and came to have the authority to punish wrong-doers.[14] In short, the Penitentes maintained both the inner and outer lives of the isolated Hispanic people during much of the nine-

Retablo of Nuestra Señora de los Dolores (Our Lady of Sorrows), the most widely portrayed saint in New Mexico. She is the mother of Christ mourning His crucifixion, bearing one or seven daggers, which symbolize the seven sorrows, in her heart. Carved by the Laguna Santero in the late eighteenth century, New Mexico.

13. The exact origin of the Penitentes is now obscure. Some early scholars believed that the Brotherhood evolved from the secular Third Order of St. Francis, originally established by the saint in Canara when an "entire village wished to abandon their homes and follow him." But both Thomas Steele and Marta Weigle, another noted authority, question this theory. See Weigle, The *Penitentes of the Southwest*. Ancient ties to Spain *were* probably involved, as "a tradition of religious self-punishment goes back at least to thirteenth century Europe."

14. There was never any centralized Penitente authority; each *morada* determined its own rules and practices.

A Penitente procession of flagellants on Maundy-Thursday in 1896; drawing by Max F. Klepper from a photograph.

teenth century. (The Penitentes are still active today. After several years of decline, membership is once again growing.)

Women were probably not part of the Brotherhood per se. But every village had women's societies which complemented the Penitentes. Some of these groups also performed penances; others served as helpers at *velorio*s, or cooked for the Brothers.[15] Today there are Penitente-related women's groups such as the *Corros* who distribute the portable altars of the Holy Family during certain festivals. The fact that Hispanas apparently did not participate directly in the Penitentes should not imply any sense of inferiority or subservience on their part. Early Hispanic women were notably independent and assertive, and they considered themselves equal to men. Their society shared this view, and court records from the period show that the average New Mexican woman was treated as an equal to men, and according to historian Janet Lecompte, "retained her property, legal rights, wages, and maiden name after marriage, like her Spanish ancestors."

15. *Velorios* are similar to wakes; they are vigils with singing and prayer, preceding the funeral.

In an area with almost no doctors, women were also respected as healers who preserved the secrets of herbal medicine and midwifery.[16] The knowledge of plants and their powers came originally from Native American medicine men and healers; gradually it passed to certain Hispanic people, who became *curanderas* (healers) and sometimes *brujas* (sorcerers).[17] This development illustrates one of the great mysteries of Hispanic society. Clearly Hispanic culture was, and is, devoutly Christian. But alongside the obvious river of Catholicism (so well represented by the Penitentes) runs another stream—that of the Indian heritage with its emphasis on the power of nature and the earth. Most nineteenth-century Hispanics depended on *curanderas* when ill, even if they might shy away from the *bruja's* realm with its mystical, sometimes frightening knowledge. In Hispanic society, Jesus Christ and the saints coexisted with powerful earth and nature spirits; the people depended on them both. At times this blending of beliefs resulted in a wider, more inclusive faith; at times it brought only deeper superstition. But even today, troubled Hispanics may consult both the priest and the *bruja*.

The persistence of Hispanic religion in the face of neglect and adversity is a telling fact. It says much not only about Hispanic devotion and determination but also about a reverence for the past, for tradition. Like the Pueblos, Hispanics generally had little concern for the future, believing that it would take care of itself if the wisdom of the past was faithfully maintained. Thus they revered their elders, *los ancianos,* people about seventy or older, who passed on the accumulated knowledge of life.

People also valued every kind of oratorical skill, from singing to poetry recitation. *Resolaneros* (sun seekers), retired men who sat in the sun during wintertime, always drew an audience of young people who took a break from work to listen to their stories, proverbs, and verses. Other elderly virtuosos staged elaborate "rhetorical duels," in which scenes from ancient and recent history, folk-sayings, and anecdotes would fly thick and fast, to the delight of listeners. At most social gatherings elders would display and hone these verbal skills. The most admired speakers could not only produce an appropriate tale or poem to fit any occasion, but could elaborate or abbreviate it in just such a way, with style and gesticulation, that it seemed a perfect comment on the situation at hand.

This type of conversation, known as "talk of the elders" was meant to teach as much as entertain. Its lessons always were: place your family and community first; follow God's will rather than self-will; try to understand and know nature; and labor to sustain your family by working the land.

Hispanics' love for song and story became part of their cultural essence. Even roundups, rodeos, and shearing time were occasions for Hispanic cowboys

Cast–off crutches and braces line the walls of a small room adjoining El Santuario de Chimayó, an adobe church built in 1816. Known for its miraculous healing powers, the sanctuary has become a mecca for pilgrims. On holy days, some believers walk or travel on their knees for miles in order to reach the church.

16. In 1844, Josiah Gregg spoke of "there being not a single native physician in the province; although a great multitude of singular cures are daily performed with indigenous roots and herbs that grow in abundance all over the country."

17. I use the feminine form here for convenience, and the masculine form elsewhere. Healers and sorcerers were and are, of either sex.

New Mexico village in 1925 (T. Harmon Parkhurst, photographer).

and sheep-shearers to display their virtuosity. Many of these men traveled from camp to camp like European troubadours, and as they worked they composed *corridos,* long dramatic songs describing notable recent events. One nineteenth-century Anglo described his impressions of these wandering poets:

> Although often illiterate, their conversational give-and-take is surprisingly bright and ready; and in the evenings they would sometimes organize plays or mock legal trials in which the command of their own language they displayed would have put to shame most educated Americans. Many times I have sat beside the campfire under the stars and listened while a couple of them sang in parts what Robert Louis Stevenson calls 'those heart-broken songs' of theirs. Gay ones too they had, sung with a style and animation no Anglo-Saxon of any class can attain . . .[18]

Some of their ballads were direct descendants of the old Spanish *romances tradicionales,* which were themselves derived from epic poems of thirteenth through fifteenth-century troubadours. The songs were passed down orally, and similar versions can still be found in Spain and New Mexico.[19]

Cuentos (folktales) were also handed down from generation to generation. Some were based on real events; some were totally fantastic. Some were reminiscent of the *Arabian Nights,* with Moorish royalty and flying carpets; others betrayed origins in India or Africa. Still others, which dwelt on the exploits of powerful witches, recalled old Pueblo tales.

> That's the way it is, Mateo, we don't need money, we need this land, this fragile piece of clay and sand and skies of unlimited stars and dreams. It's the only thing we have for the brief blessing of living from it. . . . With us, as with the lambs, we must struggle to survive until it is our turn, and even then this paradoxical gift is hard to give up. But we do not end, Mateo. Why do you think these people line the roads to the Holy Shrine? Why do you think that poor old widow constantly searches the sky for reasons? Maybe all this is for good memories, for a face that will promise hope, maybe for love. Who knows, Mateo, the key is to a door that leads to another door and then another . . .
>
> —*Orlando Romero*

There are many ways of trying to describe a people. One could use adjectives, saying that nineteenth-century Hispanics were familial, patient, and fatalistic. One could list common beliefs, such as "pain is followed by pleasure; joy by

18. The writer was an Oxford-educated Englishman who came to New Mexico in the 1800s to become a cowboy. He did not share the rigid Anglo prejudice against Hispanics so typical of the times.

19. Traditional Spanish proverbs and riddles also survived by oral transmission. In 1926, Aurelio Espinosa collected 165 New Mexican riddles and 601 proverbs, many in assonance or rhyme. He located near-exact replicas of 70 percent of the proverbs in proverb compilations from Spain.

Moving swiftly
across this arid, thirsty basin,
riding high on the shoulders
of the wind; my one dark cloud
carefully and gently uncovers
the sun for me.

I sit alone
no longer thirsty or cold.
Thankful for my patience,
saddened for my cursing,
weakened by my faltering . . . yet

A smile from my dark cloud
has washed away the tears.

—José Ortiz y Pino III, "There Is Another You"

Verbena (or vervain), native to New Mexico.

grief" or "life is sad but beautiful."[20] Such descriptions contain truth, but little life. Orlando Romero may have been correct when he pointed out that culture is often best portrayed through poetry, art, or music, rather than history. Perhaps this is especially true of Hispanic culture, for at its core, it is deeply emotional and poetic.

The following sample of northern New Mexican writing gives a taste of a real world, a culture still alive today.

> In the pelting rain I saw my Mother's petunias melt into the brownness of the earth. Nambe receives its life and passion from the sun. It rains little here. When it does rain, the inhabitants and dwellers of this ancient place take on different appearances. The forehead of the face hangs obtrusively on the brow. The color of living complexion turns gray like the sky and the eye sockets turn black like the storm. The gentleness is replaced by the heaviness of darkened spirits. It shows in their movements. Sparks fly at the darkened skies.
>
> Viable, reflexive, warm muscles are now trapped in cages. Their adobe house, or womb, is warm. But they look out with longing eyes and tired sighs; their goats, cows, horses and plows sit unmoving. In one day's rain the soul of these inhabitants will begin to gather rust.
>
> I sit by the corner fireplace, watching the piñon flames burn the air around them. My cat purrs in his dreams. His tail switches, then his leg. He dreams of the cat next door.
>
> Here in Nambe, we all dream. Some of us in the middle of the sun, some of us under black storms. My Grandfather dreams as he nervously paces the floor. He longs for his fields.
>
> My Mother sits on the rocking chair in the corner. She's looking at her book pretending she is reading. In reality, she dreams . . .
>
> —*Orlando Romero*

20. Alvin Sunseri is describing traditional Hispanics of New Mexico today. The description fits their ancestors equally well.

CHAPTER 7

AN AMERICAN TERRITORY

. . . don't be like the Americanos, they have to understand everything. It was a lesson, a miracle or a mystery. Just believe in mysteries, and you'll live a long time.

—A Hispanic grandfather answering his questioning grandson

Alli viene el ferrocarril,
Vamos á ver onde 'sta.
Ah, que gusto nos dará
Cuando lo veamos venir!

Coro: Llegando la emigracion,
"Good morning," repetiré;
"Come in! Come in!" les diré,
Vengan oir mi cancion.

De Chihuahua Franquilin[1]
Corren los Americanos,
Ganandoles el dinero
Á todos los Mejicanos.—*Coro*

Si fueras al campamiento
Onde vienen trabajando,
Yo asi me vivo cantando

The railroad is coming this way—
Let us go look at it near.
When we shall see it appear,
Ah, what a joy it will be.

Chorus: And when the tourists shall throng,
"Good morning!" I will repeat;
"Come in! Come in!" I'll entreat,
"Come on in and hear my song!"

Up from the town on the line
Come running *Americanos,*
Earning us everyone money—
Money for all us *paisanos.*—*Chorus*

Were you at the camp where they're giving
Work, and the laborers bringing—
That's just the way I live singing

(Opposite) Known in the Galisteo Basin as "the movie set," this crumbling compound in La Jara Pasture was the studio-built set for John Wayne and the cast and crew of the 1950s film "The Cowboys."

General Manuel Armijo.

Para ganar el sostento.—*Coro*	Only to earn me a living.—*Chorus*
Ni el sol ni el viento podrá Hacerme retroceder; Millas y millas correr, Para ganar nuestro bien.—*Coro*	Neither sun, neither wind shall nor could Make me turn back til I've done; Mile after mile I will run That I may win us some good.—*Chorus*
La maquina va partir, Esten toditos alerta. Vayan sacando el dinero Que ya vamos á partir.—*Coro*	The engine is going to start. Lively! Be all of you ready! Come, pull your money out—steady, For now we are going to start!—*Chorus*

—El Ferrocarril *(The Railroad)*

DOMINGO FERNÁNDEZ held the Pueblo de San Cristoval Grant for nearly a quarter-century, a period of dramatic events that transformed New Mexico. In 1828, miners discovered gold in the Ortiz Mountains, and this set off a minor rush of Anglos into the area. In 1837, New Mexicans revolted against the first taxes ever levied on them, killing Governor Albino Pérez and other officials before order was restored. Then four years later an unconventional army from Texas, now an independent republic, invaded New Mexico for mysterious purposes. The Texan force included 270 armed men and fifty merchants; their purpose may have been to take over the Santa Fe Trail trade. At any rate, the Santa Feans captured the ill-equipped and half-starved invaders and sent them down to Mexico without even a battle.

The next invasion was more serious. The energetic young United States was itching to expand, and in 1846 President Polk declared war on Mexico. Soon the U.S. Army, under Brigadier General Stephen Kearny's command, was marching down the Santa Fe Trail. Governor Manuel Armijo assembled troops and cannons in Glorieta Pass to halt the intruders, then inexplicably changed his mind and ordered his men to go home. Armijo's actions have perplexed historians, but he was a controversial figure even in his own times, a blustering man with "a reputed habit of caning his lesser subjects in the streets if they did not take off their hats quickly enough as he passed by." Known as "His Obesity" to the Missouri traders, who resented his high taxes on their wares, Armijo reputedly boasted of amassing his fortune by stealing sheep. History records that as his soldiers returned to Santa Fe, Armijo himself rode off toward Mexico, abandoning Santa Fe to the Americans.

1. Franklin, the first railroad name of El Paso.

Blooming snakeweed and purple asters.

The Sulphur Springs Stage Coach station, New Mexico, ca. 1897 (Philip E. Harroun, photographer).

Pioneer family traveling West (photographer unknown).

Guadalupe Baca de Gallegos, adopted child of a wealthy Las Vegas, New Mexico, family, told the story of her grandfather's discovery of Kearny's invasion:

> Where the . . . University now stands he saw many cannons all pointing toward the town. Immediately he rushed to town to spread the news. The town was in an uproar. Everyone, it seemed, was screaming and crying. None wanted to become Americans; all wanted to remain under the Mexican flag.

The women and children of Baca de Gallegos's family were sent to hide up in the crestón, while the head of the family, refusing to become an American, "left everything he owned and went to Mexico. All his land was confiscated and his stock killed to feed the troops." After a year he came back, regained his home and some property, and even "made friends with Kearny," whose family ended up moving in with them.

The U.S. conquest at first seemed bloodless, but the Anglo military men treated most of Santa Fe's Mexican and Indian population with contempt and abuse. The territory's first governor, Charles Bent, commenting on the frequent beatings and assaults on Hispanics, wrote, "these outrages are becoming so frequent that I apprehend consequences may result sooner or later . . . ." The governor's words were prophetic: one year later a revolt broke out at Taos Pueblo and Bent himself was killed by Mexicans and Taos men before army troops crushed the rebellion.[2]

The Treaty of Guadalupe-Hidalgo brought the war to a formal close in 1848, and New Mexico became a territory of the United States. The trickle of Anglos into the former Spanish colony now became a steady stream. "Forty-niners" passed through on their way to pan for gold in California; settlers came in covered wagons looking for work opportunities—which included everything from building roads to practicing law—on the new frontier. Soon travelers were arriving by stagecoach, which began regular service to Santa Fe in 1849.

Many colorful books have been written about the rugged westward journey on the Santa Fe Trail. Wagon trains bumped along slowly, always on the lookout for hostile Indians, covering only about 20 to 25 miles a day. One of Santa Fe's most famous immigrants, Thomas B. Catron, remembered that on his trip west, he and his party spent three whole days passing through a single buffalo herd. "The whole earth seemed to contain nothing but buffaloes," he wrote, "and a very little wagon train drawn by frightened and snorting mules."

2. Some authors believe that only Hispanics, and no Pueblos, were involved in the Taos Revolt.

Finally, change came even to the sleepy Galisteo Basin. In 1851, after twenty-four years of ownership, Domingo Fernández sold his "rustic property" to two Americans, Ethan Eaton and Alexander Reynolds, for $500.00.

Ethan Eaton, only twenty-four years old at the time of this transaction, came from a prosperous New York family; he had traveled west two years earlier in the great rush of '49. On arriving in New Mexico he prospected for gold briefly, then opened a store in Galisteo. During this period he met Marcelina Chávez, and they married the same year that he bought San Cristóbal.

Two years later, Eaton's partner, Reynolds, lost a lawsuit and had to sell all his property at auction. Eaton bought Reynolds's half of the land for $262.00 and became sole owner of the former Mexican grant, still known as the "Rancho de San Cristoval." At some point the Eatons built a home at San Cristóbal; they raised a family of nine children there. A nineteenth-century history of the territory describes one incident at San Cristóbal in the late 1850s:

> The Apache Indians ran away with 100 head of [Eaton's] livestock. [Eaton] followed with 12 men . . . overtaking the Redskins after a chase of 100 miles. All the Indians but one were killed in the fight that followed, and the lost property was restored. Colonel Eaton received a wound in the thigh from an arrowhead two and a half inches long, and it was two and a half months before he could have it removed.

A man of great "nerve and promptitude of action," Eaton later gained repute as an army commander; still later he led a vigilante force that saved the town of Socorro from outlaws.

Eaton's purchase of San Cristóbal typified a larger scenario. All over the state, former Spanish and Mexican grants were changing hands, often from communities to individuals, often from Hispanics to Anglos. The long and bitter era of New Mexican boundary disputes was now beginning.

In prehistoric times, Indians had made their pueblo boundaries clear with markers. The Spanish and Mexicans had sometimes respected these, but when they made their own grants they often used ambiguous terminology, as previously mentioned. For example, often trees or even entire mountains were used as boundary markers. And the majority of each grant was pasture land shared by the whole village. American concepts of private ownership and precisely surveyed boundaries were entirely foreign to New Mexico. As the historian Dan Murphy sums it up, "The problems of land ownership, which still plague New Mexico, were the direct result of one culture imposing its laws over another, which happened not once but twice, to thoroughly confuse the situation."

Marcelina Chavez Eaton, 1830–1920.

Colonel Ethan W. Eaton, 1827–1913. These portraits were made after the Eaton family had left San Cristóbal (photographer unknown).

As others were doing all over New Mexico, people now argued, petitioned, and litigated over the boundaries of San Cristóbal. Though there is no record of it now, Eaton likely encountered boundary problems, that is, Hispanic families living on what he considered *his* grant, very soon after his purchase. When Eaton bought the land no mention was made of any Hispanic settlers (or descendants of Fernández's companions), and Eaton believed he was entitled to sole use. In 1854 Eaton decided to petition the Surveyor General for confirmation of his grant. He finally got it in 1860, but he was given only a triangular area "from the mesita of the Lagunitas upwards as far as the spring of La Vaca." This area was Domingo Fernández's personal parcel only, and was less than one half of the total grant.

Eaton wanted the boundaries expanded. When he purchased the land in 1851, he had thought he was buying the whole grant. As things stood in 1861, old communal pasturelands could easily become public land, with Anglo homesteaders moving in to make claims. Determined to own the entire area, Eaton began a long battle to have the land resurveyed.

Union veterans of the Civil War play highball poker at Glorieta Pass in October, 1880 (Ben Wittick, photographer).

Meanwhile, people all over the territory were taking sides in a bitter conflict about to explode to the east. At Fort Union on the Santa Fe Trail, Major Henry Sibley decided to cast his lot with the newly formed Confederacy. As the first battles of the Civil War flared, Sibley went south to gather a volunteer army in Texas, and soon he was marching them up the Rio Grande. His plan was to take New Mexico for the South, then go on to capture the Colorado gold fields. His troops defeated Unionists first at Valverde, then Albuquerque. He and his men proceeded north, probably through the San Cristóbal Grant, and camped overnight in Galisteo on their way to another victory in Santa Fe. Meanwhile, a volunteer army of tough Colorado miners, galvanized by this threat, quickly assembled. They charged through winter snows from Denver to Fort Union—a trip of 400 miles—in thirteen days, joining northern troops already there.

The two armies met in Glorieta Pass in March of 1862. When the smokey battleground cleared, the Confederates seemed to have won. But unknown to the Texans, 400 Union men had climbed out of the canyon before the fighting, planning to double back on their enemy. By chance they miscalculated and emerged far behind the Confederate army, directly above its huge supply train of wagons and mules. The Union men easily overcame the few Confederate guards, then burned and destroyed everything they could find. The Texans were completely cut off from any support system, and soon they had to struggle south, defeated.

Colonel Christopher (Kit) Carson in 1864 (photographer unknown).

The Colorado Volunteers pursued the Texans to Galisteo, but the Southerners had already escaped.[3]

After this battle many soldiers left New Mexico to continue fighting in the East. The lack of army protection encouraged the Apaches and Navajos, who were already desperate in the face of encroaching Anglo culture, to increase their raids and attacks. The U.S. Army retaliated by sending in Christopher (Kit) Carson to hunt down the nomads. The Mescalero Apaches escaped from New Mexico but Carson forced the Navajos into an arid, prisonlike reservation in eastern New Mexico called Bosque Redondo. (The government plan was to retrain the Navajos as farmers.) Several years later in 1868, the sick and half-starved remnants of the tribe were allowed to return to their homeland, their raiding days over.

With the Indian threat neutralized, more Anglos streamed into the territory. By the winter of 1878 two great railroads, the Atchison, Topeka & Santa Fe and the Denver & Rio Grande Western, had simultaneously arrived in Colorado. Both were racing toward New Mexico's Raton Pass, the one and only way through the Southern Rockies. Here the famed frontiersman, 'Uncle Dick' Wootton, presided over the toll road he had built. Historian Dan Murphy tells the story:

> . . . both lines sent crews to the little town of El Moro at the foot of the Colorado side of the pass on a cold night in February 1878. While the D & RG crew lodged for the night in a hotel, the AT & SF men went on up the hill to 'Uncle Dick' Wootton's and made a deal. They moved a few shovelsful of dirt and by dawn claimed the pass by right of first construction. The total compensation paid to Wootton was a lifetime pass on the railroad and twenty-five dollars a month for groceries . . .

At first the new railroad planned to bypass Santa Fe entirely (because of the uphill climb) and go directly to Albuquerque. But Archbishop Jean Baptiste Lamy and other Santa Fe leaders were determined that their city be included on the new economic lifeline. They appealed to Santa Fe's citizens and raised the money for a branch line to a piece of land owned by the archbishop, 15 miles southwest of the city. A masonry train station was built there and a tiny village named Lamy grew up around it. Both survive today, just 6 1/2 miles north of the San Cristóbal Pueblo ruins; Amtrak and other lines now pass through daily.[4]

The railroad changed frontier life—and San Cristóbal's fate—dramatically. Now it was possible to export livestock to Eastern cities. Entrepreneurs also saw new markets for beef opening up as both government outposts and Indian reser-

3. Ethan Eaton served admirably in the war, raising Company F of the volunteer infantry, and advancing in rank to a colonel.

4. J.P. Harrington says, "Lamy and the canyon above Lamy, up which the Santa Fe railroad passes, are called in Tewa *Pi mp'oyehu'u* [or] heart water meet canyon."

The new Atchison, Topeka & Santa Fe railroad line with the engine, "Baby," at Glorieta Pass in October, 1880 (Ben Wittick, photographer).

vations grew in number. Recognizing a golden opportunity, settlers poured into New Mexico from all over the world.[5] The territory was thriving, and the competition for land, political control, and access to markets was fierce.

The story of San Cristóbal in the late 1800s reflects the rough and tumble, speculative nature of the times, when investors and entrepreneurs wheeled and dealed, making and losing fortunes. A former New Mexican of those years relates:

> That was a period, in which, if you wished to be considered a full-living and distinguished citizen, you must be tough and desperate—if not with the gun, at any rate with the poker deck, or when the boys were lined up at the brass rail. Business and professional men, cattlemen, prospective judges, senators and governors of the state, [all] gathered at the principal hotel bar and held session for two days and nights at a stretch . . . .

5. Newcomers during this era were of many nationalities. Leading the way were Chinese workers who built a great portion of the western railroads with unmatched speed and efficiency, then stayed to open businesses on the new frontier. French mountain men and traders appeared even earlier, followed by African cowboys, Polish, Slovak, and Italian miners, Japanese farmers, German and Irish settlers, German and Jewish merchants and bankers, Lebanese storekeepers, and English and Scottish ranchers, all of whom came to call New Mexico home in the 1880s.

Across from the train station, Lamy residents built Our Lady of Light Church, now fallen into disrepair, in the 1920s. Perhaps the most mysterious event in Lamy's history was the appearance of a "large balloon" one evening in 1880 shortly after the Santa Fe train pulled in. The train operator and some friends, out for a short walk before retiring, "were astonished to see a large balloon . . . monstrous in size," which "rapidly approached" from the west. The Daily New Mexican *reported on March 28: "The construction of the balloon was entirely different to anything of the kind ever seen by any of the party, being in the shape of a fish" with "fanciful characters" on the outside. "The air machine appeared to be entirely under the control of the occupants," the article continued, "and appeared to be guided by a large fan-like apparatus." The townspeople could not see the occupants, but guessed there to be eight or ten of them, and heard them calling out in an "entirely unintelligible" language, laughing, and playing occasional "strains of music." The machine "could evidently sail at any height . . . as soon after passing the Junction, it assumed a great height and moved off very rapidly toward the east." Before the visitors left, they dropped two articles: a "magnificent flower" with a slip of extremely fine paper bearing unusual, vaguely oriental-looking characters, and a cup of "very peculiar workmanship." The next day a "collector of curiosities" passed through Lamy and bought both objects for a large price, stating that the "balloon" must have come from Asia.*

Outside the Lamy train depot. This tiny station was the scene of many dramatic events. On May 7, 1890, The Daily New Mexican *headlined, "Desperadoes at Lamy—Two Men Terrorize the Town and Hold up a Number of Prominent Citizens—Also Hold up Two Trains." The suspects, "the notorious Trujillo," and Lee White, "whose reputation savors of midnight robbery and murder," robbed travelers of $47.00 and several gold watches, then caused an accidental shooting death. In the midst of the melee, one railroad baggage master approached Lee White and asked for his gold watch back. The outlaw, no doubt surprised, inquired "if he could not get along without it, and being answered in the negative, gave the watch up." The bandits then galloped off. A few years earlier, on April 22, 1881, the same newspaper reported that "warrants were issued yesterday for the arrest of four or five gamblers who have been making Lamy their headquarters . . . and have made themselves obnoxious to the public. . . . Determined to break this gang up . . . Deputy Sheriff Tony Nels went down on the train yesterday to take the wanted in out of the wet."*

Many Americans now became involved with San Cristóbal, and the grant was repeatedly mortgaged, traded, sold, bought back, explored, divided, and battled over from the 1870s to the 1920s.

One of New Mexico's most famous and powerful politicians, Thomas Benton Catron, played a major role in the saga of San Cristóbal. Brusque and aggressive, Tom Catron grew up in Missouri and fought for the south in the Civil War, then came to Santa Fe at the age of twenty-five. As a young attorney, Catron involved himself with the emerging Republican party, forming ties that would help him gradually become one of the largest landowners in U.S. history. By the 1870s he was acting as attorney for litigants in large grant cases, and beginning to acquire both land and a reputation. His admirers saw him as a man of immense energy, tenacity, and ability; his detractors, on the other hand, saw him as a master of fraud and chicanery, and referred to him as "Tomcat." Popular feeling sometimes ran strongly against Catron; once he narrowly avoided an assassin's bullet. Another time, according to an oral tradition related by biographer Victor Westphall, "he was . . . compelled to leave Mora disguised in women's clothing because certain of the townspeople objected to his role in the proceedings [during the 1876 court battle over the huge Mora Grant]." Catron eventually owned almost two million acres of land, became one of New Mexico's two original U.S. senators, and dominated New Mexico politics, law, and land deals for decades. Deeply involved with the San Cristóbal Grant from 1876 to 1907, he continued to own a small parcel of it until his death in 1921.

San Cristóbal was only one fish in a sea of disputed land grants. The wider story of the land grant struggles in New Mexico is long, complex, and controversial. In one sense the story seems simple: one nation, professing ideals of justice but following the doctrine of Manifest Destiny, conquers another. The dichotomy is apparent. Trying to uphold its idealistic side, the victor buys the conquered territories for a small sum, and promises the residents that their land rights will be respected. But the force of Manifest Destiny permeates all the events that follow.

For the sake of objectivity, it may be important to remember that nineteenth-century New Mexico after the American conquest was a remote, vast country, a hardscrabble "wild west" where a kind of frontier mentality prevailed throughout most of society. The Hispanic and Anglo cultures that met in this arena were very dissimilar. Their misunderstandings of each other began immediately, not only because of their positions as conquered and conquerors, but also because their societies and values were so different. To take a pertinent example, the Hispanic and Anglo attitudes toward land ownership and use were almost mirror opposites of each other. Their approaches to questions about how boundaries

Thomas Benton Catron in front of the Palace of the Governors in Santa Fe, ca. 1917. In the years between 1869 and 1917, Catron was New Mexico's attorney general, state legislator, U.S. District Attorney, and U.S. Senator. He and his wife Julia Walz Catron reared four sons in New Mexico. In his obituary in 1921, The Santa Fe New Mexican *described him as a "picturesque and powerful personality," who was a "pronounced 'stand-patter' of the old school." The senator's "strength was prodigious and his endurance marvelous" said the newspaper. "It was well-known that Senator Catron was a great admirer of Napoleon and had a bust of the famous general in his home. He frequently discussed the career of the little Corsican. . . ." However, "his ideal general was not Napoleon, but Cortez . . . because he declared that a study of the careers of the leading generals in history pointed to Cortez as the greatest warrior because he accomplished so much with so few men and small resources." (Wesley Bradfield, photographer)*

Horse herd and the distant Sangre de Cristo Mountains.

San Cristóbal Grant Transactions

The complex story of the San Cristóbal Grant transactions during the late nineteenth and early twentieth centuries could fill several volumes. Such an in-depth account would need to assess the aims and strategies of San Cristóbal's many owners; it would embrace the historical backdrop of the U.S.-Mexican War, the Treaty of Guadalupe Hidalgo, the Surveyor General system, the political machinations of the times, and the cultural chasm between Hispanics and Anglos. The following is only a brief chronology of the major events and sales of the era.

1869—Thomas Catron begins a partnership with Nicolás Pino, a prosperous Galisteo landowner. (In his younger days, Nicolás Pino was among the frustrated volunteers ordered back to Santa Fe by Governor Armijo when the Americans invaded. Pino was later arrested for conspiring to revolt against the American government in 1847. He opposed the Taos rebellion, however, and eventually signed an oath of allegiance to the United States.) Catron and Pino begin jointly buying small farming plots on the San Cristóbal Grant, mostly from Hispanics who claim descent from Domingo Fernández's companions. Although the deeds bear only Pino's name, Catron is also part owner.

1873—Ethan Eaton's request to have the grant resurveyed and expanded, after being mired in territorial and federal bureaucracy for thirteen years, is denied.

1874—Eaton and his wife Marcelina sell about one-third of the grant to Saron and Hattie Laughlin of San Francisco for forty-five cents an acre. Eaton mortgages his remaining portion of the grant several times, once to the famed Seligman Brothers of Santa Fe. (By this time, the San Cristóbal Grant was sometimes referred to as the Eaton Grant.)

1875—Eaton makes another appeal to have the land resurveyed, this time to the Secretary of the Interior in Washington. The Secretary decides Eaton is entitled to part of the grant, but that descendants of the original grantees (Domingo Fernández's companions) are also entitled to their portions. This decision is passed on to the New Mexico Surveyor General's office.

1876—Eaton makes his first deal with Thomas Catron, who is by then U.S. District Attorney for New Mexico. Eaton mortgages his share of the grant to Catron, borrowing money to buy about 4,500 sheep. Eaton agrees to raise the sheep and split all profits with Catron.

1876–1879—New Mexico Surveyor General Henry Atkinson begins his investigation regarding the proposed resurvey. He questions three Hispanics who were either companions of Domingo Fernández or relatives of the origi-

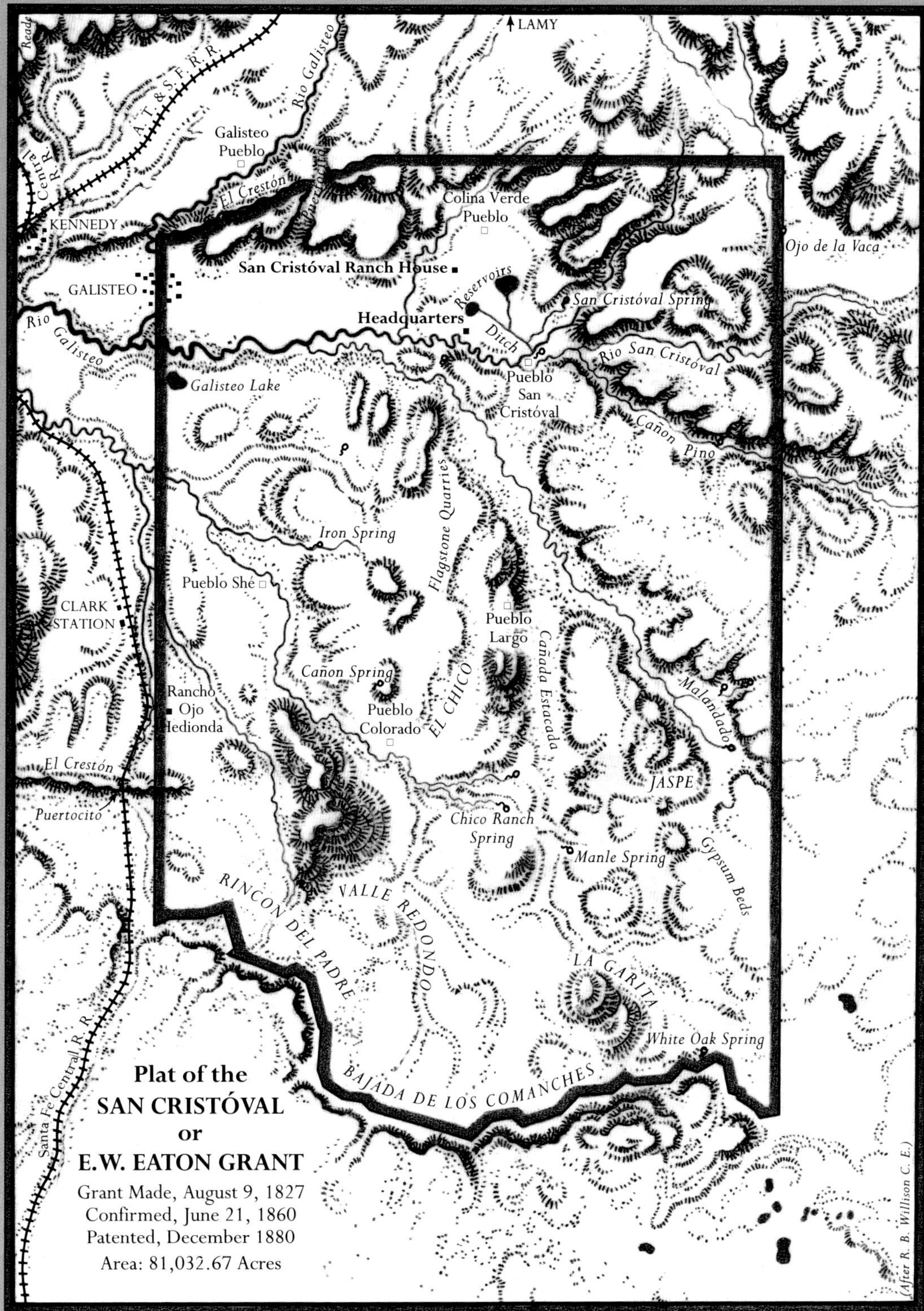
LAMY
A.T.&S.F.R.R.
Rio Galisteo
Galisteo Pueblo
El Crestón
Colina Verde Pueblo
KENNEDY
Ojo de la Vaca
San Cristóval Ranch House
GALISTEO
Reservoirs
San Cristóval Spring
Headquarters
Ditch
Rio Galisteo
Rio San Cristóval
Pueblo San Cristóval
Galisteo Lake
Cañon Pino
Flagstone Quarries
Iron Spring
Pueblo Shé
CLARK STATION
Pueblo Largo
Cañada Estacada
Cañon Spring
EL CHICO
Malandado
Rancho Ojo Hedionda
Pueblo Colorado
El Crestón
JASPE
Puertocito
Chico Ranch Spring
Manle Spring
Gypsum Beds
RINCON DEL PADRE
VALLE REDONDO
LA GARITA
White Oak Spring
BAJADA DE LOS COMANCHES
Santa Fe Central R.R.
Plat of the
SAN CRISTÓVAL
or
E.W. EATON GRANT
Grant Made, August 9, 1827
Confirmed, June 21, 1860
Patented, December 1880
Area: 81,032.67 Acres
(After R. B. Willison C. E.)

nal settlers. The three confirm that the grant was originally a large rectangle, not a smaller triangle, and give favorable testimony about the original grantees: that "they each erected a house or commenced to cultivate the land and open the springs" and that they "never abandoned their lands there except when they were driven off by the Navajo Indians." (These Hispanic witnesses may have been completely reliable. It is worth noting, however, that the court testimony they gave was crucial to the success of T. B. Catron's investments.) The Department of the Interior studies all this and finally orders the resurvey. In the Department's letter to Surveyor General Atkinson, there is extensive commentary on all parties' rights. "It is apparent from the record," the letter concludes, "that [Eaton] cannot make valid claim to the whole grant." It then goes on to uphold the rights of the original Hispanic settlers and their descendants.

1878—Eaton sells his share of San Cristóbal to Charles Guildersleeve, his son-in-law, for $1,000. Guildersleeve is a prominent Santa Fe judge, Democratic politician, and former business partner of Catron's.

1879–1880—Surveyor General Henry Atkinson makes the resurvey and formally approves the grant. The boundaries are legally expanded, and the grant is confirmed to Eaton (or to his successors, since he is no longer an owner at this point) and to "the remaining original grantees who had not forfeited their rights to the land by a non-compliance with the conditions of the grant . . . their heirs and assigns forever." Congress then issues a patent for the grant and President Rutherford B. Hayes signs it.

1880—The expanded grant is now co-owned by many parties. Saron Laughlin owns one-third, Charles Guildersleeve owns a large portion, about forty Hispanic settlers own perhaps 1,000 acres total (mostly near Galisteo), and the partnership of T. B. Catron and Nicolás Pino hold a sizeable number of miscellaneous plots.

1880–1888—Catron, now using his own name, continues buying small plots from farmers who claim descent from Domingo Fernández's companions.

April 1890—Charles Guildersleeve sells his portion of the grant to Laughlin for $1,000, leaving Laughlin as legal owner of the lion's share of San Cristóbal.

June 1890—Laughlin stocks the ranch with its first large herd of cattle. Catron and Pino, probably threatened by this development, go on the offensive. They sue Laughlin for full title to all the farming lands they have purchased. Catron itemizes a long history that traces ownership from the twenty-six original companions of Domingo Fernández to their many descendants, then to Pino and himself.

1890–1897—Laughlin replies that the twenty-six original farmers abandoned their strips of land very soon after they received them. Thus, he reasons, the whole of the grant reverted to Domingo Fernández, who sold it to Eaton, who sold it to him (Laughlin). After a seven-year battle, the court decides in Laughlin's favor.

1897—Catron appeals. By now he has completely bought out Nicolás Pino, and is fighting solely for his own interests.

1903—The court finally decides in Catron's favor, saying that the twenty-six grantees never gave up legal rights to their property, even if they departed at some point; thus, Catron is legal owner of the lands he has bought. The court adjourns to determine a precise percentage division among all the owners.

August 1903—Laughlin, defeated after a thirteen-year battle, decides to go into partnership with Catron. The two men hammer out a compromise whereby they agree that they will divide the grant in half, with a vertical line running down the middle. They plan for the western half to go to Catron, the eastern half to Laughlin. Laughlin agrees to a two-year option to buy Catron's half at $1.25 an acre, or sell it to someone else at that price (which works out to about $50,000.)

November 1903—The court announces all owners' percentages. (Catron and Laughlin hold the great majority.) The court now appoints three neutral men to travel to the grant to determine how to partition the actual land. (The Partition Statute of 1876 was passed specifically to facilitate such situations. It stated that in a case where several parties were fighting over a grant, a lawyer [in this case, Catron] could request a court division of the land.) But after three days the men report that fair division among forty-six people is impossible due to the scarcity of watered places. The court decrees that San Cristóbal must be put up for public auction.

January 30, 1904—The auction is held in front of the Santa Fe Courthouse, and Thomas Catron is the highest bidder. He buys the entire grant for $5,200.

February 5, 1904—Catron conveys San Cristóbal's eastern 40,000 acres to Laughlin, as previously agreed, for a token one dollar.

1907—After three years, Catron sells his 40,000 acres (the western half of the grant) to Laughlin for the pre-arranged $50,000. Thus, Catron, who invested only $468 in the small farms he'd bought over the years, and not much more in the actual purchase price (much of the $5,200 cost was returned to Catron, since he held a major percentage of the grant), ended by making a profit of about fifty times his original investment. (San Cristóbal was only one of Catron's many preoccupations during this 38-year period. He usually had multiple court battles and deals progressing simultaneously.)

Charles H. Gildersleeve (H. Dudensing, New York, engraver).

Windmill in West La Garita Pasture.

were defined, how ownership was proved, how resources were allocated, and whether land could be sold, could hardly have been more different. And so the two groups perceived most of the events that followed the conquest as if from across a chasm. For many poor Hispanics the period was a disaster. Anglos, on the other hand, even many poor ones, often saw themselves as pioneers bringing civilization and development to a "primitive" country and people. The legacy of the nineteenth century is felt even now, as land grant battles continue.

With the scholarly research begun in the last two decades, a bigger picture, one which places complete and detailed histories of individual grants in the context of their era, is finally beginning to emerge.

CHAPTER 8

THE COWBOY TRADITION

Day ends; come glinting campfires,
Tonight not a wind is stirred;
You can hear the boys on guard if you listen,
Singing to the herd.

—*Jack Culley*

THE GREAT AMERICAN MYTH of the western cowboy and his romantic, difficult life began not in New Mexico or Texas, but much earlier on the ancient *ranchos* of Spain. The traditions of the Spanish cowherders first traveled to the New World in the sixteenth century, when Cortéz introduced cattle to Mexico. These Spanish cows were quite unlike modern breeds; they were lean and muscular with long, dragging tails and even longer curved horns. The Spanish were chiefly interested in the animals' hides, which they exported to Spain; they used only a few cows for tallow or food (since they preferred mutton). But the "longhorn" herds began to multiply on the grassy Mexican plains and quickly grew into unmanageable millions. Soon cattle began wandering away from the *ranchos* into what would eventually be Texas. By the 1600s, herds of wild Longhorns covered these northern plains.

The first Longhorns came north in 1598 with Juan de Oñate and his colonists. *Vaqueros*, or cowboys, herded the cattle and watched them at night, using techniques they had developed among the vast Mexican herds. Oñate's cattle did not prosper and were eventually replaced by sheep, but the Mexican cowboy's skills

(Opposite) San Cristobal cowboys and neighbors "cut" mother cows from their calves before branding begins at the Galisteo corrals.

A Longhorn steer of the late 1800s (photographer unknown).

and style were highly esteemed in the new colony. Always on horseback, the impressive *vaquero* was both swifter and safer than the lowly sheepherder. His clothes, usually a wide sombrero, high boots, large spurs, and leggings (Marc Simmons reports they were originally "leather leg protectors called 'defensas' tied to each side of the saddle like fenders") caught the imagination of wealthy Hispanics, who by the 1800s began to wear elaborate versions of the outfit. Colonial men also carried on the *vaquero* tradition by competing at feats of horsemanship.

Meanwhile in southeast Texas, between three and five million Longhorns roamed freely over chaparral-covered prairies. It was inevitable that newly arriving Americans would try to take advantage of this opportunity, and by the 1860s, a combination of factors made this possible. Refrigeration and new methods of meat packing were invented, and the westward-spreading railroad created a pipeline directly to the packers. With the end of the Civil War, the army was free to control the Plains tribes, who soon became a minimal threat to Anglos and their business ventures. With vast herds of Longhorns simply there for the taking, Texans began rounding them up. They drove them north to the prairies where there was abundant grass, then continued up to southern Kansas, to "cow towns" like Abilene and Dodge City where railroad cars would carry the cattle to slaughterhouses in Chicago.

Many Mexicans were among the first trail-drive teams, and they taught the Texans everything they knew about "cowboying." They showed Americans how to roundup, to brand, to "cut" cattle out of a herd. Soon the Texans were copying the *vaqueros'* wide-brimmed hats, boots, spurs, and even *defensas,* which became chaps (from chaparral). They learned how to use *reatas* (lariats) and tame *broncos.* They used many Spanish terms, anglicizing them in the process: *jacimas* became hackamores (halters), the *caballada* became the cavyard (horse herd), the *caballerango* became the wrangler, and in far west areas, the cowboy name itself, *vaquero,* transformed into buckaroo.

More and more Texans, Easterners, and even Europeans began staking out their "customary" range areas on the public western lands. Longhorns were everywhere, but herding them together proved challenging and rough, and it bred a whole way of life which was to capture the American imagination and live on, in modified form, even until today.

No one had fences in those early days, so twice a year neighboring ranchers rounded up all their cattle, separated them according to owner, branded the new calves, and culled the cows ready for market. Roundups were hard work, but also peak social occasions where hundreds of cowboys came together from miles around, singing, playing cards, and telling stories as they waited for all the

Cowboys going to dinner, northern New Mexico, ca. 1897 (photographer unknown).

New Mexico cowboys camp for the evening, ca. 1885-1890 (photographers unknown).

ranches' chuck wagons to arrive. The roundup itself often lasted nearly a month, with cowboys scouring areas as large as 100 square miles. It was dirty, dangerous work, with jobs such as "pulling bog" (pulling stuck cattle out of mud or quicksand, then guiding the animals slowly toward the herd, to avoid weight loss). The men worked long days, always ten to fourteen hours or more.

But the truly epic feature of range life was the trail drive. From the 1860s to the 1880s cattlemen used two chief routes from Texas to Kansas—the Chisholm and the Western Trails, both far east of San Cristóbal. Another route, the Goodnight-Loving Trail, came north through Las Vegas, about 40 miles northeast of San Cristóbal; the lesser-used Santa Fe Cattle Trail came closest to the ranch, about 16 miles to the north. On any of these trails, a professional contractor for the rancher or cattle corporation would hire a master cowboy as trail boss, about ten regular cowboys, and a cook. The party would set out with a full chuckwagon and the cowboys all circling around the herd. Typically, the men covered only 12 to 15 miles a day, and 90 percent of the drive was either hot and dusty or freezing and wet. They endured a monotonous diet of fried beef, beans, bacon, biscuits, coffee, and sometimes prunes, every day for as long as the drive lasted, anywhere from two to five months. They were on horseback almost continuously, and even at night they had to take turns watching the animals. When they encountered swollen rivers, the trail boss had to choose between trying to swim across, risking men and cattle, or losing time waiting for the waters to subside. At night any sudden noise or thunderstorm could set the whole herd stampeding, and the cowboys would be up all night collecting them, only to hit the trail again at dawn. No wonder the roster of names for most drives was different at the end of the trail—worn-out men often quit mid-way, and fresh ones took their places.

John (Jack) Culley, a self-described "furriner" from England who came to New Mexico in the 1880s and lived as a cowboy and trail boss for many years, describes one drive he made:

> We were shorthanded and lost the herd every night in the pitchy dark and spent the morning gathering it again. Our beds were soaking wet. It was late fall and the rain was colder than snow . . . we'd get a dead juniper alight some nights and squat around it trying to keep warm, when we weren't with the herd.

At the end of the drive the cowboy would go on a spree in the city. Some of these "benders" were relatively harmless, but one commentator from the 1880s remembered:

> [The Cowboy's] idea of enjoyment is to fill himself full of bad whiskey, mount his mustang, tear through the streets, whooping, yelling, flourishing and firing his pistols until the streets are deserted and every house closed . . .

Then, when his money was gone, he usually headed south for his home ranch. Cowboying was seasonal work and in the winter only a few men were kept on by the ranches; the majority found other winter jobs, then came back again for spring roundup. Few men could keep trail-driving for more than ten years, for, as Martin Schmitt puts it, "it was an endless grind with worry and anxiety which only a strong physical frame could stand."

It was also an intense and unforgettable experience that changed men forever. According to John Culley's brother, also a cowboy of the 1880s, it was the high point of a way of life which "brought out all that was best in a man, and made him ashamed of the more common weaknesses."

A certain code and attitude toward life was born on the open range and the trail drives, and by the 1880s it was filtering over the entire West. As the range business boomed, outfits started driving herds into the northern states of Montana, Wyoming, Nebraska, and the Dakotas, where the animals fattened on lush grasslands. Longhorn cattle became commonplace anywhere open country existed, and so did the "Texas Cow-boys," as they were originally called. Soon Texan habits, dress, speech, and attitudes had spread over the West.

Hereford heifers and calves.

Galisteo Pasture.

Most cowboys were Southerners, but not all were white, as popular culture has depicted them. At least one-third were Mexican or black. The former were *vaqueros* or hands from south Texas and its many old Spanish ranches; the latter were slaves before the Civil War and freedmen from all over the South afterwards. There were also Indian and Hispanic cowhands. But as the cowboy traveled the West and the fact of his existence came to the attention of the rest of America, myth-makers began to idealize him as a new popular hero. As part of the idealization, he was turned into a purely white, Anglo-Saxon character.[1]

By 1890 the cattle boom was over. The prairies had become overgrazed, to the surprise of nearly everyone, and a series of droughts and bitterly cold winters killed huge numbers of animals. The cattle business struggled back, but as the railway stretched farther west, the need for long trail drives ended. Cattlemen began fencing their land with barbed wire, so soon the need for communal roundups ended, too.

Cowboy life changed as men now spent their time fixing fences and repairing windmills. They still moved cattle, branded them, and pulled them out of bogs, but the days of the 100-square-mile roundups and grueling, glorious trail drives were gone forever, after a brief heyday of only thirty years.

1. Culley points out that the average Texan of the late 1800s was deeply prejudiced against Mexicans, as a result of the battle of the Alamo. This attitude, along with the Southern prejudice against blacks, spread over the West along with other Texan beliefs. Perhaps this influenced the form that the "idealization" of cowboys took.

Late summer chamisa and purple asters.

Bronco riders at the Galisteo Rodeo.

Away up high in the Sierry Petes,*
Where the yeller pines grow tall
Ol' Sandy Bob an' Buster Jig
Had a rodeer* camp last fall.

Oh, they taken their hosses and runnin' irons
And mabbe a dawg or two,
An' they 'lowed they'd brand all the long-yered calves,
That come within their view.

And any old dogie that flapped long yeres,
An' didn't bush up* by day,
Got his long yeres whittled an' his old hide scorched,
In a most artistic way.

Now one fine day ol' Sandy Bob,
He throwed his seago* down,
"I'm sick of the smell of burnin' hair
And I 'lows I'm a-goin' to town."

So they saddles up an' hits 'em a lope,
Fer it weren't no sight of a ride,
And them was the days when a buckeroo
Could ile up his inside.

Oh, they starts her in at the Kaintucky Bar,
At the head of Whisky Row
And they winds up down by the Depot House,
Some forty drinks below.

As they was a-ridin' back to camp,
A-packin' a pretty good load,
Who should they meet but the Devil himself
A-prancin' down the road.

Sez he, "You ornery cowboy skunks,
You'd better hunt yer holes,
Fer I've come up from Hell's Rim Rock
To gather in yer souls."

Sez Sandy Bob, "Old Devil be damned,
We boys is kinda tight,
But you ain't a-goin' to gather no cowboy souls
'Thout you has some kind of a fight."

So Sandy Bob punched a hole in his seago
And he swang her straight and true,
He lapped it on to the Devil's horns,
An' he taken his dallies* too.

Now Buster Jig was a riata* man
With his gut-line coiled up neat,
So he shaken her out an' he built him a loop
An' he lassed the Devil's hind feet.

Oh, they stretched him out an' they tailed him down
While the irons was a-gettin' hot,
They cropped and swaller-forked* his yeres,
Then they branded him up a lot.

They pruned him up with a de-hornin' saw
an' they knotted his tail fer a joke,
Then they rid off and left him there,
Necked to a Black-Jack oak.

If you're ever up high in the Sierry Petes
An' you hear one hell of a wail,
You'll know it's that Devil a-bellerin' around
About them knots in his tail.

–*The Sierry Petes*[2]

Branding time.

2. Probably the most widely recited cowboy poem today, The "*Sierry Petes*" was written by Gail Gardner. Cowboy terms: **Sierry Petes:* the Sierra Prieta Mountain range near Prescott, Arizona; *rodeer:* Spanish for "rounding up." A rodeer camp is a roundup out on the range; *bush up*: hide in the bushes; *seago:* loose hemp rope; *dallies:* transliterated from the Spanish *dale vueltas*, a Mexican term that means "give it some twists," and refers to the practice of looping rope loosely (rather than tying "hard and fast") around the saddle horn; *riata:* Spanish for rope; *swaller-forked:* to make an identifying notch in the ear of cattle, in the shape of a swallowtail.

Harper McFarland (far left), Bill Grassie, Gene Thornton, Rusty McCorkell, and Apache waiting for neighbors at dawn before rounding up cattle for shipping.

Anyone who has seen a John Wayne movie probably has some notion of Western ideals, but they may have been a little different when they first bloomed in the nineteenth century. Jack Culley believes they originated in Scotland and England, particularly in the Northern border country. The people there had a long history of raiding and feuding, particularly over livestock and land. "A hard drinking, hard riding, fighting crowd they were," he says, "hardy, resourceful men and women." Many Texans and other Southerners were of English and Scottish descent, and Culley believes this heritage helped mold the early Western way of life.

The Western code, Culley says, was "fundamentally a crude one . . . open to considerable exception." The philosophy of "an eye for an eye" was the rule, and this of course led to trouble since "it was only one step from this to killing any man who seriously got in your way."

But on the other hand a spirit of genuine neighborliness also prevailed. On the open range, one's nearest "neighbor" might have been 20 miles away, but people always counted on each other for help and cooperation. The early communal roundups in that fenceless land would have been impossible otherwise.

Cattlemen and cowboys had a strong sense of honor and a disdain for legal formalities. For example, when Charles Goodnight and Oliver Loving made their historic contract that opened up the cattle trade between Texas and the northern range states, "no papers were executed and no instruments drawn; yet [the verbal agreement's] conditions bound its parties as strongly as the threads of life."

The early cowboy's life was dangerous. He had to deal with rivers "bank-high and a bilin'," untamed broncos, subzero temperatures, and more. His companions expected him to face all this resolutely and without fear. "God hates a coward" was one of the early cowboy mottoes.

Along with stoicism and courage was a tendency toward quiet reserve. Culley says that, "some of the Texans were a bit loud-mouthed, but as a general thing you never heard much noise around a cow camp." He theorizes that perhaps it was the vastness and silence of the land that discouraged "chatterboxes." But the cowboy's laconic nature was also a sign of his simplicity, his tendency to strip all things down to essentials. For example, he labeled any kind of excess "foofaraw," which meant a kind of pretentiousness or "showin' off." Foofaraw could take many forms, from fancy clothes to long goodbyes, but whenever it appeared, the cowboy response was always embarrassment or disdain. J. Frank Dobie tells the story of the cattleman who was asked what he thought of an Eastern minister's flowery Sunday sermon. "Too much mane and tail," the rancher curtly replied.

Gene Thornton, Jerry Witte, and Kenneth Scott (clockwise from top) at the Galisteo corrals.

In relations with the opposite sex, an area where the potential for "foofaraw" was high, the average cowboy was cautious and restrained. Since many Anglo cowboys were Southerners, they tended to treat women (caucasian "ladies," at any rate) with a mixture of respect and shyness.

Dances were the main form of socializing, especially on winter evenings, when little work was available. Contemporary commentators and former cowboys had varying opinions about those lively occasions. Jack Culley reports that "strict decorum prevailed" at dances. Joseph McCoy, a businessman who "opened the cattle market at Abilene, Kansas, in 1867" held a different view. McCoy says:

> these miserable beings gather into the halls of the dance house, and 'trip the fantastic toe' to wretched music, ground out of dilapidated instruments, by beings fully as degraded as the most vile. In this vortex of dissipation the average cowboy plunges with great delight. . . . To say they dance wildly or in an abandoned manner is putting it mild. . . . The cowboy enters the dance with a peculiar zest, not stopping to divest himself of his sombrero, spurs, or pistols, but just as he dismounts off his cow-pony, so he goes into the dance. A more odd, not to say comical sight, is not often seen than the dancing cowboy . . .

Suffice it to say that McCoy was describing scenes he had witnessed in Abilene (at the end of the Chisholm Trail), one of the wildest of the Wild West towns. Jack Culley was writing of dances held on the range, usually in tiny villages. His description differs considerably:

> In the gayest ballrooms I've never had such merry times as in those rough, 'dobe dance halls lighted with dim oil lamps. We'd slick the floor up with wax candles. I can still feel the pulse and rhythm of the square dances as we swung to the music of fiddle and guitar, and the "calling" of Mat McCallister . . .

Square dances and famous "callers" were immortalized in cowboy poetry of the 1880s as well:

> Don't tell me 'bout cotillions, or Germans, no sir-ee!
> That whirl at Anson City jes' takes the cake with me.
> I'm sick of lazy shufflin's, of them I've had my fill.
> Give me a frontier breakdown backed up by Windy Bill.
> McAllister ain't nowhere when Windy leads the show.
> I've seen 'em both in harness, and so I ought ter know.
> Oh, Bill, I shan't forget yer and I oftentimes recall
> That lively gaited soiree, the cowboys' Christmas ball.

Bull riding at the Galisteo Rodeo (above and left).

A horse herd with its goat. Ranchers believe that keeping a goat with horses has a calming effect on the herd.

And though a man might fall in love, showing his feeling was definitely not part of the cowboy code. Culley says, "I never remember seeing any of the boys show what you might call emotion . . . ." He goes on to say, "But they had a great feeling all of them deep down for horse and cow brute." Cowboys tended to be as tough on their animals as they were on themselves, riding horses hard, branding and castrating calves unflinchingly; but at the same time they had, and still have today, a certain empathy with animals. They observed cattle closely and, as J. Frank Dobie says, learned "cow psychology, cow anatomy, cow dietetics—cow nature in general and cow nature in particular." And they felt a responsibility, born of sympathy, to risk their comfort and sometimes their lives saving cows and calves lost in blizzards or stuck in quicksand. Some cowmen maintain that this quality is at the very heart of cowboy life, even though it rarely appeared in popular myth. In stories from the early range days, cowboys' attentiveness to animals showed up everywhere. Cattleman Culley describes his ideal horse:

> When you meet with a horse that is well-shaped and a good color; that's high-spirited yet as kind as can be; that you can bank on under all circumstances because you know he has a big heart; that's the kind of horse to tie to.

One old-time cowboy mused about cow psychology and central New Mexico in this way:

> That Pintada country is the doggonest sorriest looking layout I ever set eyes on. It ain't so much that there's no feed down there. . . . A cow raised in New Mexico gets used to doin' without much to eat. But down in that Pintada country there ain't even nuthin' for an old cow to look at! I kinda believe that it sorta helps an old cow when she's hungry, to have somethin' to look at . . .

Animals were so much a part of Western life that cattlemen and cowboys constantly used animal metaphors to describe themselves. In "The Cowboys' Christmas Ball," a nineteenth-century poem, the square dance leader begins the proceedings by calling out, "Whoa fellers, let's stampede," then goes on,

> Now fellers, stake yer pen.
> Lock horns ter all them heifers and rustle them like men,
> Salute yer lovely critters, now swing and let 'em go,
> Climb the grapevine round 'em, now all hands do-si-do.

The cowboy code even applied to Western outlaws, who were both admired and feared by law-abiding folk. Outlaws were usually cowboys themselves, and they often worked temporarily at ranches or on trail drives, unbeknownst to the bosses and other men. In fact many, like Butch Cassidy, were considered top cowhands and horsemen. They developed extraordinary skills, like the ability to gallop at breakneck speed over rocky country at night. So it was only natural that these men were, in many ways, exemplars of the cowboy code. Some, like Billy the Kid, were psychopaths who killed men at the drop of a hat, but even these were said to rarely, if ever, rob the poor or molest women. The infamous bandit Clay Allison, for example, on meeting a lady, blushed and was "far too shy to talk."

Cowboy humor tended to be terse and dry, and could appear when least expected. When the notorious Black Jack Ketcham of New Mexico was finally caught, his badly wounded arm had to be amputated. He refused anesthesia and remained stoically silent throughout the operation. Afterwards he smiled up at the surgeon and said, "Let me know if I can do the same for you someday, Doc."

Early cowboys were continuously immersed in the elements, and became very close to nature. This fact has led some recent writers to call the nineteenth-century cowboy a "romantic," or a "refugee from industrial civilization." Many *were* running from the growing cities and mechanization of the times, but such a choice could just as easily be called "sensible" as "romantic."

In any case, Culley believes that, "tough as some of our men might be, I was always aware of a certain fineness about a cow camp. We lived nearer to nature than any other class of people, and Nature has a way of refining, spiritualizing those near her."

Perhaps Culley, too, could be accused of romanticizing his early cowpunching days. Modern writers now try to dispel the mythology that has grown up around the West, emphasizing instead the ceaseless toil, monotony, and exhaustion of the cowboy's existence. Still, something drew many men and boys of the late 1800s to this difficult road. To quote Jack Culley once again,

> [some say] it was all humdrum drudgery. So it was, mostly . . . toward the end of a long day it got pretty monotonous. Yet always for me, to ride forth from camp on a fresh horse on a clear New Mexico morning . . . that never failed to stir something in me. And of all the things I have done in a long life that is the one I like best to recall.

S.N.Laughlin, registered in Castroville, California, June 3, 1890
Place on left hip or thigh, crop both ears.

B.F. Pankey, registered in Lamy, New Mexico
Place on left ribs of horses and cattle; no earmarks.

Holding brand.
Place on left shoulder of horses and cattle.

S.C. Fullerton, registered in Lamy, New Mexico
Place on left hip of cattle, left shoulder of horses.

Sawyer Cattle Company, registered in San Angelo, Texas
Place on left ribs of cattle, left hip of horses; ears cropped.

San Cristóbal Ranch Brands

San Cristóbal's first cattle arrived in June of 1890, bought by Saron Laughlin.[3] Cattle are still there today, and the cowboy way of life, in modified fashion, is also very much alive. Ranch managers and cowboys now ride pickup trucks

3. Though the Eaton family apparently ranged cattle earlier, the first official brand record was registered to Laughlin on June 3, 1890.

more than horses, returning to houses and families at night instead of camping with a bedroll. But they are still immersed in animal life, earth, water, and sky all day; they remain close to nature. Like their nineteenth-century forebears, they are still neighborly, self-reliant, and stoic; still reserved and laconic; still humorous in their dry and understated way.

CHAPTER 9

A TWENTIETH-CENTURY RANCH

When Saron Laughlin bought one-third of San Cristóbal in 1874, the *Weekly New Mexican* reported: "Mr. Laughlin is a wide awake business man, and we extend to him our best wishes, and hail his coming to our Territory with pleasure as a forerunner of an immigration of substantial men of the times, whose investments will be crowned with success . . . ." Thirty-three years later, after many court battles and compromises, Laughlin bought Tom Catron's share of San Cristóbal and finally became its sole owner. Immediately he drew up plans to subdivide the grant. He partitioned it into 4,867 tracts, and planned to sell them at $6.00 an acre. He envisioned a thriving, irrigated townsite with reservoirs, a hotel, and a schoolhouse.

But Laughlin's idea never caught on; no settlers bought his tracts. So in August of 1907 he mortgaged the grant to Catron and two other parties. Shortly after this, Laughlin sold out completely to Benjamin F. Pankey, whom the *Santa Fe New Mexican* described as "a capitalist of Topeka."[1] Pankey and his wife Flora bought San Cristóbal for $141,000 and left their home in Kansas for the unfamiliar frontier of New Mexico.

1. Part of this deal was that Pankey would cede 250 acres of prime land in and around Galisteo to Catron.

Benjamin F. Pankey in 1920 (photographer unknown).

Pankey had been a farmer in Illinois, where his first home with Flora was a one-room log house. Hard working and optimistic, he recalled later that he had never feared the future: "I had a wife who was a real helpmate. I would start ploughing at five in the morning; at nine the faithful wife would bring me my breakfast in a tin bucket." They eventually moved to Kansas, and Pankey saved enough money to go into the telephone business there, taking on the huge Bell system. He won an ensuing "telephone war" and soon after sold his business, buying San Cristóbal with the profits and immediately re-stocking the land with cattle. He also embarked on a political career, partly because he believed that "a politician on the right side of the fence in New Mexico . . . can at least get justice about his taxes." Always running as a Republican, he was elected state senator, then lieutenant governor, and finally state land commissioner. ("My, how old Pankey runs!" Thomas Catron was said to exclaim each year as he scanned the election returns.)[2] Pankey instituted several reforms as land commissioner, diminishing widespread criticism of that office.

Eventually Pankey became the largest land owner and land renter in New Mexico, and one of the state's first millionaires. He was a rotund man known for his amusing, exceptionally brief campaign speeches (perhaps one secret of his political success), and his sense of humor, which extended to his wealth. "I never knew the power of the press," he commented, "until the *Santa Fe New Mexican* printed my picture and wrote me up as a millionaire." He also liked to joke about putting cowboys in airplanes to round up all his cattle. His genial attitude served him well years later. In the 1920s a three-year drought hit New Mexico, and Pankey, along with many others, lost most of his fortune. He took the loss well, at least outwardly; "Thank God I am poor," he said, "nobody bothers me now."

When the Pankeys moved to New Mexico it was still a U.S. territory, a place that seemed very foreign to many Americans. Though some New Mexicans were pushing for statehood, the Union was resistant. New Mexican culture was older than America's, with an alien language, alien religion, and a population of "mixed breeds." The United States had never incorporated such a society and it warily put off the New Mexicans for fifty years. Many Americans agreed with John C. Calhoun when he said:

> Ours is the government of the white man. . . . Are we to associate with ourselves as equals, companions, and fellow citizens, the Indians and mixed races of [New] Mexico? I would consider such association as degrading to ourselves and fatal to our institutions.

2. Pankey and Catron clearly knew each other, not only through their land dealings, but also through the Republican Party and the Masonic Order.

This photograph, ca. 1920, may have been used to attract potential investors to San Cristóbal. The acreage figure is incorrect, however; the ranch never exceeded 81,033 acres (photographer unknown).

Five years later Colonel E. V. Sumner, the territorial governor, would echo these sentiments, saying: "The New Mexicans were thoroughly debased and totally incapable of self-government, and there is no latent quality about them that can *ever* make them respectable."

Many years passed before these attitudes began to change, but finally in January of 1912, New Mexico was admitted to the Union as a full-fledged American state.[3]

During the early years of the twentieth century Benjamin Pankey consolidated San Cristóbal, buying up plots within or near the grant from Hispanic farmers and sheepherders. From 1904 through 1911, twelve Hispanics were listed as taxpayers on government or public land within the grant, and four houses were noted. But by 1912 Pankey's name was the only name on the tax rolls. Pankey also expanded his cattle operation, building "irrigation works of every kind and nature . . . including dams, canals, ditches, laterals, headgates, and reservoirs." The *Daily New Mexican* quoted him as saying, "I will make experiments this fall in winter wheat and next spring I will experiment with other cereals and I am assured I will make a success."

But Pankey inherited serious problems when he purchased the beautiful grant. Galisteo Hispanics and others living on San Cristóbal itself had been waging a losing fight for legal confirmation of their property rights for decades. Pankey became enmeshed in these court battles, which lasted, on and off, until 1922.

3. T. B. Catron was an ardent supporter of statehood for many years, believing it would help New Mexico's economy. He worked hard toward this goal and was at least partially responsible for its success.

A ruined hearth not far from San Cristóbal Pueblo, probably from a nineteenth-century homestead.

Galisteo Land Disputes

Hispanics' battles for legal right to land near or on the San Cristóbal Grant persisted for almost a century. Many of the involved families had lived on the land for generations, farming and raising sheep. Some claimed descent from six Hispanics who were granted farm land around Galisteo in the early 1800s; others from the twenty-six compatriots of Domingo Fernández.

In 1871 several Hispanics who claimed to be heirs tried to establish firm right to their holdings around Galisteo (areas which Ethan Eaton also claimed). These Galisteo men understood the American requirement for written proof of ownership established by the Treaty of Guadalupe Hidalgo. The men produced a document they said was a copy of the grant made by Governor Alberto Maynez to their forebears in 1814. But as witnesses began to testify, a check of the Santa Fe archives revealed that Maynez was not even the governor at the time. When Maynez did take office later, the records showed he made a *verbal* grant to the petitioners in 1816, whereupon a local official had carried out the formal ceremonies of land transfer. The petitioners' document was declared fraudulent, and the case was dismissed. Apparently the Galisteo men then made a private settlement with Ethan Eaton.

Eight years later, in 1879, twenty-three Galisteo landowners learned from a publicly posted announcement about the proposed resurvey, which would make the San Cristóbal grant rectangular. Its western boundary would shift 4 miles west, cutting heavily into 7,500 acres of their pasture and timber lands. They filed a vehement protest, saying that if the plan went through, "we would be reduced to great misery and calamity and as though we were imprisoned and oppressed with only our little tracts of land, without the consolation of having liberty where to feed our animals . . . which every poor man may have for the support of his poor family." This protest had no effect on the authorities; the resurvey went ahead as planned and the patent was issued soon after.

Two years after the Catron and Pino suit against Saron Laughlin began, the same group of Galisteo citizens (joined now by Pino) sued the United States for compensation for their lost pasture and timber lands. This time they had researched the archives, and disclaimed any link with the embarrassing document of 1871. They now produced legal proof of Mexican grants from 1822, 1843, and 1846, and evidence that their families had occupied the country continuously.

But two years later, in 1894, the court rejected their claims. Only those tracts clearly outside the patented grant were confirmed and no restitution was made.

The Galisteo farmers and sheepherders continued to make use of the disputed lands anyway, and to press their claims.

When Pankey bought the grant in 1907 he had to face these thorny issues. Eventually, he decided to sue eleven of the same Galisteoans (famed *patrón* José Ortiz y Pino was now among them) for "quiet title" to the disputed lands in the Cadillal area, near Galisteo. Pankey won the case in 1916 but the Galisteo men appealed. "The case was hotly fought," according to the *Daily New Mexican,* and in 1921 the Supreme Court decided in favor of the Galisteo men. After this setback, Pankey worked out an agreement with T. B. Catron that Catron would "do all in his power to extinguish or cause to be extinguished as soon as practicable either by purchase or legal proceedings or otherwise all of said adverse claims." Catron apparently succeeded, for in 1922, the courts set the whole matter aside "for want of prosecution." According to José Ortiz y Pino III, the Catrons were responsible for the final settlement. The Río Galisteo became an official dividing line, with everything east of the river belonging to San Cristóbal, and everything west belonging to Galisteo. It seemed that at last the combatants had come to an understanding outside the courts.

After Pankey's time, various Galisteo residents again brought smaller suits against subsequent owners. It was not until the 1960s that the last of these disputes was settled.

The town of Galisteo in 1884, looking east–southeast across the San Cristóbal Ranch (J. R. Riddle, photographer).

Rodeo fans at the annual Galisteo Rodeo in August.

The Anayas' Galisteo store, famous for its home-made tamales.

Galisteo backyard sunset.

Heading out of town on Highway 41.

N.C. Nelson and crew excavating at San Cristóbal Pueblo (photographer unknown).

While Pankey and the Galisteoans were battling over disputed tracts of the ranch, an unknown archaeologist was making history at San Cristóbal Pueblo. Nels C. Nelson was a young scholar hired between 1913 and 1915 by the American Museum of Natural History to survey and excavate sites in the Galisteo Basin. Archaeology at that time was still in its infancy, but other Southwestern researchers had made considerable progress in identifying various pottery styles and correlating them to types of Pueblo ruins. Still, no one had been able to establish or prove a chronological order to the pottery types.

Nelson decided to use a new method of digging called stratigraphic excavation. Its basic premise, first developed by geologists in the early 1800s, is that lower geological strata or deposits are older than higher ones. In archaeology, this idea of digging through successive levels, rather than removing all the dirt covering a site, had been sporadically applied before, but the method was still undeveloped, and scholars, especially in the Americas, were not convinced of its value.

Nelson tried the method at several sites, but his real breakthrough came at San Cristóbal, where he found an ideal, undisturbed 10-foot-deep cultural deposit in a creek bank near the pueblo. His excavations, in 1-foot stratigraphic layers, revealed a complete sequence of pottery styles, including all the known types of the Rio Grande area. Thus, he was able to definitively establish the chronology of these styles. Nelson published his revolutionary findings in 1916, setting the stage for the use of a new digging method all over the world and for improving the future understanding of Southwestern archaeology.[4]

Soon after Nelson's breakthrough, another change came to New Mexico. In the 1920s tourists with visions of sunset panoramas and picturesque pueblos began pouring into the state. Many took the "Indian Detours" begun by Fred Harvey, the entrepreneur who built the Harvey Houses for the railways. Artists and writers came for the light and the ambiance and stayed, painting and writing about their new home. New Mexico became part of the American imagination—a romantic, unspoiled "land of enchantment."

Many thought this state enchanted for other reasons. Drilling companies were finding oil and gas in many areas, as well as minerals such as copper, zinc, lead, and potash. In January of 1924, Pankey leased the mineral rights to over 13,000 acres of San Cristóbal to Walter E. Wood of Lamy, who began drilling for both gas and oil. (Pankey also leased twelve other portions of the grant to cattle ranchers and fuel prospectors.) But no one found any oil or gas. Most of the lessees were apparently having trouble making ends meet, because the records show Pankey had great difficulty collecting any rents. Soon Pankey, too, was in serious trouble. He and his wife had mortgaged the land two years earlier, and

4. Another young archaeologist, Manuel Gamio, made similar discoveries about the value of the stratigraphic method almost at the same time as Nelson. His work took place in Mesoamerica and established the basis for a Central American ceramic chronology.

now they could not keep up their payments. M. E. Singleton and his company, Missouri State Life Insurance, foreclosed on the property and brought suit against Pankey. Pankey succeeded in obtaining a nine-month delay in the court action, during which time he brought in new investors from California and redoubled his attempts to find oil and gas. But the land yielded nothing of commercial value, and in April 1926, Pankey lost the grant to Missouri State Life and its president, M. E. Singleton.

Soon afterwards, Samuel and Minnie Fullerton and their friend Wayman Dobson traveled from Miami, Oklahoma, to see San Cristóbal. Joining forces, they purchased it in December of 1926. The partnership of Dobson and Fullerton owned the grant for twenty-two years. They held onto it through the Great Depression when all New Mexico's booming coal towns shut down, and through World War II, when Navajo "talkers" conveyed government radio messages in their unbreakable "code." World War II brought New Mexico another distinction: the world's first atomic bomb was developed at Los Alamos, 40 miles northwest of San Cristóbal, and detonated in 1945 in a desolate area about 130 miles south of the ranch.

Samuel C. Fullerton (photographer unknown).

Visitors inspect one of Pankey's newly built water tanks in the 1920s (T. Harmon Parkhurst, photographer).

An experiment in farming at Chico Pasture. The wooden house was built between 1910 and 1925 (photographer unknown).

The Chico house today. Rancher Eldon Butler and his wife lived here in the 1930s, leasing Chico Pasture for cattle. The house has been abandoned since the Butlers left in 1939.

Henry and Carolyn Singleton

Eventually Samuel Jr. took over the Fullerton share of San Cristóbal, with Wayman's siblings running the Dobson portion. In 1944 the new partners attempted an ambitious project, leasing out 39,000 acres for the "purpose of exploring, drilling, mining, and operating for oil and gas and of laying pipe lines and of building tanks, power stations and structures thereon to produce, save, and take care of said products." The drilling companies labored for two years, but their efforts were fruitless.

Perhaps discouraged by these results, the Dobson and Fullerton families sold the San Cristóbal Grant in 1948. The Sawyer Cattle Company of Texas bought a four-fifths share and the Farr Brothers, a partnership of two brothers and one son, bought the remaining one-fifth. The Farrs held onto their portion through 1952, when another land suit began, this time brought by José and Rafaela Maldonado against the grant owners and many Galisteo residents. It is unknown whether this suit had any effect on the Farrs, but a few weeks after it began, they sold all their property to the Sawyer Cattle Company.

The Sawyer Cattle Company dissolved in 1955, selling all its assets to Texas Senator William A. Blakley and his wife, Villa. The senator resumed the search for oil, gas, and minerals in 1960, but again found nothing worth commercial exploitation. Eventually the land was transferred to the Blakley-Braniff Foundation, a charitable corporation run by Blakley. The grant continued to change hands, being transferred to the Texas Scottish Rite Hospital for Crippled Children in 1964, which sold it to another Texan couple, M. W. (Buddy) Branum and his wife Betty Jo, the following year.

Henry and Carolyn Singleton now own the San Cristóbal Ranch. Dr. Singleton, who is originally from Texas, was chairman of Teledyne, Inc., from 1960 to 1990. He and his wife have lived in Los Angeles for many years. Since buying the ranch in 1986 from Buddy Branum, Dr. Singleton has purchased other ranches, and now runs a widespread cattle operation.

Cowboy: A commercial cow ranch is in business to raise calves to sell for beef. A cow's job is to have a calf as often as possible. A cowboy's job is to take care of that cow, see that that calf gets to market.

Ken Scott, ranch hand: Ranch work is more or less just a routine. A lot of it's just the same thing day after day.

Tommie Scott, ranch wife: Day in and day out and *year* in and year out.

Ken Scott: A certain time of year you do your branding and a certain time of year

> you do your shipping. . . . When your calves get up big, you know, in the fall of the year, you got to get 'em off their mothers, wean 'em. If you're not going to sell 'em, well, you still gotta wean 'em.
>
> *Tommie Scott:* It's the same thing, year in and year out, same cycle.

The people who live and work on San Cristóbal Ranch today carry on a unique way of life still tied to the land and the seasons. Their world, like that of their

The road to ranch headquarters: January and July.

Pueblo and Hispanic predecessors, revolves around weather and rain. Ample rainfall means healthier cattle at less cost to both owners and employees, and a good chance for the ranch to survive and perhaps even prosper another year.

To the outsider, a hint of romance still clings to the ranching way of life; Hollywood westerns and advertising keep this myth alive. But to the "true cowboy," ranch life has virtually no romance.[5] As Harper McFarland, San Cristóbal's Ranch manager, sums it up, "It's not like your movies, I'll say that." Cowboying is a physically exhausting job with long hours, six- to seven-day work-weeks, few holidays, and low pay.

But most cowboys and their families are fiercely proud of their way of life and rarely give it up by choice. As Jerrie Pilley, a ranch wife at San Cristóbal, explains, "The cattle and the country is your life. A cowboy will go sit on a hill; he'll say 'Well, this is God's country.' He *feels* things." The idea of taking a job in a town is anathema to most cowboys. "You learn to appreciate the land," she continues, "you appreciate the wild life. We can't take city life—the noise and the people . . . town people are just different." An older cowboy agrees: "A person that wants to be around people all the time ain't too apt to make it too long. Somebody that's kind of a lone wolf, why they're pretty well at home."

This traditional way of life with its repeating cycles is the core of the American livestock industry, which, in turn, is a much larger process tied to all sorts of seemingly unrelated worlds, such as retail clothing and pharmaceuticals. As ranching expert Harold Oppenheimer explains:

> The railroads and trucking companies move cattle, the chemical companies produce fertilizers that help to raise the feed that makes the animals grow; the farm equipment companies make it possible to work the soil; the packing companies and grocery chains process and merchandize the meat; the shoe companies and department stores retail manufactures from the by-product, leather; the drug companies produce veterinary supplies and use other by-products for humans; and practically every company on the [stock exchange] has a major market in the 20 million people tied up in the [livestock] industry.[6]

San Cristóbal is at the first level of the livestock industry—the "cow-calf operation." There are about two million cow-calf operations of widely varying sizes all over the U.S. (San Cristóbal is a fairly large one, running about 1,000 cattle, including calves and bulls, most years.) As a cow-calf producer, the ranch breeds cattle, puts the mothers and calves on grass to graze, then weans the calves at about six to seven months of age. As Henry Singleton, San Cristóbal's owner, explains:

Corrals and barn at ranch headquarters.

5. The "true cowboy" is a term of admiration among ranch people, as distinguished from the "town cowboy," an ersatz wanna-be.

6. Oppenheimer neglects to mention perhaps the most obviously related industry, fast food, as it had not burgeoned to its present state at the time of his writing.

The cycle of seasons at San Cristóbal's ranch house.

Elsie McFarland with two of her oil landscapes.

> After weaning, the calf goes on grass without its mother; the calf is referred to as a 'stocker' at this point. If you have a cow-calf operation you can take the stockers to another pasture, but most will sell their calves to other ranchers who specialize in running stockers. Historically, San Cristóbal has usually sold calves on weaning. I try to judge whether it would be better to sell them now or keep them to sell when they are larger. We've sold every time but once. This year [1990] we'll hold them over again.

Deciding whether to keep or sell the weaned calves, which usually weigh about 500 pounds, is one of many gambles the ranch owner must take. His decision depends on a lot of factors, says Singleton. "I decided to keep our calves over this winter, but we won't know until the future if it's right, if we'll have a hard winter. We could have a balmy winter, they'd do wonderfully well and gain weight, the market could rise—or the opposite could happen. You just gradually develop some kind of feeling and analysis."

The next phase for the stocker calves, whether they are on or off the ranch, is grazing by themselves, gaining in weight until they become "yearlings" that weigh about 700 pounds. By eighteen months of age, at the latest, their owner sells them to a feedlot, where they are put into pens on a full grain diet. They stay at the feedlot for about four months, until they fatten to about 1,100 pounds.

The feedlot operator then sells the cattle to a stockyard trader, who ships them to their final destination—a packing house. The animals are slaughtered and become carcasses, about 65 percent of which is usable meat. A wholesaler in an urban area buys the carcasses, divides them into cuts, and sells them to retail markets, hotels, and restaurants.

But back at San Cristóbal, the core cycle of breeding, branding, weaning, and shipping continues. The end point of this cycle—shipping day—is "the payday of the year for the ranch," says one cowboy. "They'll average each bunch [of cattle] that goes across the scale, and the total weight's what'll determine just how good we done for the year."

For a rancher like Singleton, the basic equation is straightforward; "Your input is grass and the output is beef." As on any ranch, however, much more is involved in making ends meet. Initial costs of land, equipment, and an original breeding herd, plus continuing costs of management, labor, feed, bulls, and repairs must all be figured into the balance sheet. Most ranch owners would agree that they are not in this business for profit alone. Market fluctuations and unpredictable weather make ranching a somewhat risky business, but the ranching lifestyle is a powerful compensating factor. For Singleton, who grew up on a ranch near Fort Worth, Texas, the greatest reward is "just being out in the country, the association with the land, animals, and people." As he puts it, "I like the feeling of participation, of taking care of the land . . . being one of the guys that helps to take care of the land—it's a nice feeling. I like to do it under a normal constraint: take care of the land, and have it in turn take care of the people who work on it."

A typical day for Singleton would begin at 5:30 or 6:00 a.m., the best time for telephone conversations with his ranch manager, Harper McFarland, or the managers of his other ranches. Singleton explains: "We talk about any new facilities or replacements or purchases . . . we'll talk about the cattle breeding program. . . . We go over every aspect and plan a lot. The pipelines, for example; are they wearing out? Do we need to extend them? You've got to have wells, water tanks, creeks; you have to work on them and expand them."

No day is ever routine, says Singleton. Sometimes he will drive with McFarland to check on grass or windmills, deciding about improvements or repairs. And he frequently talks to other people in the business, such as "packers, feedlot operators, etc., to discuss what kind of plans they have. I like to visit about how the year is going. There are talks with other ranchers, too. You get a lot of good ideas talking back and forth."

He pays all the ranch bills and signs all the checks, calling it "a form of discipline. Through doing the signing it's amazing how much you learn about the business. There's a reminder of each event or action behind each check." And sometimes during each day he makes time to look at trade journals or market reports. "It influences your feel," he says, "what direction you're going to go."

Only a few employees live and work on San Cristóbal's lands: the ranch manager and his wife, a couple who are caretakers, and two to three cowboys and their families. Harper McFarland and his wife Elsie have lived at San Cristóbal the longest—47 years. McFarland drove up from Texas to take over the job of ranch manager in 1948 when the Farr brothers and the Sawyer Cattle Company owned the ranch. He and Elsie raised three children at San Cristóbal, which was much different when they arrived. Elsie McFarland explains:

> The summer that we were here in '48 we had to take our laundry to town to do it and take baths in the creek. This house wasn't here, and the owner's house up there—*everybody* was in it—cowboys and the Farrs [part-owners], and their children, and Harper and I. All together. And of course there were none of the trees, you know . . . no grass . . .

Harper McFarland concurs:

Harper McFarland, ranch manager since 1948.

Bull Canyon in fall.

> Nobody wanted to work here. There just wasn't anything here really. No roads—just wood-hauling roads and wagon roads. Very little water. Weren't any fences—you had the east side and the west side. We built *lots* of fences and drilled lots of wells, for windmills. . . .

Ken and Tommie Scott

Laconic and stoic, McFarland may know more about San Cristóbal's 81,000 acres than anyone else ever has. One of New Mexico's most respected cattlemen, an expert on horses and winner of steer-roping competitions, McFarland is well known in the Galisteo Basin for helping other ranchers at branding time.

Together the people of San Cristóbal keep the cycle of ranch life flowing smoothly with the seasons. The cycle begins with breeding, when bulls (Beefmasters, Herefords, sometimes Angus and Longhorns) are introduced into pastures of heifers and older cows, which may be Herefords, Black Baldies (an Angus-Hereford cross), or Beefmaster-Hereford crosses. (Female cattle are called heifers until they are about two years old. Once they have a calf, they're "first-calf heifers"; after their first calf is weaned, they're simply called cows.) Heifers are usually about 15 months old at first breeding. Years ago heifers weren't bred until they were at least two, but today San Cristóbal, like other ranches, uses cattle that breed earlier, due to years of selection for this trait. Once a heifer has given birth, she can go on producing a calf a year until she is ten or eleven years old.

Breeding is timed so that cattle will give birth, or "calve," in spring—February through April. (Like humans, cows have a nine-month gestation period, so breeding begins in May.) Kenneth Scott, former cowboy and caretaker at San Cristóbal for over ten years, explains the cowboy's role in calving:

> The older cows don't really need help too much. Your first calf, the heifers, are the ones that need help. You put 'em in a handy pasture where you can look after 'em every day. Once or twice a day, you find a heifer that's having trouble, why you get out there, pull the calf, see that everything's goin' along alright.

Heifers are often bred with Longhorn bulls for their first calf because, as Scott explains, "the little Longhorn calf has a smooth, small head; a slim head-type, you know. They look more like a jack-rabbit than a calf when they're first born."

Loss of calves can come through miscarriage (sometimes caused by consumption of snakeweed or turpentine weed) or because of predators. Scott says, "you have a few mountain lions cuttin' along and gettin' one once in a while, and the coyotes. You have bobcats, lynx cats, and things like that in this old rough country." Calf-crop percentage, or the percent of calves who survive until weaning from a given number of cows is one of the indicators of the success of

A shallow arroyo in winter.

A road in Galisteo Pasture.

a ranch. At San Cristóbal, this figure is around 85 percent, high considering the predators and the scarcity of grass in dry years, which can cause animals not to breed.

The young calves suckle all through spring and summer, staying close to their grazing mothers. Cattle are sometimes spread over most of San Cristóbal's twenty-six pastures, though McFarland tends to run them mainly on the east side in summer. That portion of the ranch is particularly rough, with deep canyons and rocky passes; snows make it impossible to pasture livestock there in winter. This timing of rotating cattle among the pastures is an art, one which is crucial to keeping the animals healthy and preventing overgrazing. McFarland decides when to rotate based on knowledge and intuition he has gleaned from decades of observing vegetation and grazing habits. If asked to elaborate on his know-how, he says only, "It's just automatic."

Today young people go to agricultural school to learn about geology, soils, and grasses in an effort to understand more about overgrazing, part of the process of desertification that has plagued this planet for millennia. But most ranchers insist that environmentalists' fears about cattle ruining land are exaggerated and unjustified.

A young ranch manager in New Mexico, Jeff Bilberry, echoes McFarland's sentiments: "You can go to school and learn all about grasses, but when is it time to move the cattle? It's a gut feeling. There's no way in the world I could ever explain it." He continues, "Most environmentalists are so far away from the land, they don't understand. We have to live and co-exist with nature out here. We slit our own throat if we don't. Old-timers always told me: 'If you take care of the land, she'll take care of you. And if you take care of a cow, she'll take care of you.'"

When pressed, Bilberry admits that an economic crunch could push a rancher to overgraze; someone "might lean on it a little bit, to hold things together [temporarily]. But when you lean on the land it will ask to give it back, and the land is harder to pay back than a banker—it demands more. So you try and pay attention."[7]

Meanwhile, the cows and calves lead a relatively peaceful existence until late spring. When the calves are between one and four months old, the time comes for branding.

The "Spring Works," or branding time, is one of the two most intense periods of the year (the other being the "Fall Works"). The Spring Works used to be a communal time when neighbors met for visiting as well as working, the women all bringing food. Today at ranches like San Cristóbal, male neighbors still come to help, but only for a few days, and ranch wives who have not taken

7. Many New Mexico cattlemen are familiar with the philosophy of Australian Allan Savory, an ecologist who conceived the idea of Holistic Resource Management (HRM). HRM involves moving the cattle in an entirely new way with the aim of eliminating overgrazing. Many New Mexicans feel it only works in areas with more rainfall. Bilberry says, "It wrecked several ranches I know of—you've got to move cattle in a more common sense way. Maybe it works better in Australia."

outside jobs make midday meals for the men.

At San Cristóbal, the Spring Works begin around May 1. They require about three days from each week and continue for three to four weeks. (The rest of the week must be devoted to the usual round of tasks). McFarland and his cowboys begin by spending one to two days rounding up cattle from one or more pastures. Neighbors usually help with the larger pastures; on the small ones, McFarland and his cowboys work alone. Years ago the men had to scour the brush, finding and rounding up every cow-calf pair individually; now they simply drive a feed truck with a "sirene" into the pasture and turn it on. The cattle, trained by feed deliveries during the winter, run to the truck; if their calves are old enough to follow, they come too. But sometimes the men must spend a whole day finding and rounding up stray calves, and sometimes the cattle, realizing they won't be fed, refuse to follow the truck. Sooner or later the cowboys, all expert herdsmen, succeed in driving the entire herd into one of the three main corrals on the ranch. The next morning McFarland, his hands, and two to ten neighbors (depending on the size of the job) gather before dawn at ranch headquarters. They load up horse trailers and head for the corrals, where they drive the mother cows out of the pens, leaving only the calves inside. Then they form a team that includes: (1) one roper, to rope the calves, (2) two flankers, who hold the calves down, (3) one man who brands, (4) one man who castrates the bull calves and earmarks the heifer calves (at San Cristóbal this marking consists of a quarter circle in the left ear and a crop and underbit in the right ear), (5) one man who de-horns the bull calves and year-brands the heifer calves, and (6) one man who vaccinates. Usually there are two to three teams of flankers, holding a series of calves down in assembly line fashion, prepared for the main branding team.

All of these procedures have become customary and are considered necessary for either health, profit, or convenience. Branding is still essential; though cattle are rarely stolen nowadays, they still wander into neighbors' pastures. Also, state law now mandates branding, without which cattle cannot legally be sold. Castration is done to aid the growth of bull calves; steers simply have better meat and more of it. The de-horning practice started in crowded feedlots, where four cattle must eat from the same trough; horned animals knock others away from the food. Cropping the ears of heifers is another means of identification, like branding, making the females easier to pick out in a herd. Arlin Talbot, a ranch hand at San Cristóbal, says, "If your crew is on the ball, that calf won't be on the ground more than two to three minutes. It's just something that has to be done if you're going to be associated with ranch life."

When the branding is over, the cowboys release the dazed calves into the

The Spring Works: roping and branding calves at the Galisteo corrals.

larger herd and stand watch to make sure they all "mother up" properly. When all the cow-calf pairs are reunited, they are put out to pasture again, where the calves' wounds heal in a few days.

Meanwhile, McFarland and his crew begin the process again, rounding up cattle from one pasture after another until all San Cristóbal's calves have been branded.

The branding portion of these days is usually over by noon. Typically, McFarland, cowboys, and neighbors then all head back to headquarters, where one of the ranch wives has prepared a large dinner. Ken and Tommie Scott recall their many branding meals:

> *Ken Scott*: Main thing an ol' cowboy wants to eat is baked beans and potatoes.
>
> *Tommie Scott:* Pot roast and peach cobbler, that's all they want. I've done a *lot* of that.

Unloading a horse trailer before branding.

Jerrie Pilley echoes those sentiments: "A cowboy don't like to sit down to just a salad, or a baloney sandwich." Even for everyday meals, she cooks mostly beef, potatoes, home-baked bread, and sometimes home-grown vegetables.

Most cowboys consider the Spring Works the most strenuous time of the year. But as they end, the men begin other jobs like grading the dirt roads, and the cycle of life continues. Summertime brings welcome rain; huge thunderclouds appear in July and August and many warm days are punctuated by showers. Grass is usually abundant and there is rarely any need to put out extra feed for the cattle. But as always, says Ken Scott, "the main thing is to get out early before your cattle get out, stray off, go on their way grazing and stuff like that. You can find 'em better in the morning."

So cowboys rise at 4:30 or 5 a.m., setting out by 6:30 or 7. With twenty-six pastures to watch, and close to 150 miles of road to maintain, there is always work to do in summer. The actual list of tasks the San Cristóbal cowboy performs is impressive: he fixes windmills (of which there are thirty-eight), maintains five electric water pumps, repairs miles of fences, "doctors" cattle and horses, calves heifers, shoes horses, breaks horses, grades roads, and of course ropes, herds, and brands cattle. He performs jobs only a cowboy could know about, as Arlin Talbot describes: "You'll see cattle chewing on deer horns or bones, for the minerals—then they get bones stuck in their throat. You have to tie them down and dislodge it." Like ranch hands all over the U.S., this jack-of-all-trades qualifies as a veterinarian, engineer, and heavy machinery operator (as well as a herdsman), though like cowboys everywhere, he is rarely recognized or valued for all these skills.

Arlin Talbot, San Cristóbal cowboy.

As summer turns to autumn, the "Fall Works" approach. By October 1 at the latest, McFarland and his hands begin rounding up cows and calves, cutting old and sick cows out of the herd, weaning the calves and weighing them, and usually shipping off the sold calves. At San Cristóbal, this process can work one of two ways, depending on whether the owner, Henry Singleton, decides to sell the calves on weaning or keep them to sell the next year.

If the calves are going to be kept, McFarland and the cowboys begin rounding up livestock one or two pastures at a time. First they herd the animals into a set of pens, separating the calves from the cows. Then they divide the steer calves from the heifer calves, and weigh each group separately. (Calves are sold by the pound, with steers commanding a higher price—at this writing about 96 cents per pound versus 90 cents per pound for heifers.) The men then drive all the calves into a "holding trap" (a small pasture of about 300 to 800 acres). This is where the calves will be weaned—a process lasting eight to twelve days. The calves cry or "bawl" for several days, "walking the fence" as they search for their mothers. Even though they are fed by the cowboys, they still lose 20 to 25 pounds during this weaning time.

When one group of calves is weaned, the ranch hands herd them into a new pasture to "go on grass" and regain their lost weight. The men then round up another one or two pastures and the process continues until all the ranch calves are weaned, weighed, and "put on grass" to grow into yearlings. This process could take as long as a month.

Even if the ranch keeps all of the calves, a few older cattle are always sold at shipping time. Between eight and twelve years of age, cows' teeth wear down to the point where they can no longer chew grass. "An old cow she'll just go down," says Ken Scott, "she'll get poor, she won't stay fat." So ranchers cull such cattle, along with crippled, sick, or "white-eyed" cows, and sell them while they still command a price. ("Dry" cows, those which don't produce a calf, are usually sold when this is discovered, in spring.)

But often the ranch sells its calves at weaning time. When this choice is made, McFarland and his cowboys still round up one area at a time, but they herd the cattle into several northern pastures near the Galisteo pens (which have a set of scales), and the animals remain there until shipping day. Shipping day, like the spring branding days, begins with neighbors and ranch hands gathering at headquarters in the pre-dawn darkness. Horse trailers loaded, they head to the pens, where they separate the calves from the cows, divide the steers from the heifer calves, weigh the two groups separately, and load them onto shipping trucks, all before noon. (They must wean and ship the calves the same day because of the dramatic weight loss that begins at weaning.) "I always have mixed feelings when we're loading," writes rancher Linda Hasselstrom, "pride at the quality of the cattle and their condition, and a sadness at seeing cows I've worked over, and calves I've saved, go off to their fates."

This apparent contradiction, of real caring and empathy for cattle, which is often one of the signs of a good rancher or cowboy, with an acceptance of sending them off to a brutal end, is for ranch people simply part of a larger reality. Being so close to nature, they constantly witness its harshness as well as its beauty. When they eat a steak, they tend to recognize that it was recently part of a living cow, whereas city dwellers may forget this. For ranch people, the bottom line is survival and practicality, and so, when shipping day arrives, their feelings take a back seat.

Even children get used to these facts of life early. T. C. Pilley, age twelve, has been bottle-feeding young calves, or "dogies" who have lost their mothers, for several years. His mother Jerrie says, "Sure, that bothers T. C. He knows in the fall they're gonna get shipped off. Because you become real close to the animals. You work with them every day."

"I'm used to it now," T. C. says, "'cause I've raised a bunch of them. But then I can buy nice clothes for school."

A ranch manager south of San Cristóbal recalled some similar feelings as a child. Jeff Bilberry says, "I had lots of pet calves as a kid. But it's a lot easier [seeing them shipped off] when they're making you a hundred dollars a head. Course when you're losing a hundred dollars a head on them," he continues ruefully, "you *want* 'em to get their heads cut off, those sorry rascals."

Once the calves are shipped (or moved into their own pastures) the usual rhythm of ranch life resumes as the cowboys herd the remaining cattle back to winter pastures. "Replacement heifers," culled from the calves to become part of the breeding herd, are generally herded to their own pasture so cowboys can help them when February comes.

San Cristóbal winters can be harsh, with heavy snows, fierce winds, and temperatures dipping into the teens. But even in winter the weather remains typically New Mexican, that is, unpredictable. The coldest snowy morning can turn into a sun-filled afternoon, with the earth dry again by evening.

In winter San Cristóbal's cowboys bring feed to the cattle—grain cake with salt and 20 percent protein—and break ice on the ponds and water tanks. They also continue their perennial tasks of repairing windmills and fences.

There is work to do even during the heaviest snowstorm; the men simply trudge the short distance from their homes to the maintenance shop, and spend the day indoors making repairs. But since winter days are shorter, ranch hands often have more evening hours to spend with their families and to work on hob-

Wesley Layman, ranch caretaker, finishing an original sculpture.

Wesley and Cathy Layman, San Cristóbal's caretakers.

bies that may bring in extra money. San Cristóbal's people create everything from silver spurs to wood carvings to porcelain dolls.

Despite the long hours and back-breaking work, ranch life holds its people. Sometimes they may stay from necessity—not being trained for any other trade—but the truth is that cowboys more often *leave* this life due to economic necessity. When they stay, it is because they value their way of working and their way of life, because ranching is one of the last occupations where people live close to the land, coming to feel a part of it, coming to know it in their bones. "This is home," says Jeff Bilberry, gesturing toward the countryside. "It's where your heart is, it's what you know."

"We're never bored," writes Linda Hasselstrom, "seeing the same scenery over and over only seems to make us notice more, so that we spot any change in the landscape, and any interesting animal behavior." Animals still abound at San Cristóbal: hawks, eagles, crows, coyotes, bobcats, antelope, snakes, cottontails, jackrabbits, and skunks. Even bears appear occasionally. Trappers used to come onto the ranch in winter to trap coyotes, according to Ken Scott. "They sell the hide," he reports, adding, "Lot of these women's fur coats, you know the fur collar?—that's an ol' coyote hide."

"I'll always have a pet, like an antelope or deer or crow, that I become real close to," says Jerrie Pilley, "you appreciate the animals." Most valued of all is the horse. "Your better cowboys are the people that really take pride in their horses," comments one ranch hand, "because the better the horse, the better the job you can do working cattle." "Breaking" horses to ride is an art based on emotional attunement, as one cowboy explains:

> All horses and cattle can tell if you're tense or scared, and a little ol' colt, he can figure out if a man really likes him—they sense that real quick. He'll get to likin' you and he'll just mother right up to a man, and figure as long as he's comin' to you, he's O.K. And that really helps 'em come around.

Ranch life also holds its people because of the closeness they often feel to each other and to their families. Neighbors almost always help each other in many small ways besides branding and shipping. Even if they are 20 miles apart, neighbors know implicitly that they can count on each other. Jeff Bilberry points out that the ranching community "is a broad world, too"; he says that he could go to any ranching or farming community and "in ten minutes feel like we're all old friends—we have so much in common." Seeing the alienation in modern cities on television and in movies, ranch people are acutely appreciative of their world, where they still leave their doors unlocked, know everyone for miles

Terry Pilley, ranch hand and silversmith.

The McCorkell family (clockwise from top), Peggy, Jody, Gip, and Jake, getting ready to leave for the school bus stop.

around, and welcome travelers. Bilberry reports that the modern pace is slowly reaching rural people, too, and they are busier, go to town more, and generally have less time and money for get-togethers than they once did. Often, says one cowboy, it's just a case of "too much month at the end of the money."

Perhaps most important to ranch people are the advantages for family life. On most ranches, children grow up steeped in traditional values, like the worth of hard work. Children's days are often as long as their parents' since they commonly travel several miles to meet the school bus, then ride 20 to 40 miles to school. San Cristóbal's children must leave home by 6:30 a.m. to meet their bus 6 miles north on US 285; they don't return to that bus stop until 4 p.m. Children are expected to help their parents with adult work also, and from thirteen years of age onward, to perform as well as a woman or man. "It's a way of life that demands that you be responsible to yourself and others," says Bilberry. He believes that kids "get a college education in agriculture by the time they're seventeen" because "there's a vast wealth of things to learn from on a ranch." Children become intimate with nature, observing and studying everything from the nest-building habits of swallows to heifers giving birth, and they feel at home in the wild. Jerrie Pilley says she doesn't worry when her young son goes exploring in the hills behind their home. T. C. agrees, "It's just like a big ol' playful back yard. You can go out and try'n catch bunnies or somethin'."

"A country kid gets bored with a mall," says his mother, "and vice-versa."

Children sometimes go with their fathers when they work; on occasion wives who don't have outside jobs come, too. Ken and Tommie Scott recall their ranching days together:

> *Ken:* After our kid got up big enough to go to school, after I'd go out maybe and feed a pasture or two of cattle, you know, I'd come back by the house . . . she'd have the housework done and the kid off to school, so she'd go with me. We'd windmill or fix fence or feed or whatever we had to do.
>
> *Tommie:* We just kind of got in the habit of working together, you know. I knew what he was gonna do and he knew what I was gonna do . . .
>
> *Ken:* Yep. We worked at it.
>
> *Tommie:* That's the reason I've got all these wrinkles—too much outdoors. But I've always loved it out there.

Another Southwestern cowboy explains:

> That's one of the nicest things about this job, to me, is that the whole family can go and help. . . . everyone can be involved. That way, well, if something goes

Arlin Talbot teaches his son Brandon the basics.

San Cristóbal reservoir in December.

> wrong at work and you come home a little bit cranky, they know just what it's about. . . . The more you do together, the more you'll really understand each other, and appreciate each other, and therefore you just get closer.

Bilberry says, "I'll take other hands' kids with me [when I work] too. On ranches kids learn from each others' parents. It's like that African saying: 'It takes a whole village to raise a child.'" When children observe their parents or other adults performing tasks the children would like to learn, they tend to admire and respect the adults. Perhaps this partially explains the continued use of "sir" and "ma'am" in rural conversations; a sense of respect for elders still evolves fairly naturally on many ranches.

In spite of the admiration young people may feel for their parents' work, many are now leaving ranches for better salaries. Thus much of the old hard-won knowledge about livestock and the range, passed down from father to son, is being lost. "You can't learn it in a book," says Bilberry. He encourages young people to stay on ranches, or at least in the rural community. "There are lots of opportunities for ranch kids," he says, "lots of ag-related businesses you can set up." Possibilities include farming, veterinary work, wind-milling, horse training, raising feed, rodeo work, and jobs in other levels of the livestock industry.

The love that many ranch families feel for their way of life shows in a desire that their children follow in their footsteps, that their sons become cowboys or ranch managers, too. Arlin Talbot, for example, says of his sons, "I would love for them to do it, yes, if they enjoyed it. But I wouldn't pressure anyone—you have to want to do it. Myself, I wouldn't trade it for any other kind of lifestyle." Asked to explain, he replies, "I do this for myself—it gives me peace of mind. I get on my horse and can disappear into another world in thirty minutes."

Ken Scott agrees, remembering, "If you enjoy it, why there's nothing *more* enjoyable than gettin' on an ol' pony and riding' off across the hills, lookin' after the cattle, checkin' the water, checkin' your fences. I've always been an outside boy. I've worked inside very, very little in my life."

Despite the lack of recognition or reward, ranch people are proud of the way they live, treasuring the simplest things the most. One hand, asked his goal, replied, "I'd like to be remembered as a good cowboy." And Jerrie Pilley says simply, "I value just being by myself in God's country. It makes me real excited to hear a cowboy bringin' in a herd of cattle and hearin' the dogs bark, and being real close to my family."

EPILOGUE

IN THE SUMMERS OF 1990 AND 1991, a crew of archaeologists and laborers worked quickly to unearth what they could from the San Cristóbal land bordering US 285 south of Lamy. State construction crews followed close behind them, widening the narrow road.[1]

What the archaeologists found was both significant and unique: an ancient site with at least fifteen pithouses, many adjacent storage pits, two kivas, and over forty human burials. Tree-ring dates from some of the pithouse beams indicate that the structures were built as early as A.D. 1204 to 1224.[2]

These round or oval pithouses were small—about 2 to 4 meters in diameter, often with a floor hearth in the center. Small bands of seasonal hunters probably used them for sleep and shelter only, living mainly outside. There is evidence that the structures were fairly easy to build, and that their owners frequently abandoned them, perhaps because the walls collapsed during unoccupied seasons, or, in some cases, because of a death in the family (some bodies were found placed on floors with the house filled in over them). Apparently these early hunting families used their abandoned homes as trash middens, or dumps, and

1. The Waste Isolation Pilot Project, known as WIPP, will, as of this writing, be using US 285 as their route from Los Alamos to Carlsbad, New Mexico.

2. Both kivas and nine of the pithouses were originally excavated in 1956 by Bertha Dutton, working for the Museum of New Mexico, and then reburied. Much of the data gleaned from this early excavation was subsequently lost. As for the estimated dates of 1204 to 1224, archaeologist and project director, John Ware, points out that old logs from that period conceivably could have been used at a later date, but that the difference probably would have been only a few years. The Office of Archaeological Studies, Museum of New Mexico, conducted the excavation sponsored by the New Mexico State Highway and Transportation Department. Information on this excavation was contributed primarily by John Ware in 1991.

Office of Archaeological Studies' crew excavating at LA 3333 along US 285.

built new pithouses nearby.

Since they dug down several feet to bedrock for their floors, the pithouse remains now reveal three distinct layers. At the bottom is the pale green shale floor. Next comes a layer of reddish brown silt, somehow deposited there by either man or the elements. The third layer—mottled and multicolored with many flecks of charcoal—is the trash layer, composed of animal bones, broken pottery, burned remains of food, wood, and charcoal, and a few rocks. It is within this trash layer that most of the human skeletons have been found.

The skeletons are those of a smallish people buried on their backs, their torsos twisted so the knees are drawn up to one side. Their heads are turned in the same direction as their knees. When one of their tribe died, the pithouse dwellers often dug out part of an old trash pit, or used one that was only partially full, wedging the body into the small space in a flexed position, then filling it up with more refuse. (Unbroken pots and other objects were sometimes buried with the body.)

To our modern eyes, such a practice appears strange, even shocking, and certainly disrespectful to the dead. But ancient Native Americans' attitude toward trash was probably quite different from ours. First, the amount of their refuse was only a tiny fraction of ours, and all of it, except food remains, had probably been used for a long time. John Ware, archaeologist with the Museum of New Mexico and field director of the excavation, theorizes that just as modern witches require personal belongings to influence the owner, the pithouse people may have believed that objects they used absorbed their energy or contained some of their power. Thus, their "trash" needed to be treated properly, perhaps even honored or kept from enemies. Ware points out that whereas today we find refuse repellent and want to distance ourselves from it, early Native tribes may have viewed it as an extension of themselves. In all ancient pueblos, including the Anasazi, the dead were often buried in trash middens.[3]

But the whole truth about these pithouse dwellers is still a mystery. Ware says they were probably Southern Tewa, but there is no way we can be sure. "We can't dig up languages," he says ruefully. Many findings from the dig may someday yield conclusions instead of perplexity: for example, the male skeleton whose rounded vertebrae showed his advanced age in spite of perfect teeth; or the high incidence of head and arm injuries, most likely the result of battle.[4]

The Galisteo Basin as a whole has been referred to by the New Mexican media as an "archaeological time bomb waiting to explode." Besides the six pueblos on San Cristóbal land, there are four others in the basin: Galisteo, San Lázaro, San Marcos, and Pueblo Blanco. Archaeologist Jonathan Haas has called these ten pueblos "an incomparable national resource surpassing Chaco Canyon,

3. Ware points out that prehistoric Pueblos also buried their dead "on and under house floors, occasionally in kivas, and also, perhaps, in other areas where archaeologists have never looked."

4. Regarding the source of this conflict, Ware theorizes that "the eastern Galisteo Basin witnessed a major influx of population during the early decades of the thirteenth century resulting in increased competition for resources. Cultural and geographic 'frontiers' are typically associated with high levels of conflict. After the frontier is settled, things tend to sort out and conflicts subside. This may explain why trauma rates are much lower in the burial population from San Cristóbal, 100 to 200 years later."

Mesa Verde, and any of the known monuments." The large size of the pueblos, most of which have two to three stories and thousands of rooms, partly accounts for their significance. But perhaps even more important to scholars is the fact that some were inhabited during the Spanish period. With proper excavation, these ruins could open a new world of information about the Tanos and their lives, both before and after the Spanish *entradas,* and also answer mysteries about the Pueblo Revolt and the towns' ultimate abandonment.

Five of the six San Cristóbal pueblos are now covered with dirt and cactus. They are difficult to locate for the untrained observer, appearing only as gentle mounds slightly raised above the generally broken terrain. Any illegal would-be excavators would soon be observed by cowboys on their rounds. But at San Cristóbal Pueblo some partially excavated walls are still barely visible. This site, and its adjoining petroglyph area, are quite vulnerable. Visitors routinely bypass the "no trespassing" signs to hike up to the intriguing rock art in its striking setting. Most respect the Tanoan art and the land, but the possibility of vandalism is disturbing.

The Singleton family is making plans to create a conservancy to protect San Cristóbal Pueblo and its petroglyph site. The land will remain in its natural state, but the area will be fenced and protected. Visitors will be welcome, but they will be asked to sign in and out, and pay a token fee toward the preservation of the site. In this way the rock art may be saved from the harm some other sites have suffered.

US 285 near Lamy.

Not far from the pithouse dig and the advancing highway crew, the San Cristóbal petroglyph rocks provide many places where one can sit and watch the progress of bright orange machines moving back and forth on the newly paved highway.

It is October and the air is cool. I lean against a huge flat boulder, black with volcanic age. It has nooks and crevices where snakes have lived for centuries; swallows have built their nests here. Shadows play over the piñons and dirt in front of me and I glance up. There is nothing. The shadows reappear and I crane my neck, looking almost into the sun. Two ravens are dancing, gliding on air currents above my head. They touch wings lightly, separate, then touch again, their black shapes breaking the pattern of white and blue.

So close, they seem almost like an omen. Or perhaps they are just studying me. Like this place, they're a mystery.

The wind is becoming serious. It rushes over the land, now from the south-

west, now the north. It spills through the arroyo, flattening the gramma grass, fluttering the cottonwoods. Most of the trees have turned golden green. One, changing faster than the rest, glitters yellow in the sun.

I imagine the Tanos coming down to the creek in this weather, filling their pots, then hurrying back to the pueblo, to windowless, thick-walled rooms, where fires are already burning.

The rhythms of nature are still strong here. Others before us who loved this land—the Tanos, the Spanish, the early Hispanics, the pioneer Anglos—all are now part of the mystery. We are the caretakers now!

CITATION AND QUOTATION CREDITS

COPYRIGHT MATERIAL

The poems "Song of the Sky Loom" (p. 23), "The Cloud–Flower Lullaby" (p. 28), "Lake Song of the Tewa K'osa" (p. 31), "Initiation Chant" (p. 33), "Song of the Hunter's Wife" (p. 42), and "Song of Avanyu, the Storm Serpent" (p. 61) from *Songs of the Tewa* by Herbert J. Spinden, copyright © 1976, are reproduced by permission of Sunstone Press, P.O. Box 2321, Santa Fe, New Mexico, 87504–2321.

The Raingod Ceremony (pp. 33–42) from *Seeking Life* by Vera Laski is reproduced by permission of the American Folklore Society from the *Memoirs of the American Folklore Society*, 50, 1959. Not for further reproduction.

"La Mentira" (p. 87), "El Viejo" (p. 131), "Las Columnas" (p. 144), and "El Ferrocarril" (pp. 153–154) from *The Land of Poco Tiempo* by Charles F. Lummis, copyright © 1952, are reproduced by permission of the University of New Mexico Press, Albuquerque.

The extracts on pp. 148, 150, and 153 from *Nambe—Year One* by Orlando Romero, copyright © 1976, are reproduced by permission of Tonatuik–Quinto Sol International, Berkeley, California, and the author.

Extracts in Chapter 6 from *We Fed Them Cactus* by Fabiola Cabeza de Baca, copyright © 1954, appear courtesy of the University of New Mexico Press, Albuquerque.

The untitled poem on p. 149 from *There Is Another You* by José Ortiz y Pino III appears courtesy of José Ortiz y Pino III, Galisteo, New Mexico.

Extracts in Chapter 8 from *Cattle, Horses, and Men (of the Western Range)* by John H. (Jack) Culley, copyright © 1940, are reproduced by permission of John Henry Culley III and the University of Arizona Press, Tucson.

The poem "Sierry Petes" (pp. 182–183) is reproduced by permission of Gail Steiger, for the estate of Gail Gardner.

Extracts in Chapter 9 from *Ranch Album* appear courtesy of Gail Steiger (producer–director).

CHAPTER 1. THE EARLY GALISTEO BASIN

8 Many scholars believe early Paleoindians: Cordell 1984:122.
produced results that may: *Time* 1990.
Paleoindians were clearly: Lang 1977:12.
12 Obsidian tools were found: ibid.:12–16.
to supplement gathered foods: Cordell 1984:173–174.
numerous hunting lookout stations: Lang 1977:18–19.
ancient tribes here moved: Lang 1992, personal communication.
art . . . reveals "strong cultural ties": Lang 1977:21.
a trade route: ibid.:22.
13 much of their technological knowledge: Plog 1979:128.
They abandoned . . . their lower–elevation towns: Lang 1992, personal communication.
"there is really no question": ibid.
15 "to accommodate periodic influxes": Judge 1984:2, 9.
16 (caption) The diverse Pueblo languages: Hale and Harris 1979:170–177.
"people, not cultures, moved": Plog 1979:130.
a strong "Anasazi cast": Lang 1977:23.
But after about 1300: Ford et al. 1972:30–31.
similar customs and ceremonies: Dozier 1966:3.
Tano . . . meaning "near the sun": Ortiz 1979:280.
for at least 2,000 years: Ford et al. 1972:31–32.
18 "Historical and ethnological data": Dozier 1966:3.

Citations to Footnotes

7 (fn1) Harrington 1916:486–488.
(fn3) Richard W. Lang 1992, personal communication.
8 (fn4) Evidence of man . . . disputed, however: Cordell 1984:128.
12 (fn5) The term "Anasazi": Plog 1979:108.
(fn6) "by the A.D. 500s": Lang 1992, personal communication.
13 (fn7) Plog theorizes that and "variation in rainfall": ibid. 1979.
18 (fn8) "at about 1300": Cordell 1984:106.

CHAPTER 2. THE SOUTHERN TEWA

22 "mythical ordering of life": Highwater 1982:91
27 The outermost ring of this world: Ortiz 1969:18–21.
"Earth mother earth navel": ibid.:21
30 "in out of the darkness": ibid.:32.
The Water–Giving Ceremony: ibid.:33–37.
31 Summer or Winter: Dozier 1970:207–208, Laski 1959:3–4.
32 Tewas become *Patowa* . . . cure for illness: Ortiz 1969:86–87.
33 in former times Kachinas lived: Wright 1986:11.
The Raingod Ceremony: Laski 1959:34–59.
42 "A council meeting is one–half talk": Waters 1970:14.
44 "'to sing' often means": Spinden 1976:23.
46 "all help one another": Parsons 1939:111.
"Women," Ortiz says: Ortiz 1979:284.
Tewas were . . . gradually "made": ibid.:287.
"It is hard work": ibid.:288
47 "each participant gives up": Laski 1959:74
"we are all in one nest": Waters 1970:17.
The same eternal "breath": Wright 1986:20.
underneath is a human spirit: ibid.:22.
Makowa, Makawasendo: Hewett and Dutton 1945:22.
Sun Old Man: Wright 1986:18.
50 "In all social relations": Bunzel 1932:480.
"An Indian treats the stranger kindly": Dumarest 1919.
"The child or children dance": Dozier 1970:179.
51 "huge red welts appear" and "mood of the occasion": Ortiz 1969:42–43.
"to save their lives": Parsons 1939:470.
One is the lack of privacy: ibid.:4.
"Witch" is "the most abusive . . .": ibid.:67.
"envious, jealous, retaliatory . . .": ibid.:63.
"to keep clear of pernicious influences": ibid.:107.
52 "modest . . . polite, well–behaved . . .": Roediger 1961:20.
"highly developed ceremonial war": Schaafsma 1990:16.
The Southern Tewa at San Cristóbal built: Bandelier 1890–1892:103–105, vol. 2.
54 "As we were going through this province": Hammond and Rey 1929:119–120.
They pulled up their ladders: ibid.
55 The Hano people: Dozier 1966:97.

"Hano songs and dances": Schaafsma 1990:23.

58 Southern Tewa built at least five other villages: Nelson 1914.

Colina Verde: Lang 1977:224–225.

Archaeologists have recently discovered: J. Ware 1992, personal communication.

Citations to Footnotes

22 (fn1) "Until about a century ago . . .": Dozier 1970:81.

"Tewa scalps are called . . .": Parsons 1939:171, 351.

Among the Plains Indians: La Flesche 1939.

(fn2) This simplified account: Ortiz 1969:13–16.

23 (fn3) *Song of the Sky Loom*: Spinden 1976:94.

The Sacred Pipe: Black Elk 1971:25.

27(fn4) the *Tsave Yoh*: Ortiz 1969:76.

(fn5) Ortiz reports that: Ortiz 1979:20.

Lang comments that: Lang 1992, personal communication.

28 (fn6) *The Cloud-Flower Lullaby*: Spinden 1976:80.

Parsons comments that: Parsons 1939:403.

30 (fn8) *Midwinter Ceremony*: Yava 1978:44.

Albert Yava says the chant: ibid.

(fn9) There is some question: Ortiz 1969:147–148.

31 (fn10) *Lake Song:* Spinden 1976:120.

(fn11) Ortiz makes interesting: Ortiz 1969:16–17.

(fn12) Ortiz says there is: ibid.:97.

32 (fn13) This description of the *Towa é*: ibid.:61–77.

(fn14) That the *Patowa* were "made": ibid.:79–119.

(fn15) Ortiz describes the Northern Tewa: ibid.:81.

33 (fn16) *Initiation Chant*: Spinden 1976:87.

37 (fn20) "backward speech": Parsons 1939:103.

40 (fn22) "Scant or diminutive offerings": Parsons 1939:94–95.

41 (fn23) Laski explains that: Laski 1959:149.

42 (fn24) *O yi ka* is the goddess: ibid.:164.

(fn25) *Song of Hunter's Wife:* Spinden 1976:102.

While her husband hunts: ibid.:124.

43 (fn26) Ahlee James heard: James 1927:112–115.

44 (fn27) Pueblo music in general: Herzog 1936:238–417.

(fn28) This tale was related: James 1927:97–103.

47 (fn29) "Be as brave as . . .": Laski 1959:65–66.

(fn30) The traditional Tewa relay: Parsons 1939:393.

50 (fn31) Dozier says, "The child . . .": Dozier 1970:179.

52 (fn32) After the 1680 rebellion: Lang 1992, personal communication.

(fn33) "bristling with protective": Schaafsma 1990:21.

CHAPTER 3. THE PETROGLYPHS

61 *Song of Avanyu:* Spinden 1976:99

"Rio Grande Style": Schaafsma 1980:243–299.

Kachina masks, ceremonial figures: Schaafsma 1992, personal communication.

Certain petroglyphs date from: Lang 1977:23.

Images from this period: Schaafsma 1980:160.

A few San Cristóbal petroglyphs: Lang 1992, personal communication.

According to Polly Schaafsma: Schaafsma 1992, personal communication.

62 "measures to invoke or coerce": Parsons 1939:xi.

"of the Tewa winter solstice": ibid.:186.

Sometimes designs were pecked: Young 1988:173–176.

"beneficial imagery": Schaafsma 1991, personal communication.

And Tewas apparently created: Young 1988:164.

"are relatively weak beings," and Traditional Pueblos believe: ibid.:169–170.

Mexican culture seems . . . in Mesoamerica and Mexico: Schaafsma 1980:237.

63 "the paintings of their houses": Bolton 1930:178.

"white washed and painted with colors": ibid.:182.

"rock drawings are but an echo": Schaafsma 1980:251.

Despite this "involutedness": ibid.:299.

But Schaafsma believes the opposite: ibid. 1991, personal communication.

64 (caption) Martineau's theory about such: Martineau 1973:47–48.

64 Essentially, scholars see Pueblo: Schaafsma 1992, personal communication.

(It is interesting that Zunis . . .): Young 1988:175, 182.

Schaafsma, for example, says: Schaafsma 1992, personal communication.

65 (caption) They depict Avanyu and "iconographically distinct": Schaafsma 1994, personal communication.

"god of life . . ." and "seen combined with his twin brother . . .": Schaafsma 1980:238.
Between the two serpents: Fewkes 1903:1–126.

66 (caption) ducks, birds, that played . . . associated with healing: Schaafsma 1980:134.
Human figures holding staffs: ibid.:223.

67 (caption) "in the Pueblo world": ibid. 1980:192.
Bear paws are among the sacred: Laski 1959.
(caption) "cloud terraces": ibid.

68 (caption) "a good journey": Martineau 1973:160.
(caption) the Arrow Swallowers, a Warrior Society: Sims 1963:218.
Carol Patterson–Rudolph has: Patterson–Rudolph 1988.

69 (caption) Zunis of the late nineteenth century: Stevenson 1904:439.
Jane Young believes that Zunis: Young 1988:164.
(caption) Schaafsma believes that: Schaafsma 1992, personal communication.
(caption) This four–horned creature . . . typical bear paws: ibid. 1994, personal communication.
"Insects depicted may have": ibid. 1980:233, citing Parsons 1939:191–192 and Castañeda 1974:96–97.
Warriors also appealed: Young 1988:160–162.

71 (caption) "play his flute to melt": Schaafsma 1980:141, citing Parsons 1938:337–338 and Wellmann 1970:1678–1682.
Some also consider him: Schaafsma 1980:136–141.

72 (caption) may indicate water or rain: Martineau 1973:28.

73 (caption) Bears are patrons . . . become people: Parsons 1939:189.
star designs: Schaafsma 1990:10
"The stars . . . have more": Parsons 1939:963.
The morning star connotes war: Schaafsma 1990:11–12.
Star faces may symbolize . . . in many kiva murals: Schaafsma 1980:295–296.
The cornstalk, chiseled . . . by a different artist: ibid. 1994, personal communication.

74 (caption) The two black masks: Schaafsma 1992, personal communication.
war and scalping were related . . . rain–bringers and fetishes: Parsons 1939:171.
"Though in his life": ibid.:350.
Among the Tewa: ibid.:351.
these are often seen: Schaafsma 1992, personal communication.
At Zuni, only certain: Young 1988:191–192.

75 (caption) Two horned snakes like these: Schaafsma 1980:298.
Schaafsma says that several: ibid. 1994, personal communication.
Young, speaking of the Zuni: Young 1988:179.
Hehea, an ancient and widely depicted: Fewkes 1903:74.

77 (caption) The figure in the pointed cap: Schaafsma 1980:238.
There is evidence that: ibid.:217.
Some scholars think this deity: Ellis and Hammack 1968.
Schaafsma says the shield: Schaafsma 1992, personal communication.
Curved–in horns denote Kachinas: Ortiz 1993, personal communication.

78 (caption) Warrior images . . . bear claws: Schaafsma 1994, personal communication.

79 (caption) All are part: ibid.

Citations to Footnotes

63 (fn3) "multivocality": Young 1988:202, 228.

CHAPTER 4. THE SPANISH *ENTRADAS*

82 "I have already said": Covey 1961:92.
"We traveled in that region": ibid.:106.
". . . we [Cabeza de Vaca and his companions]": ibid.:147–148.

86 An oral tradition and "he sat up, dog–fashion": Bandelier 1890–1892:116–117.
"Kirauash" and "Querechos": ibid.:119.

87 *La Mentira* (The Lie): Lummis 1952:173–174.
"Recent arrivals in Mexico": Inglis 1982:11.

88 "all Spain's wars became . . .": Brown 1969:27.
75 to 134 inhabited pueblos: Schroeder 1979:254.

89 "under the jurisdiction of Cicuye": Hammond and Rey 1940:259.
"staged a minor rebellion": Dozier 1970:44.

"mainly by burning at the stake": Spicer 1962:155.
91 "Four pueblos were discovered": Hammond and Rey 1927:50.
"threatened to gather three thousand": ibid.
"local natives dropped a big rock": Kessell 1987:39.
Tanos were thus responsible: Simmons 1979a:178.
92 "as the pueblo was large" and "The news of what had happened": Hammond and Rey 1927:116–120.
"marching three leagues": Hammond and Rey 1929:119–120.
95 "acted in the same manner" and "the people were so frightened": ibid.
"a complete weakling who": Brown 1969:60.
96 The Spaniards dedicated their chapel . . . become obedient vassals: Twitchell 1911:321; Espinosa 1933:151.
"defending them [the Pueblos]": Hammond and Rey 1953:344.
"so far as the Holy Catholic faith": Twitchell 1911:322–323.
99 "Now the Indians have to provide": Hammond and Rey 1953:693.
"were sentenced to have one foot": Spicer 1962:157.

Citations to Footnotes

83 (fn2) The Pueblos called these . . . 'Teyas': Bandelier 1890–1892:118, vol. 2.
"Caddoan–related dog nomads": Schaafsma 1990:17.
(fn3) Schaafsma, following a theory: ibid.:19
"drought was probably": Lang 1992, personal communication.
87 (fn5) Conjecture about Estévan's death: Baldwin 1926:193; Shepard 1970:111–114.
(fn6) Not all of Coronado's: Steiner 1989:132.
(fn7) Their ruling ideal was honor: Brown 1969:33.
89 (fn9) Dr. Frances Levine: Levine 1992, personal communication.
91 (fn10) Most modern scholars agree: Schroeder 1979:236–254.
(fn11) "Lay officer of the Inquistion. . .": Kessell 1987:41.
95 (fn12) Most Southwestern authorities: Schroeder 1979:248, table 5.
96 (fn13) "by 1545 . . . one–quarter": Steiner 1989:138–151.

CHAPTER 5. A REMOTE COLONY

101 "another ten leagues to the north": Hodge et al. 1945:67.
102 "who had had considerable experience": Scholes 1937:86.
The first priest . . . Juan de Rozas: Hodge et al. 1916:198–199.
The next day thunderclouds: Espinosa 1933:147–148.
early churches' walls were built: Prince 1915:228.
By 1621 Fray Pedro de Vergara . . . Fray Alonso de Estremara: Hodge et al. 1945:270.
103 (caption) Sister María de Jesús: Brown 1969:137.
106 Clemente succeeded in uniting: Sánchez 1989:41.
In 1661 . . . a San Cristóbal woman: Scholes 1942:74.
"twenty–two Indians from Galisteo": ibid.:48–49.
"washing of hides": ibid.:49.
107 At the convento of Galisteo: ibid.:111.
"the Pueblo [mission] interpreter": ibid.:60.
"to invoke the powers of the devil": ibid.:62.
"These scoundrel friars say": ibid.:61.
108 "[These nomads] often go": Hammond and Rey 1940:258.
"gentle people, not cruel": ibid.:262.
110 The court ordered that: Sánchez 1989:41–42.
Luckily the governor decided: ibid.
Among them were . . . Tano leaders: Sando 1979:194–197.
The conspirators would usually meet: ibid.:195.
112 "The captains of the Tagnos": Hackett 1942:62.
113 "a deerskin thong with two knots": ibid.:4.
"very far away toward: and "Indians of San Cristóbal": ibid.:5.
"armed and giving war whoops": ibid.:98.
"God and Santa María were": ibid.:13.
The white one meant: ibid.:14.
114 "they had the mandate": ibid.:16.
115 The people of San Cristóbal: Bandelier 1890–1892:103–105, vol. 2.
Along with the Indians of San Lázaro: Schroeder 1991:5.
117 "audacity, boldness, impudence": Hackett 1942:14.
Pedro Garcia's testimony: ibid.:62.
Galisteo's "father custodian" and "to kill the custodian, the fathers": ibid.:24.
Perhaps August 13 had been: Silverberg 1970:116.
118 Also, Joe Sando, the Jemez historican . . . and ". . . the one

above beyond the clouds": Sando 1979:54.
"perform miracles and foretell" and "a 'god' that might be. . .": Dozier 1970:69.

119 "they were unwilling to participate": Hackett 1942:96.

120 "lamentable tragedy" and "This miserable kingdom": Hackett 1942:94.
"remote beyond compare": Kessel 1989:168.
"commenced to shout furiously" and "very clever": Espinosa 1942:81–83.
"pelts of animals": Bailey 1940:50.
"for the royal crown": Espinosa 1942:145.
"they were received joyously": Bailey 1940:64.
"craft, skill, and sagacity": Espinosa 1942:306.

122 "blasphemous declarations": Bailey 1940:125–129.
"wanted only to wage open battle": ibid.:148.

123 "sierra of Chimayo, where": Espinosa 1988:177.
"it is known they are instigating": ibid.:171.
"true martyrdom," "irritation and obstinacy," and "the senseless ones": ibid.:172, 178, 231.
The Indians then set: Hodge et al. 1916:248.
Tanos united with groups: Schroeder 1991:10.

125 Some fled to the Plains: ibid.:10–11.
In 1706 . . . Nuestra Señora de los Remedios: ibid.:12.
"They are enduring even more": Adams and Chavez 1956:217.

126 the Galisteo burial book: Chavez 1957:232.
"The ancient people of Galisteo": Harrington 1916:484–485.
They formulated a complex system . . . mixed heritage: Bustamante 1989:70–74.

128 They remained stationed: Elkus 1974.

Citations to Footnotes

108 (fn2) "Here we were met": Hammond and Rey 1953:747–748.

110 (fn4) The Pueblo author Joe Sando: Sando 1979:196.
(fn5) According to some sources: Hackett 1942:62.

113 (fn7) Hackett gives the date: ibid. 1942:12–13, 98.

114 (fn8) Whether the colonists lasted: ibid.
(fn9) Otermín says that: ibid.:101.
"a movement which": Worchester 1975:27.

115 (fn10) "No doubt some": Levine 1992, personal communication.

123 (fn11) These descriptions are from: Espinosa 1942:210.

125 (fn12) Yava, a Hopi–Tewa: Yava 1978:26–35.

128 (fn13) Aragon was the first: Elkus 1974:66.
(fn14) According to José Ortiz y Pino III: Ortiz y Pino 1990, personal communication.

CHAPTER 6. A MEXICAN GRANT

132 "All classes abandoned themselves": Duffus 1930:165–166.

134 "a descendant of the conquerors": Land Grant Records, New Mexico State Records Center and Archives, Santa Fe, reel 14, frame 823.
All quotations and material about Domingo Fernández's quest for the San Cristóbal Grant, which are not otherwise cited, can be found on frames 823 to 844 of reel 14, Land Grant Records of New Mexico, New Mexico State Records Center and Archives, Santa Fe.

137 "On the north, by the summit": Bowden 1969:275.
"pulled up weeds": Surveyor General's Office, New Mexico, vol. 4, Miscellaneous Documents of the U.S. Senate. 3d session 45th Congress, pp. 1282–1293.
138Witnesses later testified: letter from J. A. Williamson, Commissioner of the U.S. Dept. of the Interior to Henry M. Atkinson, Surveyor General 1879 (on file with landowner).
"From the time I was three": Cabeza de Baca 1954:11, 14–15.

139 The San Cristóbal settlers . . . in many ways: Ortiz y Pino III 1990, personal communication.
"The hunters formed a group": Cabeza de Baca 1954:42.

142 "The inhabitants appear" and "In justice to them": Marmaduke 1911:1–10.
Many Americans found it shocking: Lecompte 1981:18.
"at the common labor": Jackson 1966:401, vol. 1.
"decidedly polite": Drumm 1926:210–212.
"Visited Galisteo, which contains": Elliott 1883:241–242.

143 "rich and poor worshipped together": Lecompte 1981:19.
"flour, biscuits, woven blankets": Simmons 1979a:61.
The lone Hispanic guide: ibid.:61–62.
"When he was a": Cabeza de Baca 1954:65.

144 *Las Columnas*: Lummis 1952:68.

In 1849 there were: Chavez 1957:258–262.

145 "wanted it to come out": Jaramillo 1941:26.
"spiritual administration in": Pino and Carroll 1942:50.
But the Brotherhood's aim: Steele and Rivera 1985:6.
Brothers dedicated their lives: Cabeza de Baca 1954:55.

146 But every village had women's societies: Weigle 1987:25.
"retained her property": Lecompte 1981:19.

147 women were also respected: Steele and Rivera 1985:9; Cabeza de Baca 1954:59.
But even today, troubled Hispanics: Ortiz y Pino III 1993, personal communication.
Like the Pueblos, Hispanics: Simmons 1979b:2–3.
Thus they revered their elders: Briggs 1987:245.
Resolaneros (sun seekers): Simmons 1979b:2–3.
"rhetorical duels" . . . situation at hand: Briggs 1987:246–248.
"talk of the elders": ibid.:246.

148 Many of these men traveled: Cabeza de Baca 1954:24.
"Although often illiterate": Culley 1940:292.
Cuentos (folktales) were also: Ortiz y Pino III 1983:7.
"That's the way it is, Mateo": Romero 1976:168.
"pain is followed" and "life is sad": Sunseri 1979:144.

150 Orlando Romero may have: Romero 1992, personal communication.
"In the pelting rain": Romero 1976:50.

Citations to Footnotes

131 (fn1) "One of the most popular": Lummis 1952:176–177.
132 (fn2) "bartering for peace": Levine 1992, personal communication.
139 (fn5) This tradition of "usufruct": Van Ness 1987:190.
143 (fn11) *Comancheros:* Cabeza de Baca 1954:47–49.
145 (fn13) "entire village wished": Weigle 1970:5–13
"a tradition of religious": Brewer and McDowell 1990:44.
147 (fn16) "There being not a single": Gregg 1954:143.
148 (fn19) In 1926, Aurelio: Espinosa 1926:135.

CHAPTER 7. AN AMERICAN TERRITORY

153 ". . . don't be like the Americanos": Romero 1976:56.
El Ferrocarril: Lummis 1952:180–182.

154 The Texan force . . . even a battle: Murphy 1985:67–69.
"a reputed habit": Duffus 1930:175.

156 "Where the . . . University": Weigle 1987:39.
"left everything he owned" and "made friends with Kearny": ibid. 1987:39, 128.
"These outrages are becoming": Sunseri 1979:102.
"The whole earth seemed": Westphall 1973:22.

157 In 1851, after twenty–four years: Land Grant Records, New Mexico State Records Center and Archives, reel 17, frame 847.
Eaton bought Reynold's half, and "Rancho de San Cristoval": Land Grant Records, New Mexico State Records Center and Archives, reel 14, frames 850, 857.
"The Apache Indians ran away": Anonymous 1895:268–269.
"nerve and promptitude of action": ibid.
"The problems of land": Murphy 1985:83.

159 "from the mesita": Land Grant Records, New Mexico State Records Center and Archives, reel 14, frame 847, 935.
He and his men proceeded north: Hall 1960:141–142.
The Texans were completely: Murphy 1985:76–80.

160 The Colorado volunteers pursued: Hall 1960:176.
". . . both lines sent crews": Murphy 1985:87.

161 "That was a period": Culley 1940:63.

164 "according to oral tradition": Westphall 1973:43.
The Hispanic and Anglo attitudes . . . could hardly have been more different: Van Ness and Van Ness 1980:3–11.

166 brief chronology of the major events and sales: Miscellaneous documents from several sources on file with the landowner.
In his younger days, Nicolás Pino: Vigil 1980:49–50.

168 "they each erected a house," "never abandoned their lands," and "It is apparent": letter from U.S. Dept. of the Interior to Henry M. Atkinson, directing resurvey of the San Cristoval or Eaton Grant, July 14, 1879 (on file with landowner).
"The remaining original grantees": Land Grant Records, New Mexico State Records Center and Archives, reel 13, frame 1100.

Citations to Footnotes

156 (fn2) Some authors believe: Levine 1990, personal commu-

nication.

160 (fn3) Ethan Eaton served: Anonymous 1895:268–269.
(fn4) "Lamy and the canyon": Harrington 1920.
161 (fn5) Newcomers during this era: Steiner 1989:134–136.

CHAPTER 8. THE COWBOY TRADITION

173 "Day ends; come glinting": Culley 1940:193.
By the 1600s, herds: Taylor and Maar 1983:17–18.
174 "leather leg protectors": Simmons 1979b:94.
Meanwhile in Southeast Texas . . . their business ventures: Taylor and Maar 1983:18.
Soon the Texans were copying . . . transformed into buckaroo: Culley 1940:5, 110; Taylor and Maar 1983:20.
177 From the 1860s to the 1880s . . . 16 miles to the north: Beck and Haase 1969:39.
"We were shorthanded": Culley 1940:70.
178 "[The Cowboy's] idea of enjoyment": Dodge 1882:609–618.
"it was an endless grind": Schmitt 1956:93.
"brought out all that was best": Culley 1940:323.
"Texas Cow–boys": Savage 1975:33.
179 Most cowboys were Southerners . . . the South afterwards: Taylor and Maar 1983:20.
As part of the idealization: ibid.
182 "Away up high in the Sierry Petes": Gardner 1985:3–5.
184 "A hard drinking, hard riding": Culley 1940:99.
"fundamentally a crude one" and "it was only one step": ibid.:244–245.
"no papers were executed": Haley 1936:147.
"bank–high and a bilin'" and "God hates a coward": Culley 1940:206.
"some of the Texans": ibid. 1940:319.
"foofaraw": Sinclair 1982:3.
"Too much mane and tail": Dobie 1964:94.
186 "Strict decorum prevailed": Culley 1940:326.
"opened the cattle market": Savage 1975:17.
"These miserable beings gather": McCoy 1874:132–142.
"In the gayest ballrooms": Culley 1940:326.
"Don't tell me 'bout cotillions": Chittendon 1985:17–19.
188 "I never remember seeing" and "But they had a great feel ing": Culley 1940:322.
"cow psychology, cow anatomy": Dobie 1964:32.
And they felt a responsibility . . . popular myth: Taylor and Maar 1983:27.
"When you meet with a horse": Culley 1940:166.
"That Pintada country": ibid.:281.
"The Cowboys' Christmas Ball": Chittendon 1985:18.
Outlaws were usually cowboys . . . cowhands and horsemen: Culley 1940:53.
189 "far too shy to talk": ibid.:221.
"Let me know if": ibid.:46–47.
"refugee from industrial civilization": Taylor and Maar 1983:27.
"tough as some of our men": Culley 1940:322.
"[some say] it was all humdrum": ibid.:189.
(caption) Brands from *Santa Fe County Brand Book: 1853–1889*, New Mexico. State Records Center and Archives, Santa Fe.

Citations to Footnotes

179 (fn1) Culley points out: Culley 1940:21–22.
183 (fn2) *The Sierry Petes*: Gardner 1985:3–5.
189 (fn3) Though the Eaton family: *Santa Fe County Brand Book*: *1853–1889*, p. 225. New Mexico State Records Center and Archives.

CHAPTER 9. A TWENTIETH–CENTURY RANCH

193 "Mr. Laughlin is a wide awake": *Weekly New Mexican*, 1874, History Library, Museum of New Mexico, Santa Fe.
"a capitalist of Topeka": *Santa Fe New Mexican*, August 15, 1907, History Library, Museum of New Mexico, Santa Fe.
194 "I had a wife who," "a politician on the right side," "I never knew the power," "Thank God I am poor": Santa Fe New Mexican, June 1, 1929 (obituary), History Library, Museum of New Mexico, Santa Fe.
"Ours is the government": Sunseri 1979:99.
195 "The New Mexicans were": ibid.:97.
"irrigation works of every kind": Deed of Trust, October 6, 1916, recorded in Book Q—Mortgages, 73. Recorded October 20, 1916, Santa Fe County Records (document on file with the landowner).
"I will make experiments": *Daily New Mexican*, August 22, 1908, History Library, Museum of New Mexico, Santa Fe.
196 "we would be reduced": Protest of Ramon B. Chávez,

Nicolas Pino against resurvey of San Cristobal Grant, made to Surveyor General on August 24, 1879 (document on file with landowner).

197 "The case was hotly fought": *Daily New Mexican*, January 14, 1921, History Library, Museum of New Mexico, Santa Fe.
"do all in his power": Quitclaim Deed of May 9, 1921, signed by Saron and Hattie Laughlin, to the First National Bank of Santa Fe. Recorded in Book P–1 Quit Claim Deeds, p. 394, July 2, 1921, Santa Fe County Records (document copies on file with landowner).

200 His name was Nels C. Nelson: Willey and Sabloff 1980:85–88.

201 They held onto it . . . 130 miles south of the ranch: Murphy 1985:103–114.

204 "purpose of exploring": Oil and Gas Lease, February 8, 1944, filed September 26, 1945, Book G, Contracts, p. 54, Santa Fe County Records (document copies on file with landowner).
It is unknown whether this suit: Warranty Misc. Deeds, 502–504, Santa Fe County Records; and case #24867, February 25, 1952, District Court, Santa Fe (document copies on file with the landowner).
The grant continued to change hands: Warranty Deeds, November 18, 1955, Book 112, Misc. Deeds, 158–161; October 1962, Book 195 Misc. Deeds, 210–212; September 1964, Book 217 Misc. Deeds, 455–457; Dallas County Records, Dallas, Texas (document copies on file with landowner).
"A commercial cow ranch": *Ranch Album*, Anonymous.
"Ranch work is more or less": K. and T. Scott 1988, personal communication. All other comments by K. and T. Scott in this chapter were recorded in 1988.

207 "It's not like your movies": Harper McFarland 1988, personal communication. All other comments by H. McFarland in this chapter were recorded in 1988.
"The cattle and the country": Jerrie Pilley 1994, personal communication. All other comments by J. Pilley in this chapter were recorded in 1994.
"A person that wants": *Ranch Album*, Chuck Harvard.
"The railroads and trucking companies": Oppenheimer 1976:16.

212 "After weaning, the calf": Henry Singleton 1991, personal communication. All other comments by H. Singleton in this chapter were recorded from 1991 to 1994.
The feedlot operator . . . hotels and restaurants: Oppenheimer 1976:17.
"the payday of the year": *Ranch Album*, Anonymous.

213 "The summer that we were here": E. McFarland 1988, personal communication.

218 "You can go to school": Jeff Bilberry 1994, personal communication. All other comments by J. Bilberry in this chapter were recorded in 1994.

219 "If your crew is": Arlin Talbot 1994, personal communication. All other comments by A. Talbot in this chapter were recorded in 1994.

222 "I always have mixed": Hasselstrom 1987:17.

223 "I'm used to it now": T. C. Pilley 1994, personal communication.

224 "We're never bored": Hasselstrom 1987:6.
"Your better cowboys": *Ranch Album*, Harry Chiantaretto.
"All horses and cattle can tell": ibid.

226 "That's one of the nicest things": ibid.

229 "I'd like to be remembered": *Ranch Album*, John Chiantaretto.

Citation to Footnotes

200 (fn4) Another young archaeologist: Willey and Sabloff 1980:85–88.

218 (fn7) Many New Mexico cattlemen: Lasater and Kingsbery 1987.

EPILOGUE

231 These round or oval pithouses: Ware and Akins 1992:3.

232 the high incidence of head and arm injuries: ibid.:8.
"archeological time bomb" and "an incomparable national resource": *The New Mexican*, November 1, 1987, Section B, 1, History Library, Museum of New Mexico, Santa Fe.

Citation to Footnotes

232 (fn4) "the eastern Galisteo Basin": John Ware 1991, personal communication.

PHOTOGRAPH AND ILLUSTRATION CREDITS

All photographs, except where noted, copyright © Christina Mednick.

CHAPTER 1. THE EARLY GALISTEO BASIN

8 map by Deborah Reade, Santa Fe, New Mexico
9 map by Deborah Reade, Santa Fe, New Mexico
14 map by Deborah Reade, from *Chaco Canyon, a Center and Its World,* photographs by Mary Peck, essays by S. H. Lekson, J. R. Stein, and S. J. Ortiz, copyright © 1994, appears courtesy of the Museum of New Mexico Press, Santa Fe
15 courtesy Museum of New Mexico, neg. nos. 6152, 68796
17 map by Deborah Reade, Santa Fe, New Mexico, after Roediger 1961 and Schroeder 1979

CHAPTER 2. THE SOUTHERN TEWA

29 courtesy Museum of New Mexico, neg. no. 143728
33 courtesy Museum of New Mexico, neg. no. 144709
34 courtesy Museum of New Mexico, neg. no. 21608
36 courtesy Museum of New Mexico, neg. no. 134736
38 limited edition poster reproduced by permission of the artist and the copyright holder, Bien Mur Indian Market Center, Albuquerque
45 courtesy Museum of New Mexico, neg. no. 143735
46 by permission of the University of California Press, from *Ceremonial Costumes of the Pueblo Indians. With a New Introduction,* copyright © 1991 Regents of the University of California (Introduction), © 1941, 1969 Virginia More Roediger Johnson
47 by permission of the University of California Press, from *Ceremonial Costumes of the Pueblo Indians. With a New Introduction,* copyright © 1991 Regents of the University of California (Introduction), © 1941, 1969 Virginia More Roediger Johnson
48 courtesy Museum of New Mexico, neg. nos. 143716, 143727
49 courtesy Museum of New Mexico, neg. nos. 144515, 143709
51 courtesy Museum of New Mexico, neg. no. 49463
54 courtesy Museum of Indian Arts and Culture/Laboratory of Anthropology (MIAC/LOA); Largo Glaze Polychrome

jar, MIAC/LOA, Santa Fe (21521/11); Abiquiu Black–on–gray bowl, MIAC/LOA (32010/11); Galisteo Black–on–white bowl, MIAC/LOA (43679/11); Espinosa Glaze Polychrome jar, School of American Research Collections in the Museum of New Mexico (8586/11); Cundiyo Smeared Indented jar, School of American Research Collections in the Museum of New Mexico (8775/11)

55 from "Pueblo Ruins of the Galisteo Basin, New Mexico," by N. C. Nelson, *Anthropological Papers of the American Museum of Natural History,* vol. 15(1), 1914

56 courtesy Museum of New Mexico, neg. no. 46101

57 courtesy Museum of New Mexico, neg. no. 37924

CHAPTER 3. THE PETROGLYPHS

62 courtesy Museum of New Mexico, neg. no. 37014

70 courtesy Museum of New Mexico, neg. no. 74524

CHAPTER 4. THE SPANISH *ENTRADAS*

82 from map of the world in *Ptolemy Atlas,* Venice, 1548. In *Coronado's Quest: The Discovery of the Southwestern States* by A. Grove Day, copyright © 1940 Regents of the University of California, copyright © renewed 1968, A. Grove Day

83 from *Historia General de las Indias* by Gómara, 1554. In *Coronado's Quest: The Discovery of the Southwestern States* by A. Grove Day, copyright © 1940 Regents of the University of California, copyright © renewed 1968, A. Grove Day

87 by permission of Texas Western Press, University of Texas at El Paso. In *Riders across the Centuries: Horsemen of the Spanish Borderlands,* copyright © 1984, drawings and text by José Cisneros

88 copyright © Rijksmuseum–Stichting Amsterdam, neg. no. 6325

89 copyright © National Portrait Gallery, London, reg. no. 347

95 copyright © Museo del Prado, Madrid. All rights reserved. Total or partial reproduction is prohibited

96 by permission of Texas Western Press, University of Texas at El Paso. In *Riders across the Centuries: Horsemen of the Spanish Borderlands,* copyright © 1984, drawings and text by José Cisneros

97 map by Deborah Reade, Santa Fe, New Mexico, after Beck and Haase 1969

98 courtesy Museum of New Mexico, neg. no. 58320

CHAPTER 5. A REMOTE COLONY

102 copyright © Museo del Prado, Madrid. All rights reserved. Total or partial reproduction is prohibited

103 courtesy of Bancroft Library, University of California, Berkeley

105 courtesy Museum of New Mexico, neg. no. 12321

108 courtesy Museum of New Mexico, neg. no. 2114

110 courtesy Museum of New Mexico, neg. no. 143718

113 gift of the Historical Society of New Mexico to the Museum of New Mexico, Museum of International Folk Art, Santa Fe (A.5.56–25)

116 map by Deborah Reade, Santa Fe, New Mexico, after Beck and Haase 1969

119 courtesy Museum of New Mexico, neg. no. 143719

120 courtesy Palace of the Governors, Museum of New Mexico, Santa Fe, neg. no. 11409

123 courtesy of the collections of Spanish Colonial Arts Society at the Museum of International Folk Art, Museum of New Mexico, Santa Fe (L.5.54–13)

124 courtesy of the Collections of the International Folk Art Foundation at the Museum of International Folk Art, Museum of New Mexico, Santa Fe, copyright © 1993, Blair Clark, photographer

126 map by Deborah Reade, Santa Fe, New Mexico, after Beck and Haase 1969

CHAPTER 6. A MEXICAN GRANT

133 courtesy Museum of New Mexico, neg. nos. 22468, 144638

134 courtesy Museum of New Mexico, neg. no. 45011

138 courtesy of the Collections of the International Folk Art Foundation at the Museum of International Folk Art, Museum of New Mexico, Santa Fe, copyright © 1993, Blair Clark, photographer

139 courtesy Museum of New Mexico, neg. no. 68820
140 courtesy Museum of New Mexico, neg. no. 67224
142 courtesy Museum of New Mexico, neg. no. 71218
143 courtesy Museum of New Mexico, neg. no. 56166
144 courtesy of the Collections of the Museum of New Mexico, Museum of International Folk Art, Santa Fe (A.64.19–1)
145 courtesy of the Spanish Colonial Arts Society, Inc., at the Museum of International Folk Art, Museum of New Mexico, Santa Fe (L.5.52–6), Blair Clark, photographer
146 courtesy Museum of New Mexico, neg. no. 8168
148 courtesy Museum of New Mexico, neg. no. 6938

CHAPTER 7. AN AMERICAN TERRITORY

154 courtesy Museum of New Mexico, neg. no. 50809
156 courtesy Museum of New Mexico, neg. nos. 9372, 15069
157 courtesy Museum of New Mexico, neg. nos. 122151, 122150
159 courtesy Museum of New Mexico, neg. no. 86873
160 courtesy Museum of New Mexico, neg. no. 58388
161 courtesy Museum of New Mexico, neg. no. 15780
165 courtesy Museum of New Mexico, neg. no. 13309
167 map by Deborah Reade, Santa Fe, New Mexico
169 courtesy Museum of New Mexico, neg. no. 152217

CHAPTER 8. THE COWBOY TRADITION

174 courtesy Museum of New Mexico, neg. no. 44204
175 courtesy Museum of New Mexico, neg. no. 5324
176 courtesy Museum of New Mexico, neg. nos. 5127, 72346

CHAPTER 9. A TWENTIETH–CENTURY RANCH

194 courtesy Museum of New Mexico, neg. no. 50440
195 courtesy Museum of New Mexico, neg. no. 12725
197 courtesy Museum of New Mexico, neg. no. 76053
200 courtesy Museum of New Mexico, neg. no. 46539
201 courtesy of Polly Griffin, Muskogee, Oklahoma
201 courtesy Museum of New Mexico, neg. no. 12731
202 courtesy Museum of New Mexico, neg. no. 12729

REFERENCES CITED

Adams, Eleanor B., and Fray Angélico Chavez (translators and annotators). *The Missions of New Mexico 1776: A Description by Fray Francisco Atanasio Dominguez.* University of New Mexico Press, Albuquerque, 1956.

Anonymous. *An Illustrated History of New Mexico.* Lewis Publishing Company, Chicago, 1895.

Bailey, Jesse B. *Diego de Vargas and the Reconquest of New Mexico.* University of New Mexico Press, Albuquerque, 1940.

Baldwin, Percy M. "Fray Marcos de Niza and His Discovery of the Seven Cities of Cíbola." *New Mexico Historical Review* 1, no. 1(1926):193.

Bandelier, Adolph F. *Final Report of Investigations among the Indians of the Southwest United States, Carried on Mainly in the Years from 1880–1885.* 2 vols. J. Wilson and Son, Cambridge, Massachussetts, 1890–1892.

Beck, Warren A., and Ynez D. Haase. *Historical Atlas of New Mexico.* University of Oklahoma Press, Norman, 1969.

Black Elk. *The Sacred Pipe*, edited by Joseph Epes Brown. Penguin Books, New York, 1971.

Bolton, Herbert E. *Spanish Exploration in the Southwest 1542–1706.* Charles Scribners Sons, New York, 1930.

Bowden, J. J. "Private Land Claims in the Southwest." Master of Laws in Oil and Gas thesis, Southern Methodist University, College Station, Texas, 1969.

Brewer, Robert, and Steve McDowell. *The Persistence of Memory: New Mexico's Churches.* Museum of New Mexico Press, Santa Fe, 1990.

Briggs, Charles L. "Getting Both Sides of the Story: Oral History in Land Grant Research and Litigation." In *Land, Water, and Culture: New Perspectives on Hispanic Land Grants,* edited by Charles L. Briggs and John R. Van Ness, pp. 217–265. University of New Mexico Press, Albuquerque, 1987.

Brown, Dale. *The World of Velázquez: 1599–1660.* Time–Life Books, New York, 1969.

Bunzel, Ruth L. *Introduction to Zuni Ceremonialism.* Bureau of American Ethnology Annual Report 47. Smithsonian Institution, Washington, D.C., 1932.

Bustamante, Adrian H. "Españoles, Castas, y Labradores: Santa Fe Society in the Eighteenth Century." In *Santa Fe: History of an Ancient City,* edited by David Noble, pp. 65–77. School of

American Research Press, Santa Fe, New Mexico, 1989.

Cabeza de Baca, Fabiola. *We Fed Them Cactus.* University of New Mexico Press. Albuquerque, 1954.

Carroll, H. Bailey, and J. Villasana Haggard (editors). *Three New Mexico Chronicles.* The Quivira Society, Albuquerque, 1942.

Castañeda, Carlos. *Tales of Power*. Simon and Schuster, New York, 1974.

Chavez, Fray Angélico. *The Archives of the Archdiocese of Santa Fe, 1678–1900.* Academy of American Franciscan History, Washington, D.C., 1957.

Chittendon, Larry. "The Cowboys' Christmas Ball." In *Cowboy Poetry: A Gathering,* edited by Hal Cannon, pp. 17–19. Gibbs M. Smith, Layton, Utah, 1985.

Cordell, Linda S. *Prehistory of the Southwest*. Academic Press, Harcourt, Brace, Janovich, Orlando, Florida, 1984.

Covey, Cyclone (translator and annotator). *Cabeza de Vaca's Adventures in the Unknown Interior of America*. University of New Mexico Press, Albuquerque, 1961.

Culley, John H. (Jack). *Cattle, Horses, and Men (of the Western Range).* University of Arizona Press, Tucson, 1940.

Dobie, J. Frank. *Cow People*. Little, Brown and Company, Boston, Toronto, 1964.

Dodge, Richard I. *Our Wild Indians: Thirty–three Years' Personal Experience among the Red Men of the Great West*. A. D. Worthington and Company, Hartford, Connecticut, 1882.

Dozier, Edward P. *Hano: A Tewa Indian Community in Arizona*. Holt, Rinehart, and Winston, New York, 1966.

———. *The Pueblo Indians of North America*. Holt, Rinehart, and Winston, New York, 1970.

Drumm, Stella M. (editor). *Down the Santa Fe Trail and into Mexico: The Diary of Susan Shelby Magoffin, 1846–1847*. Yale University Press and Oxford University Press, New Haven, Connecticut, and London, 1926.

Duffus, P. L. *The Santa Fe Trail*. Longman, Green and Company, Toronto, 1930.

Dumarest, Noel. *Notes on Cochiti, New Mexico.* American Anthropological Association Memoirs 6(3), Lancaster, Pennsylvania, 1919.

Elkus, Jim. "Galisteo: 1500–1900." Unpublished senior honors thesis, Colorado College, Colorado Springs, 1974.

Elliott, Richard S. *Notes Taken in Sixty Years*. R. P. Studley and Company, St. Louis, Missouri, 1883.

Ellis, Florence H., and Laurens Hammack. "The Inner Sanctum of Feather Cave, a Mogollon Sun and Earth Shrine Linking Mexico and the Southwest." *American Antiquity* 33(1968): 25–44.

Espinosa, Aurelio M. "Spanish Folk-Lore in New Mexico." *New Mexico Historical Review* 1, no. 2(1926):135.

Espinosa, Gilberto (translator). *History of New Mexico by Gaspar Pérez de Villagrá*. Quivira Society, Los Angeles, 1933.

Espinosa, J. Manuel. *Crusaders of the Rio Grande*. Institute of Jesuit History, Chicago, 1942.

——— (translator and editor). *The Pueblo Indian Revolt of 1696 and the Franciscan Missions in New Mexico: Letters of the Missionaries and Related Documents*. University of Oklahoma Press, Norman and London, 1988.

Fewkes, Jessie W. *Hopi Katcinas Drawn by Native Artists*. Twenty–first Annual Report of the Bureau of American Ethnology. Government Printing Office, Washington, D.C., 1903.

Ford, Richard I., Albert H. Schroeder, and Stewart L. Peckham. "Three Perspectives on Puebloan History." In *New Perspectives on the Pueblos*, edited by Alfonso Ortiz, pp. 19–39. University of New Mexico Press, Albuquerque, 1972.

Gardner, Gail. "Sierry Petes." In *Cowboy Poetry: A Gathering,* edited by Hal Cannon, pp. 3–5. Gibbs M. Smith, Layton, Utah, 1985.

Gregg, Josiah. *Commerce of the Prairies*. University of Oklahoma Press, Norman, 1954.

Hackett, Charles W. (editor), and C. Shelby (translator). *Revolt of the Pueblo Indians of New Mexico and Otermin's Attempted Reconquest, 1680–1682*. 2 vols. Coronado Cuarto Centennial Publications. University of New Mexico Press, Albuquerque, 1942.

Hale, Kenneth, and David Harris. "Historical Linguistics and Archeology." In *Handbook of North American Indians*, vol. 9, *Southwest*, edited by Alfonso Ortiz, pp.170–177. Smithsonian Institution Press, Washington, D.C., 1979.

Haley, J. Evetts. *Charles Goodnight, Cowman and Plainsman*. University of Oklahoma Press, Norman, 1936.

Hall, Martin H. *Sibley's New Mexican Campaign.* University of Texas Press, Austin, 1960.

Hammond, George P., and Agapito Rey. *The Gallegos Relacion of the Rodriguez Expedition to New Mexico.* El Palacio Press, Santa Fe, New Mexico, 1927.

———. *Expedition into New Mexico Made by Antonio de Espejo 1528–1583.* The Quivira Society, Los Angeles, 1929.

———. *Narratives of the Coronado Expedition.* University of New Mexico Press, Albuquerque, 1940.

———. *Juan de Oñate: Colonizer of New Mexico 1595–1628,* vol. 1. University of New Mexico Press, Albuquerque, 1953.

Harrington, John P. *The Ethnogeography of the Tewa Indians.* Twenty–ninth Annual Report of the Bureau of American Ethnology, pp. 486–488. Washington, D.C., 1916.

———. "Old Indian Geographical Names around Santa Fe, New Mexico." *American Anthropologist* 22, no. 4(1920):341–359.

Herzog, G. "A Comparison of Pueblo and Pima Musical Styles." *Journal of American Folklore* 49(1936):238–417.

Hasselstrom, Linda. *Windbreak: A Woman Rancher on the Northern Plains.* Barn Owl Books, Berkeley, California, 1987.

Hewett, Edgar L., and Bertha P. Dutton. *The Pueblo Indian World.* University of New Mexico Press, Albuquerque, 1945.

Highwater, Jamake. *The Primal Mind: Vision and Reality in Indian America.* Meridian, New York, 1982.

Hodge, F. W., G. P. Hammond, and A. Rey (editors and translators). *Fray Alonso de Benavides Revised Memorial of 1634.* University of New Mexico Press, Albuquerque, 1945.

Hodge, F. W., C. F. Lummis (editors), and Mrs. E. Ayer (translator). *The Memorial of Fray Alonso de Benavides, 1630.* Edward E. Ayer, Chicago, 1916.

Hordes, Stanley M. "A History of Santa Fe." In *Santa Fe: History of an Ancient City,* edited by David G. Noble, pp. 1–7. School of American Research, Santa Fe, New Mexico, 1989.

Inglis, G. Douglas. "The Men of Cíbola: New Investigations on the Francisco Vázquez de Coronado Expedition." *Panhandle–Plains Historical Review* 55(1982):1–24.

Jackson, Donald (editor). *The Journals of Zebulon Montgomery Pike, with Letters and Related Documents.* 2 vols. University of Oklahoma Press, Norman, 1966.

James, Ahlee. *Tewa Firelight Tales.* Longmans, Green and Company, New York and London, 1927.

Jaramillo, Cleofas M. *Shadows of the Past.* The Seton Village Press, Santa Fe, New Mexico, 1941.

Judge, James. "New Light on Chaco Canyon." In *New Light on Chaco Canyon,* edited by David G. Noble, pp. 1–12. School of American Research Press, Santa Fe, New Mexico,1984.

Kessell, John L. *Kiva, Cross, and Crown: The Pecos Indians and New Mexico, 1540–1840.* University of New Mexico Press, Albuquerque, 1987.

——— (editor). *Remote Beyond Compare: Letters of Don Diego de Vargas to His Family from New Spain and New Mexico, 1675–1706.* University of New Mexico Press, Albuquerque, 1989.

La Flesche, Francis. *War and Peace Ceremony of the Osage Indians.* Bulletin 101, Bureau of American Ethnology. Smithsonian Institution, Washington, D.C., 1939.

Lang, Richard W. *Archeological Survey of the Upper San Cristobal Arroyo Drainage, Galisteo Basin, Santa Fe County, New Mexico.* Report prepared for New Mexico State Planning Office, Santa Fe, 1977.

Lasater, Laurie, and Bob Kingsbery. *Welcome to the New Cattle Industry.* Kingsbery Communications, San Antonio, Texas, 1987.

Laski, Vera. *Seeking Life.* Philadelphia American Folklore Society, Philadelphia, 1958.

Lecompte, Janet. "The Independent Women of Hispanic New Mexico, 1821–1846." *The Western Historical Quarterly* 12, no.1 1981).

Lummis, Charles F. *The Land of Poco Tiempo.* University of New Mexico Press, Albuquerque, 1952.

Maketa, Jacqueline D. (editor). *Legacy of Honor.* University of New Mexico Press, Albuquerque, 1986.

Marmaduke, M. M. "Santa Fe Trail—Journal." *Missouri Historical Review* 6, no. 1(1911):1–10.

Martineau, LaVan. *The Rocks Begin to Speak.* K.C. Publications, Las Vegas, Nevada, 1973.

McCoy, Joseph G. *Historic Sketches of the Cattle Trade of the West and Southwest.* Ramsey, Millett and Hudson, Kansas City, Missouri, 1874.

Murphy, Dan. *New Mexico: The Distant Land.* Windsor Publications, Northridge, California, 1985.

Nelson, Nels C. *Pueblo Ruins of the Galisteo Basin, New Mexico.* Anthropological Papers of the American Museum of Natural History, vol. 15, pt. 1 (1914).

Oppenheimer, Harold L. *Cowboy Economics*. The Interstate Printers and Publishers, Danville, Illinois, 1976.

Ortiz, Alfonso. *The Tewa World: Space, Time, Being, and Becoming in a Pueblo Society*. University of Chicago Press, London and Chicago, 1969.

———. "San Juan Pueblo." In *Handbook of North American Indians*, vol. 9, *Southwest*, edited by Alfonso Ortiz, pp. 278–295. Smithsonian Institution Press, Washington, D.C., 1979.

Ortiz y Pino III, José. *The Last Patrón*. Sunstone Press, Santa Fe, New Mexico, 1981.

———. *Curandero: A Cuento*. Sunstone Press, Santa Fe, New Mexico, 1983.

———. *There Is Another You*. Self–published booklet, Galisteo, New Mexico, no date.

Parsons, Elsie Clews. "The Humpbacked Flute Player of the Southwest." *American Anthropologist* 40, no. 2(1938):337–338.

———. *Pueblo Indian Religion*. 2 vols. University of Chicago Press, Chicago, 1939.

Patterson–Rudolph, Carol. "Navajo/Tewa Battle Petroglyph Analysis." Unpublished paper presented to the Australian Rock Art Research Association, 1988. On file, Laboratory of Anthropology, Museum of New Mexico, Santa Fe.

———. *Petroglyphs and Pueblo Myths of the Rio Grande*. University of New Mexico Press, Albuquerque, 1991.

Plog, Fred. "Prehistory: Western Anasazi." In *Handbook of North American Indians*, vol. 9, *Southwest*, edited by Alfonso Ortiz, pp. 108–130. Smithsonian Institution Press, Washington, D.C., 1979.

Prince, L. Bradford. *Spanish Mission Churches of New Mexico*. Torch Press, Cedar Rapids, Iowa, 1915.

Ranch Album. Documentary film. Gail Steiger, producer–director, Eugene Polk and Richard Menschel, executive producers. Sharlot Hall Historical Society of Arizona, Prescott, 1987.

Roediger, Virginia M. *Ceremonial Costumes of the Pueblo Indians*. University of California Press, Berkeley, 1961.

Romero, Orlando. *Nambe—Year One*. Tonatiuh–Quinto Sol International, Berkeley, California, 1976

Sánchez, Joseph P. "Twelve Days in August: The Pueblo Revolt in Santa Fe." In *Santa Fe: History of an Ancient City*, edited by David Noble, pp. 39–52. School of American Research Press, Santa Fe, New Mexico, 1989.

Sando, Joe S. *The Pueblo Indians*. The Indian Historian Press, San Francisco, 1976.

———. "The Pueblo Revolt." In *Handbook of North American Indians*, vol. 9, *Southwest*, edited by Alfonso Ortiz, pp. 194–197. Smithsonian Institution Press, Washington, D.C., 1979.

Savage, William Jr. (editor). *Cowboy Life: Reconstructing an American Myth*. University of Oklahoma, Norman, 1975.

Schaafsma, Polly. *Indian Rock Art of the Southwest*. University of New Mexico Press, Albuquerque, 1980.

———. "War Imagery and Magic: Petroglyphs at Comanche Gap, Galisteo Basin, New Mexico." Unpublished manuscript, 1990. On file, Laboratory of Anthropology, Museum of New Mexico, Santa Fe.

Schmitt, Martin F. (editor). *The Cattle Drives of David Shirk from Texas to the Idaho Mines, 1871 and 1873*. Champoeg Press, Portland, Oregon, 1956.

Scholes, France V. *Church and State in New Mexico, 1610–1650*. University of New Mexico Press, Albuquerque, 1937.

———. *Troublous Times in New Mexico*. University of New Mexico Press, Albuquerque, 1942.

Schroeder, Albert H. "Pueblos Abandoned in Historic Times." In *Handbook of North American Indians*, vol. 9, *Southwest*, edited by Alfonso Ortiz, pp. 236–254. Smithsonian Institution Press, Washington, D.C., 1979.

———. "A Brief History of San Lázaro and San Cristóbal Pueblos." Unpublished manuscript, 1991. On file, Laboratory of Anthropology, Museum of New Mexico, Santa Fe.

Shepard, Elizabeth. *The Discoveries of Estevan the Black*. Dodd, Mead, and Company, NewYork, 1970.

Silverberg, Robert. *The Pueblo Revolt*. Weybright and Talley, New York, New York, 1970.

Simmons, Marc. "History of Pueblo–Spanish Relations to 1821." In *Handbook of North American Indians*, vol. 9, *Southwest*, edited by Alfonso Ortiz, pp. 178–193. Smithsonian Institution Press, Washington, D.C., 1979a.

———. *People of the Sun: Some Out–of–Fashion Southwesterners*. University of New Mexico Press, Albuquerque, 1979b.

Sims, Agnes C. "Rock Carvings, a Record of Folk History." In *Sun Father's Way*, edited by Bertha P. Dutton, pp. 215–220. University of New Mexico Press, Albuquerque, 1963.

Sinclair, John. *Cowboy Riding Country*. University of New Mexico Press, Albuquerque, 1982.

Spicer, Edward H. *Cycles of Conquest: The Impact of Spain, Mexico and the United States on the Indians of the Southwest, 1533–1960*. University of Arizona Press, Tucson, 1962.

Spinden, Herbert J. *Songs of the Tewa*. Sunstone Press, Santa Fe, 1976.

Stanislawski, Michael B. "Hopi–Tewa." In *Handbook of North American Indians*, vol. 9, *Southwest*, edited by Alfonso Ortiz, pp. 587–602. Smithsonian Institution Press, Washington, D.C., 1979.

Steele, Thomas J., and Rowena A. Rivera. *Penitente Self–Government: Brotherhoods and Councils, 1797–1947*. Ancient City Press, Santa Fe, New Mexico, 1985.

Steiner, Stan. *The Waning of the West*. St. Martin's Press, New York, 1989.

Stevenson, Matilda C. *The Zuni Indians: Their Mythology, Esoteric Fraternities, and Ceremonies*. Twenty–third Annual Report of the Bureau of American Ethnology in the Years 1901–1902. Smithsonian Institution, Washington, D.C., 1904.

Sunseri, Alvin R. *Seeds of Discord: New Mexico in the Aftermath of the American Conquest 1846–1861*. Nelson–Hall, Chicago, 1979.

Taylor, Lonn, and Ingrid Maar. *The American Cowboy*. Exhibit book, Library of Congress, Washington D.C., March 26–October 2, 1983.

Time. "Mistaken by Millenniums." June 11(1990):55.

Tobias, Henry J. *A History of the Jews in New Mexico*. University of New Mexico Press, Albuquerque, 1990.

Twitchell, Ralph E. *Leading Facts of New Mexican History*, vol. 1. Torch Press, Cedar Rapids, Iowa, 1911.

Van Ness, John R. "Hispanic Land Grants: Ecology and Subsistence on the Uplands of Northern New Mexico and Southern Colorado." In *Land, Water, and Culture: New Perspectives on Hispanic Land Grants*, edited by Charles L. Briggs and John R. Van Ness, pp. 141–214. University of New Mexico Press, Albuquerque, 1987.

Van Ness, John R., and Christina Van Ness (editors). *Spanish and New Mexican Land Grants in New Mexico and Colorado*. Center for Land Grant Studies and the Colorado Humanities Program. Sunflower University Press, Manhattan, Kansas, 1980.

Vigil, Maurilio E. *Los Patrones: Profiles of Hispanic Political Leaders in New Mexico History*. University Press of America, Washington, D.C., 1980.

Waters, Frank. *The Man Who Killed the Deer*. Washington Square Press, New York, 1970.

Ware, John A., and Nancy J. Akins. "LA 3333: An Early PIII Pithouse Village in the Eastern Galisteo Basin." Paper presented at the 65th Annual Pecos Conference, Pecos, New Mexico, August, 1992. On file with authors, Office of Archaeological Studies, Museum of New Mexico, Santa Fe.

Wellmann, K. F. "Kokopelli of Indian Paleology: Hunchbacked Rain Priest, Hunting Magician, and Don Juan of the Old Southwest." *Journal of the American Medical Association* 212, no. 10(1970):1678–1682.

Weigle, Marta. *The Penitentes of the Southwest*. Ancient City Press, Santa Fe, New Mexico, 1970.

——— (editor). *Two Guadalupes: Hispanic Legends and Magic Tales from Northern New Mexico*. Ancient City Press, Santa Fe, New Mexico, 1987.

Westphall, Victor. *Thomas Benton Catron and His Era*. University of Arizona Press, Tucson, 1973.

Willey, R. Gordon, and Jeremy A. Sabloff. *A History of American Archeology*. W. H. Freeman and Co., San Francisco, California, 1980.

Worchester, Donald E. "The Apaches in the History of the Southwest." *New Mexico Historical Review* 50, no. 1(1975):27.

Wright, Barton. *Pueblo Cultures*. Iconography of Religions series, section 10, North America, fascicule 4. E. J. Brill, Leiden, Netherlands, 1986.

Yava, Albert. *Big Falling Snow: A Tewa–Hopi's Life and Times and the History and Traditions of His People*, edited by Harold Courlander. Crown Publishers, Inc., New York, 1978.

Young, M. Jane. *Signs from the Ancestors: Zuni Cultural Symbolism and Perception of Rock Art*. University of New Mexico Press, Albuquerque, 1988.

General Reading

Bailey, L. R. *Indian Slave Trade in the Southwest.* Westernlore Press, Tucson, Arizona, 1966.

Forrest, Earle R. *Missions and Pueblos of the Old Southwest: Their Myths, Legends, Fiestas, and Ceremonies, with Some Accounts of the Indian Tribes and Their Dances; and of the Penitentes,* vol. 1. Arthur H. Clark Co., Cleveland, Ohio, 1929.

Leonard, Irving A. *The Mercurio Volante of Don Carlos de Sigüenza y Góngora: An Account of the First Expedition of Don Diego de Vargas into New Mexico in 1692.* The Quivira Society, Los Angeles, 1932.

Ortiz, Alfonso (editor). *Handbook of North American Indians,* vol. 9, *Southwest.* Smithsonian Institution Press, Washington, D.C., 1979.

Prince, L. Bradford. *A Concise History of New Mexico,* 2d edition. The Torch Press, Cedar Rapids, Iowa, 1914.

Steele, Thomas J., S. J. *Santos and Saints: The Religious Folk Art of Hispanic New Mexico.* Ancient City Press, Santa Fe, New Mexico, 1982.

Sweet, Jill D. *Dances of the Tewa Pueblo Indians.* School of American Research Press, Santa Fe, New Mexico, 1985.

Thomas, Alfred B. *The Plains Indians and New Mexico 1751–1778,* vol. 11, edited by George P. Hammond. Coronado Cuarto Centennial Publications. University of New Mexico Press, Albuquerque, 1940.

Index

A

Abiquiu Black-on-gray bowl, 54 (photo)
Abstract Style, 61
Acoma Pueblo, 98 (photo)
 assault on, 99
Agriculture, adoption of, 12
Aguilar, Nicolás de, 106
Allison, Clay, 189
Altar screen, 138 (photo)
Anasazi, 12-13, 12n5
 migration of, 16
Anayas' store, 198 (photo)
Anglos (Anglo-Americans), 132n3, 153, 171, 234, 148n18
Anthropomorphs, petroglyphs of, 75
Apaches, 108, 108n2, 108 (photo), 120, 122, 123, 126
 attacks by, 107, 110, 115, 157, 160
 Pueblo Revolt and, 112, 114n9, 120
 slaves and, 125
Aragón, Juan: grant for, 128, 128n13
Aragón, Rafael
 painting by, 123
 santo by, 113
Arbizu, José, 123
Armijo, Manuel, 154
 Fernández and, 137
 San Cristóbal Grant and, 166
Arrow Swallowers, 68
Ash Youth, 27
Atchison, Topeka & Santa Fe, 160, 161 (photo)
Atkinson, Henry: San Cristóbal Grant and, 166, 168
Atsinakwi, 64
Avanyu, 61n1
petroglyph of, 65
 song of, 61

B

"Baby" (railroad engine), 161 (photo)
Baca de Gallegos, Guadalupe, 156
Bandelier, Adolph, 86, 95n12
Bartolomé, 119
Bear, petroglyph of, 69, 73
Bear Society, 32, 67
Beast God of the Zenith, 69
Becknell, William, 132-33, 134
Benavides, Alonso de, 102
 on Galisteo, 101
Bent, Charles, 156
Bernal, Juan: Pueblo Revolt and, 112, 113
Bilberry, Jeff, 223
 ranching and, 218, 224, 226, 229
Billy the Kid, 189
Birds, petroglyph of, 71, 73
Birthing figure, petroglyph of, 77
Blakley, Villa, 204
Blakley, William A., 204
Blakley-Braniff Foundation, 204
Blazing star (*Mentzelia* sp.), 50 (photo)
Blue Corn Woman, 21, 30
Blue Flower, 44n28
 story by, 44-46
Bolsas, Antonio, 110, 120, 122
Branding, 183 (photo), 219, 220 (photo), 221
Brands, sample, 189
Branum, Betty Jo, 204
Branum, M. W. (Buddy), 204
Breeding, 215, 218
Bronco riders, 182 (photo)
Brujas (sorcerers), 147, 147n17
Buffalo, petroglyph of, 68
Buffalo Dance, costume from, 47 (illustration)
Bull Canyon, 214 (photo)
Bull riding, 186 (photo), 187 (photo)
Bunzel, Ruth: on ideal Pueblo type, 50
Butler, Eldon, 203

C

Cabeza de Baca, Fabiola, 143
 on childhood, 138
Cabeza de Vaca, Alvar Núñez, 81-82, 83, 87, 87n5
Caciques, 46, 54, 102, 102n1, 110(photo), 119
Calhoun, John C.: on New Mexicans, 194
Calves, 215, 218, 219, 221, 222, 223
 selling, 212
Canyon Ceta, 24-25 (photo), 53 (photo)
Canyon Ceta reservoir, 93 (photo), 137 (photo)
Carboneli, Antonio, 123
Carson, Christopher (Kit), 160, 160 (photo)
Cassidy, Butch, 189
Castañeda, Pedro de, 88
 on Apaches, 108
 on Pecos, 89
Castaño de Sosa, Gaspar: colonization and, 95
Catholic church (Galisteo), 141 (photo), Lamy, 162
Catholicism
 Penitentes and, 147
 Pueblos and, 105-6
 spread of, 102, 105-6
Catron, Julia Walz, 165
Catron, Thomas Benton, 156, 165 (photo), 193, 193n1
 Laughlin suit and, 197
 Pankey and, 194, 194n2
 San Cristóbal Grant and, 164, 166, 168, 169
 statehood and, 195n3
Cattle, 178 (photo), 189, 190 (photo), 191, 207
 introduction of, 173
 selling, 212
 types of, 215
Ceremonial mask, Hopi, 107 (photo)
Cerro Pelón, 3
Chaco Canyon, 12-13, 12n6, 14 (map), 232
 importance of, 15
Chamisa, 180-81 (photo)
Chapel ruins, 104 (photo)
Charles V, 88, 88 (painting)
Chávez, José Antonio, 138
Chico Pasture, 202 (photo), 203 (photo)
Chief Raingod, 40, 41
Childhood, 138
 training during, 50-51
Chisolm Trail, 177, 186
Cholla (*Opuntia* sp.), 42 (photo)
Cisneros, José: illustration by, 87, 96
Clemente, revolt by, 106
Cloudbeings, 3
Cloud Boys, 47
Cloudflower, 37
Cloud-Flower Lullaby, The, 28
Clowns, 35, 36 (photo), 37, 39, 41, 51
 cold, 32
 initiation chant of, 33
 snakes and, 75
 warm, 22, 31n10, 32
Cochití, raid by, 122
Colina Verde, 7, 58, 83
Colorado Volunteers, 160
Comanche Gap, petroglyphs at, 51n33, 78, 79
Comanche Peace Treaty, 143
Comancheros, 143, 143n11
Comanches, 126, 128, 143 (photo), 143n11
 attacks by, 125
 Galisteo Basin and, viii
 Hispanics and, 143
 slaves and, 108
Convento, 103, 107
Corn Dance, 44
Corn-Mother-Sky-Father, 68
Corn Priests, 74
Corridos, 148
Corros, 146
Cortéz, cattle and, 173
Cowboys, 172 (photo), 173-74, 175 (photo), 176 (photo), 182 (photo), 183 (photo), 186 (photo), 187 (photo), 191, 220 (photo), 223
 equipment of, 174
 humor of, 189
 life of, 177-78, 179, 184, 189, 207
 socializing by, 186, 188
 terms of, 183n2
 true, 207n5
 See also Vaqueros
"Cowboys' Christmas Ball, The" (poem), 188
Crow Wing, 62
 on community/cooperation, 46
Cuentos (folktales), 148
Culley, John (Jack), 173
 on cowboys, 177, 178, 179n1, 186, 188, 189
 on Western ideals, 184
Cundiyo Smeared Indented jar, 54 (photo)
Curanderos (healers), 128n14, 147
Curtis, Edward S.: photo by, 29, 33, 45, 48, 49, 110, 119

D

Daily New Mexican
 on Lamy, 162, 163
 on Pankey, 195
 San Cristóbal Grant and, 197
Dances, 133 (illustration)
 banning, 107
 cowboys and, 186
Dark Star Man, 47
Dawn Youths, 47
Death God, 65
Deer, petroglyphs of, 43 (photo)
Deer Dancer, 46 (illustration)
Denver & Rio Grande Western, 160
Dishta, Duane: painting by, 38
Dobie, J. Frank, 184, 188
Dobson, Wayman, 201, 204
Domínguez, Francisco Atanasio: on Tano, 125-26
Dozier, Edward P., 30n9, 118
 on cradleboards, 50n31
 on Tewa cultures, 18, 18n9
Dry Food People, 31, 31n12, 32
Ducks, petroglyphs of, 66

Dutton, Bertha: excavation by, 231n2

E
Earth Navel, 37
Earth Old Woman, 47
Eaton, Ethan W., 157 (photo), 160n3, 196
 cattle and, 189n3
 San Cristóbal Grant and, 157, 159, 166, 168, 169
Eaton, Marcelina Chávez, 157, 157 (photo)
Eaton Grant, 7, 166, 167 (map)
El Ferrocarril (The Railroad), 153-54
Elk, petroglyphs of, 43 (photo)
El Santuario de Chimayó, 147 (photo)
El Viejo (The Old Man), 131
Encomienda system, 103
Entradas, 83, 91n10, 95, 233
Epidemics, 110n3, 126
Espejo, Antonio de, 91n11, 95
 on Piros, 63
 on Pueblo people, 54
 Southern Tewa and, 54
 travels of, 91-92
 on Zia, 63
Espinosa Glaze Polychrome jar, 54 (photo)
Estancias, 81
Estévan, 82, 87
Estremara, Alonso de, 103
Evening Star, 47

F
Fall Works, 218, 222
Farr Brothers, 204, 213
Fernández, Domingo, 134, 136, 137, 138, 143, 157
 Galisteo and, 196
 San Cristóbal Grant and, 154, 159, 166, 168, 169
First Mesa, 55, 125
Flute players, petroglyph of, 71
Food Offering Prayer, 35
Fortress wall, 86 (photo)
Francisco the white-eyed, 136
Fullerton, Minnie, 201
Fullerton, Samuel C., 201, 201 (photo), 204
 brand of, 189
Fullerton, Samuel C., Jr., 204

G
Galisteo Basin, 3, 117, 128, 139, 197
 Anasazi in, 16
 attacks on, 110
 explorers and, 88
 land disputes in, 196-97
 pottery from, 54 (photo)
 Pueblo Revolt and, 111, 118
 story of, vii, 7, 8, 12
 surveying/excavating in, 200
Galisteo Black-on-white bowl, 54 (photo)
Galisteo Black-on-white ceramics, 18n8
Galisteo Pasture, 179 (photo), 217 (photo)
Galisteo Rodeo, 182 (photo), 198 (photo)
Gallegos, Hernan: on Piedra Quita, 91
Gamio, Manuel: discoveries by, 200n4
Garcia, Pedro, 117, 119
Gardner, Gail: *Sierry Petes* and, 183n2
Glorieta Pass, 159 (photo), 161 (photo)
 battle at, 159-60
Goodnight, Charles: cattle trade and, 184
Goodnight-Loving Trail, 177
Great Goodness, 41
Great Spirit, 23
Grinding holes, 32 (photo)
Guildersleeve, Charles H., 169 (photo)
 San Cristóbal Grant and, 168

H
Haas, Jonathan, 232-33
Hackett, Charles W., 113n7, 119
Handprints, 67 (photo)
 petroglyphs of, 71, 75
Hano (Thano), 18, 55, 58, 125
 chiefs of, 57 (photo)
 songs/dances of, 55
Harrington, J. P.: on Lamy, 160n4
Harvey, Fred: "Indian Detours" and, 200
Hasselstrom, Linda: ranching and, 223, 224
Hayes, Rutherford B.: San Cristóbal Grant and, 168
Healers, 147, 147n17
Hearth ruins, 196 (photo)
Heart of the Sky God, 73, 74
Hehea, 75
Hidalgo, Pedro: Pueblo Revolt and, 113
Hidalgos, 87, 87n7
Hish-í, 58
Hispanics, 133 (photo), 137, 138-39, 142 (photo), 171, 234
 Anglo prejudice toward, 148n18
 culture of, 150
 Galisteo and, 142-43, 144
 Indians and, 139n7
 property rights of, 195, 196-97
 San Cristóbal and, 132, 139, 144, 195, 196-97
Hopi, 123
 ceremonies/pantheon of, 63
 language, 16
 priests, 70 (photo)
Horned beings, petroglyph of, 73
Horned mask, pictograph of, 72
Human figures, petroglyphs of, 66, 68, 75
Humpback, 71
Hunt Chief, 21-22, 30
Hunter-gatherers, 8, 12
Hunting lookout station, 13 (photo)
Hunt Society, 32

I
"Indian Detours," 200
Indian paint brush *(Castilleja* sp.), 22 (photo)
Inglis, C. Douglas: on hidalgos, 87
"Initiation Chant of the Kwirana K'osa, The," 33, 33n16
Inquisition, 96n13, 106
Isleta Pueblo mission, 105 (photo)

J
James, Ahlee, 43n26, 44n28
James, Thomas, 132
Jaramillo, Cleofas, 145
Jaramillo, Colonel and Mrs. Venseslao, 140 (photo)
Jemez Mountain bands, obsidian tools for, 12
Jornada Mogollon, 63
Juan of Galisteo, Pueblo Revolt and, 110, 111, 113
Judge, W. James: on Chaco Canyon, 15

K
Kachinas, 33, 39, 40, 41, 51 (illustration), 73, 77
 petroglyph of, 74
Kachina Society, 32, 32n15, 62
Kearny, Stephen, 154, 156
Keres, 51n32, 120, 123
 Pueblo Revolt and, 115
Keresan language, 16, 43
Ketcham, Black Jack, 189
Kidder, A. V.: on Anasazi, 12n5
Kiowa-Tanoan languages, 16
Kirauash, 86
Kivas, 52, 58
 entrance to, 34 (photo)
 excavation of, 231
Knifewing, 69
Kokopelli, 71
Kossa (warm clowns), 22, 31n10, 32
Kwirana (cold clowns), 22, 32

L
"La Baile" (dancing), 133 (illustration)
La Familia Sagrada, bulto of, 124
Laguna Santero, retablo by, 145
La Hermandad de Nuestro Padre Jesús Nazareno (Brotherhood of our Father Jesus). See Penitentes
La Jara Pasture, 152 (photo)
Lake Song of the Tewa K'osa, 31
La Mentira (The Lie), 87
Lamy, 160n4, 162 (photo)
 train depot, 163 (photo)
Lamy, Jean Baptiste, 144n12, 160
Lang, Richard W., 8n3, 12, 51n32, 83n3
 on Anasazi, 12n6, 16
Largo Glaze Polychrome jar, 54 (photo)
Las Columnas (The Crosses), 144
Laski, Vera, 39n21
 on cursing words, 41n23
 on Pueblo dances, 47
 on Raingod Ceremony, 33, 35, 37, 39-42
Laughlin, Hattie: San Cristóbal Grant and, 166
Laughlin, Saron N.
 brand of, 189
 Catron-Pino suit and, 197
 cattle and, 189, 189n3, 191
 ranching by, 193
 San Cristóbal Grant and, 166, 168, 169
Lecompte, Janet, 139n8, 146
Levine, Frances, 132n2
 on pueblo organization, 89n9
 Pueblo Revolt and, 115n10
Little-Brother-Older-Than-I, 35
Little Twin Brother, 35, 35n18
Longhorns, 173, 174, 174 (photo), 178, 215
López, Francisco, 91
López de Mendizábal, Bernardo, 107
 petitions against, 106
"Los Moros y los Christianos," 96
Loving, Oliver: cattle trade and, 184

M
McCoy, Joseph: on cowboy socializing, 186
McFarland, Elsie, 212 (photo)
 on ranch life, 213
McFarland, Harper, 184 (photo), 213 (photo)
 on cowboys, 207
 ranching and, 213, 215, 218, 219, 221, 222
Made People (Towa é), 22, 27, 31, 32, 32nn13, 14, 35n18, 37, 44, 51
Makawasendo, 47
Makowa, 47
Maldonado, José, 204
Maldonado, Rafaela, 204
Manifest Destiny, 164
María de Jesús, Sister, 103 (illustration)
Marmaduke, M. M., 139, 142
Martineau, LaVan: on petroglyphs, 64, 68
Martinez, Alonso: dance ban by, 107
Masked Raingod, 37
Masks
 painted, 74
 petroglyph of, 71, 72, 73, 75
Maynez, Alberto, 196
Medicine Man, 26, 47n29, 67, 87n5, 147
Medicine Society, 32
 bears and, 73
 songs of, 43-44
Melgares, Facundo, 134, 136
Mesa Verde, 13, 233
Mesa Verde Black-on-white ceramics, 18n8
Midwinter Ceremony, chant song from, 30
Mishongnovi Pueblo, 70 (photo)
Missionaries, 103
Montezuma, 118
Moon Old Man, 47
Moradas, 145, 145n14
Mora Grant, 164
Morning Star, 47, 65, 77
Mudheads, 71, 73

Murphy, Dan
San Cristóbal and, 157
on Wootton, 160

N
Nambe, Tewas in, 16
Navajos, 122, 126
attack by, 110, 160
Pueblo Revolt and, 114n9
Navajo "talkers," 201
Nels, Tony, 163
Nelson, Nels C., 200 (photo)
map by, 55
San Cristóbal and, 200
New Light on Chaco Canyon (Judge), 15
New Mexico State Highway and Transportation Department, excavation by, 231n2
New World, 82 (map)
Niza, Marcos de, 87, 88
Northern Tewa, 18n9, 22, 122
Catholicism and, 102
language of, 16
Pueblo Revolt and, 114
Nuestra Señora de Guadalupe (Our Lady of Guadalupe), 138
Nuestra Señora de los Dolores (Our Lady of Sorrows), retablo of, 145
Nuestra Señora de los Remedios, 125

O
"Offering at the Waterfall, An" (Curtis), 33 (photo)
Office of Archaeological Studies, Museum of New Mexico, excavation by, 231n2
Oñate de Salazar, Juan de, 96, 96 (illustration), 99, 108n2
cattle and, 173
conquest of 97 (map)
on Galisteo Basin, 108
One-horned serpents, petroglyph of, 76, 77
Oppenheimer, Harold, 207n6
on ranching, 207
Origin myths, 22n2
Ortiz, Alfonso, 28n7, 30n9
on Dry Food People, 31n12
on shrines, 27n5
Tewa origin myth and, 22n2
on Tewa women, 46
on *Towa é*, 32n13
Ortiz Mountains, 3, 84-85 (photo), 127 (photo)
gold in, 154
Ortiz y Pino, José, 143, 143n9, 10
Laughlin suit and, 197
San Cristóbal Grant and, 197
Ortiz y Pino, José, III, 128n14, 143n10, 197
poem by, 149
Otermín, Antonio de, 113n6, 114n9
Pueblo Revolt and, 112-15, 117-20
Our Lady of Light Church, 162 (photo)
Overgrazing, 218, 218n7
Oxua, 33

P
Paleoindians, Galisteo Basin and, 8, 12
Pankey, Benjamin F., 193, 193n1, 194 (photo)
brand of, 189
Catron and, 194, 194n2
ranch of, 195 (photo), 201 (photo)
San Cristóbal Grant and, 195, 197
trouble for, 200-201
Pankey, Flora, 193, 194
Parraga, Diego: sexual abuse by, 106
Parrot, petroglyph of, 63 (photo)
Parsons, E. C., 73
on backward speech, 37n20
on Crow Wing, 62
on Pueblo behavior, 51
on Pueblo songs, 28n6
Partition Statute (1876), 169
Pataragueyes, 92
Patowa, 32nn14, 15, 44
Patterson-Rudolph, Carol, 64n4
on petroglyphs, 68
Payastiamo, 118
Payatiabo, 118
Pecos, 51n32, 120, 123
Pueblo Revolt and, 115, 117, 118
Penitentes, 144-45, 146, 146 (illustration)
Catholicism and, 147
origins of, 145n13
songs of, 144
Peralta, Pedro de, 99
Pérez, Albino, 154
Pérez de Luxán
Espejo and, 92
San Cristóbal and, 95
Petroglyphs, vii-viii, 12, 43 (photo), 63 (photo), 64, 64, (photo), 65 (photo), 66 (photo), 68 (photo), 70 (photo), 71 (photo), 73 (photo), 74 (photo), 75 (photo), 76 (photo), 77 (photo), 78 (photo), 79 (photo), 233
dating, 61
defined, 64n5
interpreting, 3-4, 63
Philip II, 89-90, 89 (painting), 95, 96
Philip III, 95, 95 (painting), 101
Philip IV, 101, 102 (painting), 103
Pictographs, 62 (photo), 64, 64n5
Piedra Quita, 91, 91n10
Pike, Zebulon, 134, 142
Pilley, Jerrie
on cowboys, 207
ranching and, 221, 224, 226, 229
Pilley, T. C., 223
ranching and, 226
Pino, Nicolás: San Cristóbal Grant and, 166, 168
Piros, 54, 63
Pithouses, 12, 58, 232
excavation of, 231
Plains Indians
raids by, 107
slaves and, 108
Plog, Fred
on Anasazi abandonment, 13n7
on migration, 16
Pocos, 92
Po-he-yemu, 113, 114, 118
Polk, James K., 154
Popé, 110, 111
authority of, 115
P-o p-oe, 43
Prayer feather, 33 (photo)
Prayers, 43, 44
Prayer sticks, 106 (photo)
Priests, 74
Hopi, 70 (photo)
Tewa, 26
Provincial Deputation of New Mexico, 136
Puaray, 89, 92
Pueblo Blanco, 232
Pueblo Bonito
kivas at, 15 (photo)
wall at, 15 (photo)
Pueblo Colorado, 7, 24-25 (photo), 58, 67, 69, 72, 83
Pueblo Cultures (Wright), diagram from, 27
Pueblo languages, 16 (diagram), 17 (map)
Pueblo Largo, 7, 58, 67, 69, 72, 83
Pueblo Revolt (1680), viii, 110-21, 116 (map), 233
Southern Tewa and, 52
Spanish records and, 81n1
Pueblos, vii, 8, 54
Galisteo Basin and, viii
religion and, 105-6, 110
Teyas and, 83n2
Pueblo Shé, 7, 58, 83
Pyramids, 67 (photo)

Q
Querechos, 86
Quetzalcoatl, 65, 73, 75, 77
Quivira, 89

R
Railroads, 160-61
Rain collector, 13 (photo)
Raingod Ceremony, 33, 35, 37, 39-42
Ramon of the Pueblo of Pojoaque, 136
Ranch life, 213, 215, 218, 221-24, 226-27, 229
Rancho del Pueblo de San Cristoval, 7, 132, 157
Ranchos, 81, 113, 173
Raton Pass, 160
Real Alencaster, Joaquín del: Pike and, 134
Repartimiento, 103
Reredos, 138 (photo)
Resolaneros (sun seekers), 147
Retablos, 145
Reynolds, Alexander, 157
Rio Grande Style, 61, 63
Rock art, see Petroglyphs
Rodeo, 198 (photo)
Rodríguez, Agustín, 91
Roediger, Virginia M.: illustration by, 46, 47
Romances traditionales, 148
Romero, Orlando, 139n6
quote of, 148, 150
Roundups, 174, 177
Royal Edict (1813), 137
Rozas, Juan de, 96, 102
Runner kachina, 51 (illustration)

S
Sacred Pipe, The (Black Elk), 23n3
San Antonio (St. Anthony of Padua), 91, 138
San Antonio de Padua and Ruego del Nos, carving of, 91
Sánchez, Jorge: carving by, 91
San Cristóbal, 7, 55 (map), 91n10, 92, 139, 232-33
attacks on, 110
boundaries of, 159
excavation at, 200 (photo), 231
explorers and, 88, 89
history of, viii, 8, 26-27
petroglyphs at, 61, 62
Pueblo Revolt and, 111, 112, 119
room block at, 59 (photo)
San Cristóbal (St. Christopher), *retablo* of, 123
San Cristóbal Canyon, 10-11 (photo), 136 (photo)
San Cristóbal Creek, 26 (photo)
San Cristóbal Grant, 128n14, 154, 159, 167 (map)
boundaries of, 9 (map), 137
dispute over, 164, 171
establishment of, viii
Hispanics and, 196-97
transactions surrounding, 166, 168-69
San Cristóbal Ranch, ix, 58, 128, 132, 206 (photo), 207 (photo), 208 (photo), 209 (photo), 210 (photo), 211 (photo), 216 (photo)
location of, vii
names of, 7
San Cristóbal reservoir, 228 (photo)
Sando, Joe, 118
on Pueblos, 110n4
Sandstone walls, 84-85 (photo)
San Francisco (St. Francis) de Asís, 91, 102, 138
statue of, 113
Sangre de Cristo Mountains, 166 (photo)
San Ildefonso, 16, 126

San Juan de los Caballeros, 96
San Juan Pueblo
clowns at, 36 (photo)
Tewas in, 16
San Lázaro, 8, 92, 115, 123, 232
explorers and, 88
San Marcos, 8, 232
explorers and, 88
San Miguel (St. Michael) the Archangel, 138
San Rafael, Archangel, 138
Santa Clara, Tewas in, 16
Santa Fe New Mexican
on Catron, 165
on Pankey, 193, 194
Santa Fe thistle (*Cirsium* sp.), 23 (photo)
Santa Fe Trail, 134, 134 (illustration), 134n4, 159, 177
travel on, 154, 156
Santa Gertrudis (St. Gertrude), 138
Santa María, Juan de, 91
Santo Domingo Pueblo, 86
Santos, 145
Savory, Allan: HRM and, 218n7
Sawyer Cattle Company, 204, 213
brand of, 189
Scalp Chief, 22
Scalp Society, 32
bears and, 73
Schaafsma, Polly, 61n2, 69, 83nn2, 3
on Hano songs/dances, 55
on *Patowa*, 32n15
on petroglyphs, 51n33, 61, 62, 63, 64, 65, 67, 77, 78
on Teyas, 83n2
on two-horned serpents, 75
Schmitt, Martin: on cowboys, 178
Scott, Kenneth, 185 (photo), 204, 215 (photo)
on cowboys, 215
ranching and, 221, 222, 224, 226, 229
Scott, Tommie, 204, 205, 215 (photo)
ranching and, 221, 226
Seeking Life (Laski), 33
Seh t'a, 31, 31n11
Seligman Brothers, San Cristóbal Grant and, 166
Seven Cities of Cíbola, 83, 87, 88
Shields, petroglyph of, 69, 76, 78
Shrines, 27n5, 58
Sibley, Henry, 159
Sichumovi, chiefs of, 57 (photo)
Sierry Petes, The (Gardner), 182-83, 183n2
Simmons, Marc, 174
Singleton, Carolyn, 204, 204 (photo)
Singleton, Henry, 204, 204 (photo), 207, 212-13
ranching and, 222
Singleton, M. E.: Pankey and, 201
Sipapu, 27
Sipofene, 21, 22, 27, 30n8, 31, 32n14
Sky God, 77
Sky Old Man, 47
Slavery, 82, 103-4, 106, 108, 125, 128
Smoke Prayer, 33
Snakes, 61, 62
clowns and, 75
petroglyph of, 71, 75, 76, 77, 79
Song of the Hunter's Wife, 42
Song of the Sky Loom, 23
Songs, 28n6, 43-44
Sorcerers, 147, 147n17
Sotuqnang-u, 77
Southern Tewa, (see also Tanos) vii, 18n9, 22, 51n32, 232
aggressiveness of, 52, 54-55
Catholicism and, 102
Espejo and, 54
explorers and, 89
language of, 16
migration of, 18
petroglyphs of, 52
Pueblo Revolt and, 52
towns of, 8
Spider Woman, 27
Spinden, H. J., 33n16, 44
Spirits, ancestral, 28
Spring Works, 218, 219, 220 (photo), 221
Star Kachina, 73
Stars, petroglyph of, 71, 73, 74, 79
Statehood, 195, 195n3
Storage pits, excavation of, 231
Storm Serpent, song of, 61
Sulphur Springs Stage Coach station, 156 (photo)
Summer Chief (*Poetunyo*), 22, 30, 31, 33, 37, 40, 46
Summer Initiation, 47n29
Summer People, 22, 30, 31, 51, 52
relay race with, 47n30
Summer Society, 32, 102n1
Summer spirits, 28
Sumner, E. V.: on New Mexicans, 195
Sun Old Man, 47
Symbols, repeating, 75

T

Talbot, Arlin, 219, 222 (photo), 227 (photo)
ranching and, 221, 229
Tanoan languages, 16, 54
Tanos, (see also Southern Tewa) 91, 122, 123, 136, 233, 234
Catholicism and, 138
described, 125-26
Pueblo Revolt and, 112-15, 117, 119, 120
raids on, 107
Taos Revolt, 156, 156n2, 166
Tesuque, Tewas in, 16
Tewa language, 16
Tewas, viii, ix, 4, 45 (photo), 63, 83, 122, 123
ceremonies of, 30, 33-42, 47, 51
costumes of, 46 (illustration) 47 (illustration)
children of, 28, 30-31
ideals of, 23
migration of, 21
personalities of, 51-52
Pueblo Revolt and, 113
Texas Scottish Rite Hospital for Crippled Children, 204
Thano. See Hano
Tiwa language, 16
Tlaloc, cult of, 62
Towa é, 22, 27, 31, 32, 32nn13, 14, 35n18, 37, 44, 51
Towa language, 16
Trash People, 31
Trash pits, 232
Treaty of Guadalupe Hidalgo (1848), 156, 166, 196
Treviño, Juan Francisco: raid by, 110
Tribes, eighteenth-century, 126 (map)
Trujillo, 163
Tsave Yoh, 27, 27n4
Tupatú, Luis, 120
Turkey hunt, petroglyph of, 69
Turquoise trade, 15
Tuteveni, 64
Two-horned snakes, petroglyphs of, 75
Tze-Man Tu-o, 7, 7n1, 58

U

Utes, 126
raid by, 122
Uto-Aztecan languages, 16

V

Vaqueros, 173, 179
equipment of, 174
See also Cowboys
Vargas, Diego de, 120 (painting), 122, 123, 123n11, 125
Vásquez de Coronado, Francisco, 87 (illustration), 87n6, 91
exploration by, 87, 88-90
Verbena (vervain), 150 (photo)
Vergara, Pedro de, 102
Villandrano, Rodrigo de: painting by, 102
Villa of Santa Cruz, 123
Villar, Nicolás de, 107
Visitas, 103

W

Walpi, chiefs of, 57 (photo)
Ware, John, 231n2, 232
Warrior figures, petroglyph of, 72
Warrior Society, 52, 68
War Society, 32, 74
bears and, 73
Waste Isolation Pilot Project (WIPP), 231n1
Watchtowers, 58
Water-collecting holes, 32 (photo)
Water-Giving Ceremony, 30, 30n9
Waters, Frank: on Pueblo elders, 42
Water Serpent, 62
Weed People, 31
Weekly New Mexican, on Laughlin, 193
Western Trail, 177
West La Garita Pasture, 170 (photo)
Westphall, Victor: on Catron, 164
Whipper kachina, 51 (illustration)
White, Lee, 163
White Bluffs, 40 (photo), 53 (photo), 121 (photo)
White Corn Maiden, 21, 30
White Mountain Apaches, 108 (photo)
Wild Horse Mesa, 127 (photo)
Wind Old Woman, 47
Winter Chief (*Oyike*), 22, 31, 33, 37, 40, 41, 42n24, 46
Winter Initiation, 47n29
Winter Men, 37, 41, 42
Winter People, 22, 30, 33, 51, 52
relay race with, 47n30
Winter Society, 32, 102n1
Winter spirits, 28
WIPP. See Waste Isolation Pilot Project
Witches, 51
Women's Society, 22n1, 32, 74
Scalp Chief and, 22
Wood, Walter E., 200
Woolly Indian wheat (*Plantago* sp.), 30 (photo)
Wootton, "Uncle Dick," 160
Worchester, Donald: Pueblo Revolt and, 114n9
Wright, Barton: diagram from, 27

X

Xavier, Francisco: Pueblo Revolt and, 112, 114, 115, 117, 119
Xayeh, 28, 31

Y

Yam-p'-ham-ba, 7, 7n1, 32, 46, 58
described, 26-27
travelers and, 83
Yava, Albert, 30n8
on Tewa, 125n12
Yellowhouse Pasture, 84-85 (photo)
Yema, LeRoy Kewan: illustration by, 51
Yope, Cristóbal, 110
Young, Jane, 62, 69
on multivocality, 63n3
on symbols, 75
Younger-Brother-Older-Than-I, 35n18
Yucca Old Man, 47

Z

Zaldivar, Vicente de, 99
Zia, 63
Zuni, 51
ceremonies/pantheon of, 63
language, 16